GOLFIN' & GOOFIN'

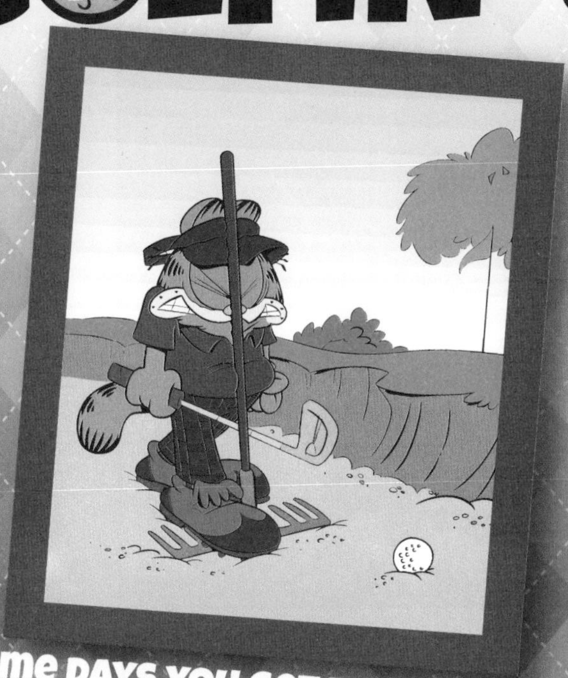

Some days you get the course. *MOST* days the course gets you.

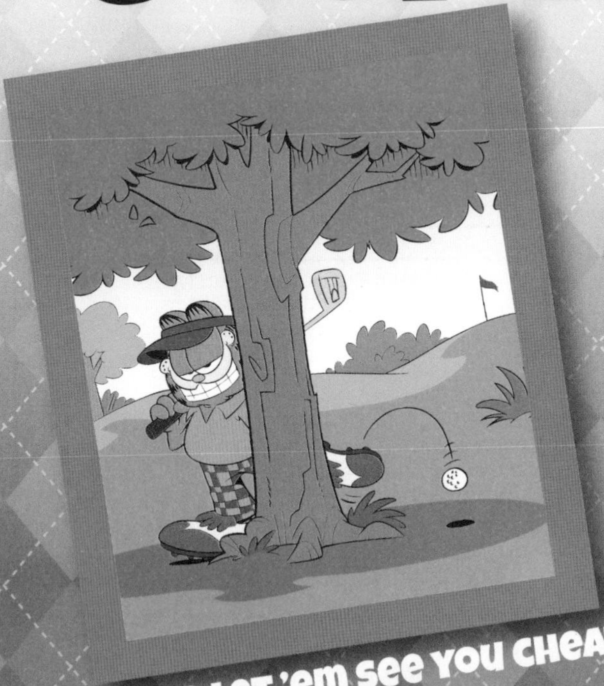

Never let 'em see you cheat.

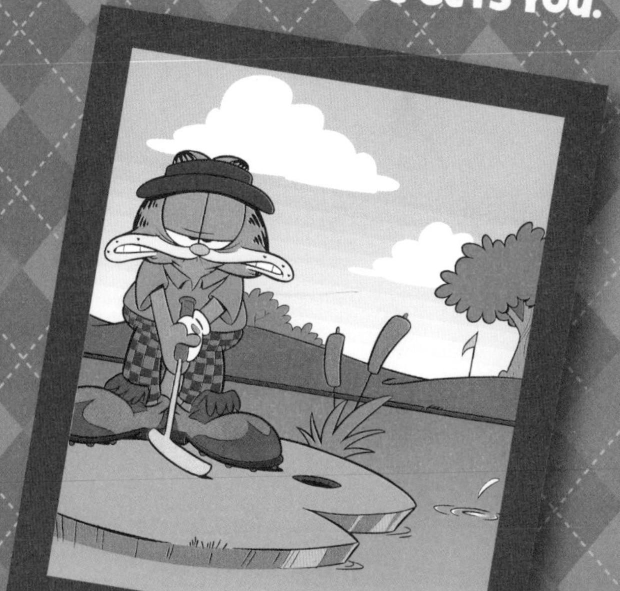

I've got my "golf face" on.

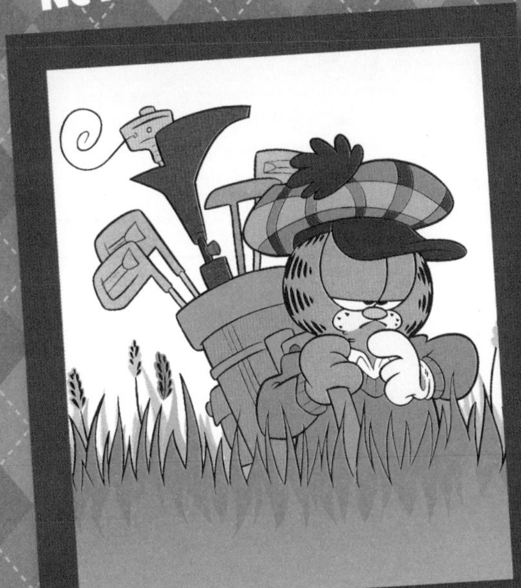

Should I use the wedge or the weedwhacker?

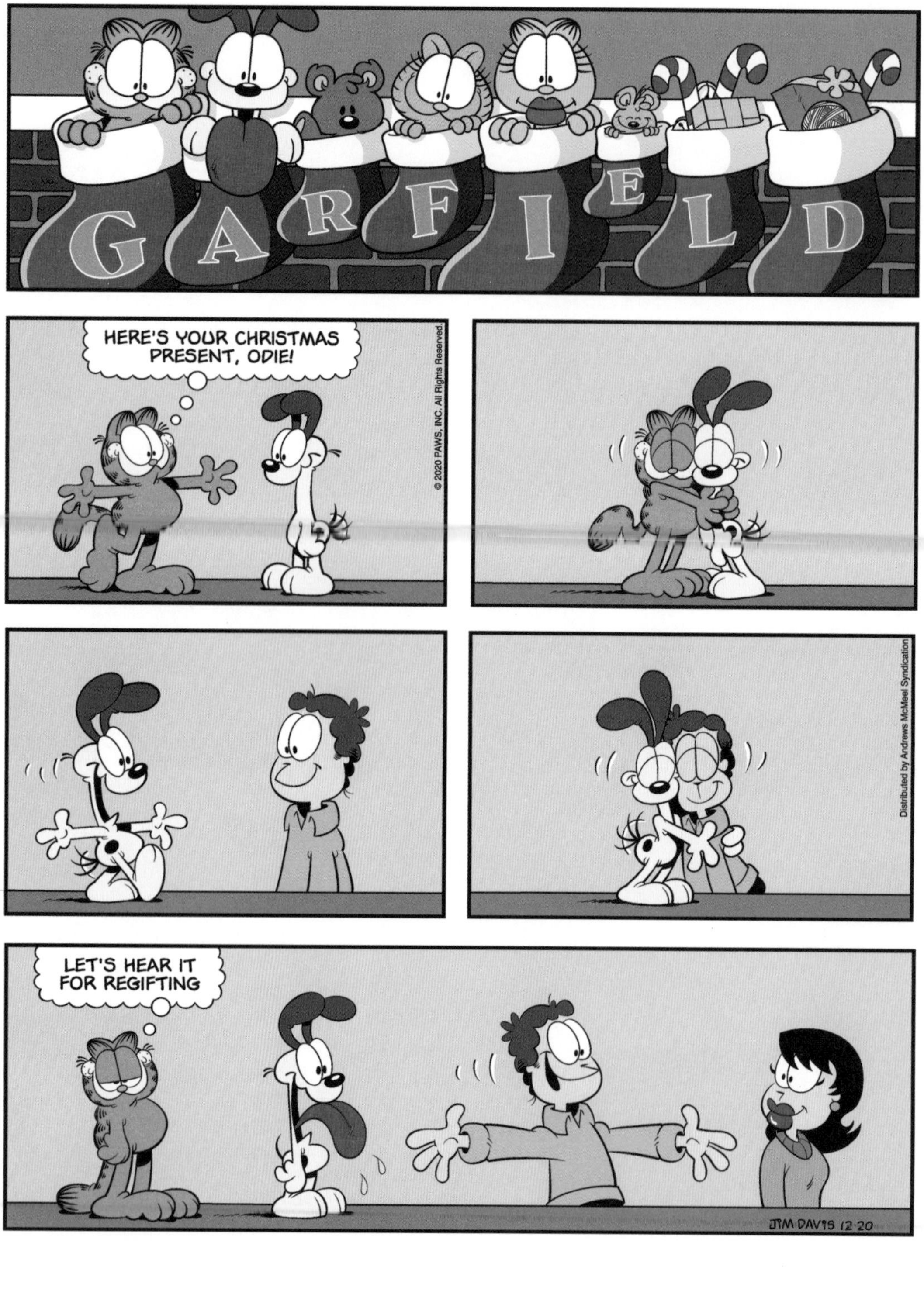
GARFIELD
HERE'S YOUR CHRISTMAS PRESENT, ODIE!
© 2020 PAWS, INC. All Rights Reserved.
Distributed by Andrews McMeel Syndication
LET'S HEAR IT FOR REGIFTING
JIM DAVIS 12·20

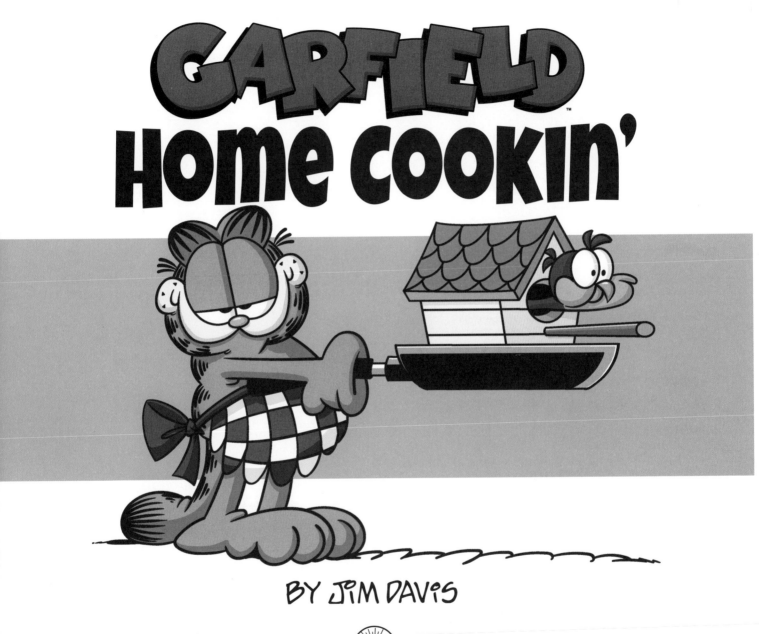

GARFIELD HOME COOKIN'

BY JIM DAVIS

Random House Worlds ● New York

A Random House Worlds Trade Paperback Original

Published in the United States by Random House Worlds, an imprint of Random House,
a division of Penguin Random House LLC, New York.

All of the comics in this work have been previously published.

ISBN 978-0-593-59919-8
Ebook ISBN 978-0-593-59920-4

Printed in China on acid-free paper

randomhousebooks.com

9 8 7 6 5 4 3 2 1

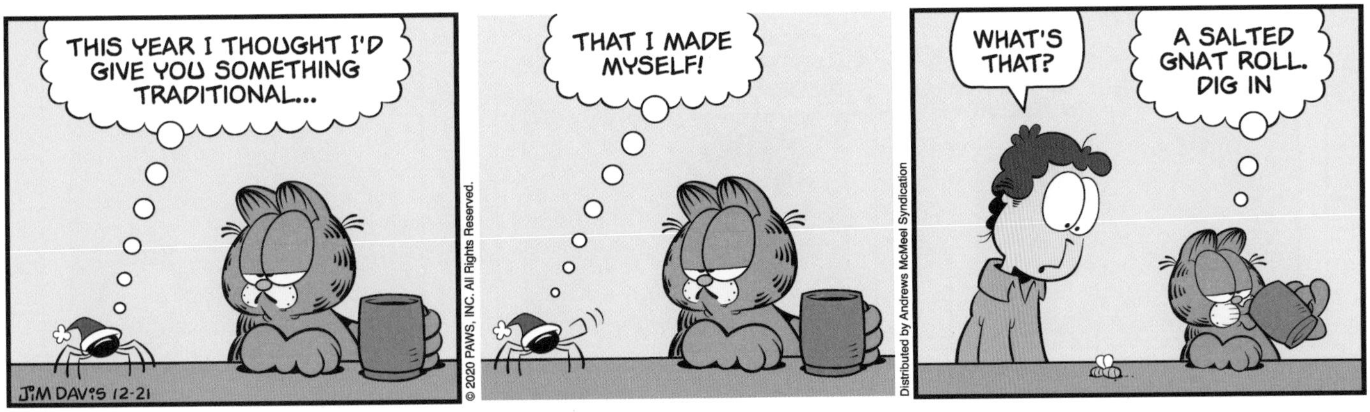
THIS YEAR I THOUGHT I'D GIVE YOU SOMETHING TRADITIONAL...
JIM DAVIS 12-21
© 2020 PAWS, INC. All Rights Reserved.
THAT I MADE MYSELF!
Distributed by Andrews McMeel Syndication
WHAT'S THAT?
A SALTED GNAT ROLL. DIG IN

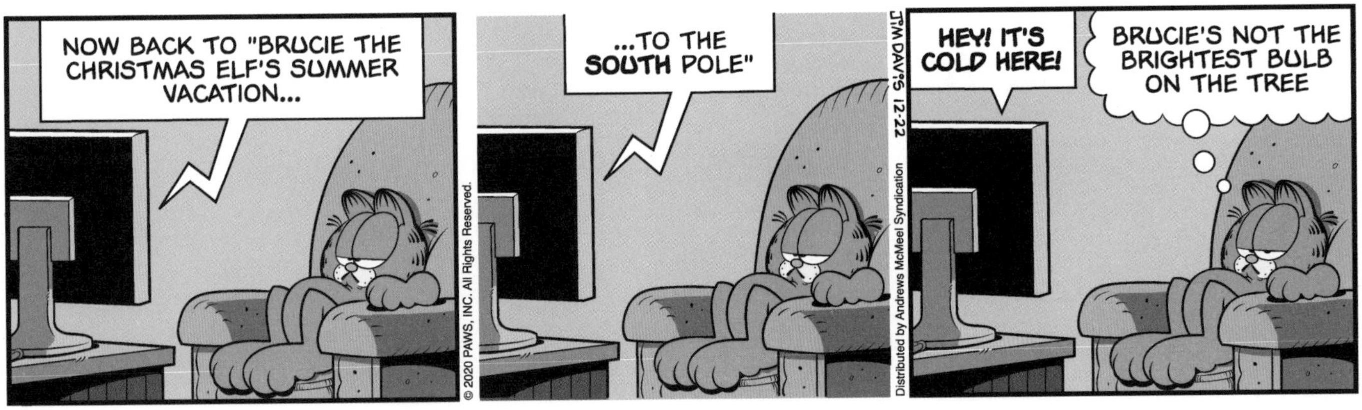
NOW BACK TO "BRUCIE THE CHRISTMAS ELF'S SUMMER VACATION...
© 2020 PAWS, INC. All Rights Reserved.
...TO THE **SOUTH** POLE"
JIM DAVIS 12-22
Distributed by Andrews McMeel Syndication
HEY! IT'S COLD HERE!
BRUCIE'S NOT THE BRIGHTEST BULB ON THE TREE

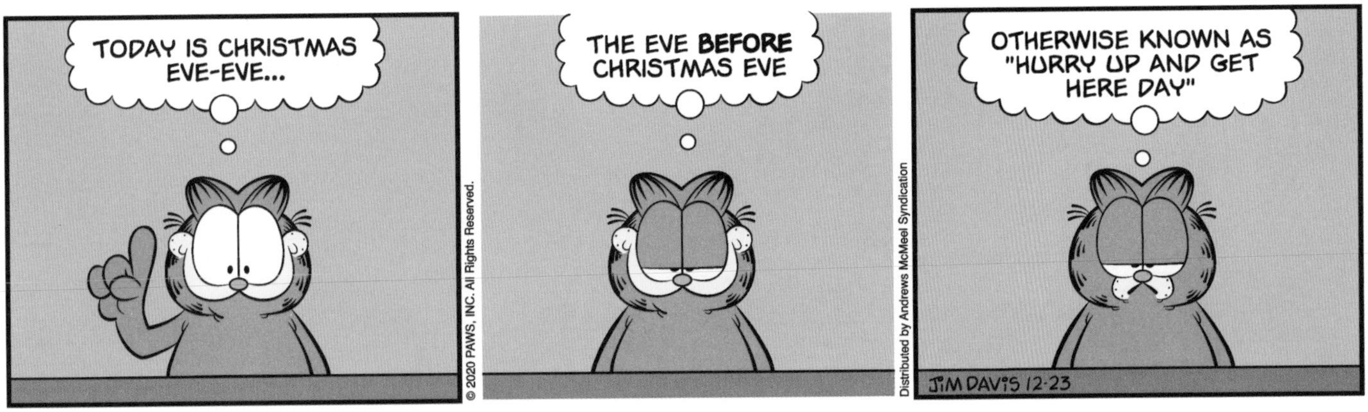
TODAY IS CHRISTMAS EVE-EVE...
© 2020 PAWS, INC. All Rights Reserved.
THE EVE **BEFORE** CHRISTMAS EVE
Distributed by Andrews McMeel Syndication
OTHERWISE KNOWN AS "HURRY UP AND GET HERE DAY"
JIM DAVIS 12-23

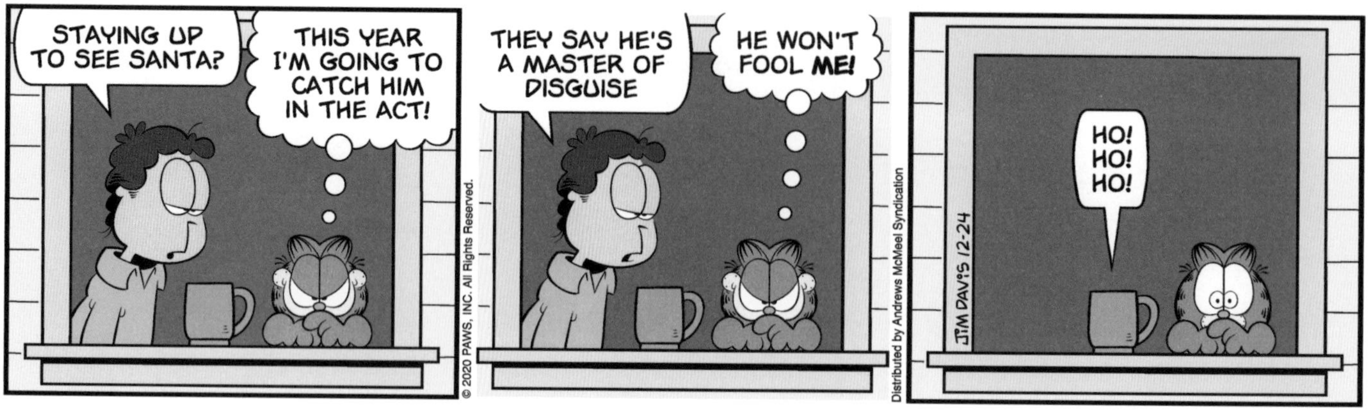
STAYING UP TO SEE SANTA?
THIS YEAR I'M GOING TO CATCH HIM IN THE ACT!
THEY SAY HE'S A MASTER OF DISGUISE
HE WON'T FOOL **ME!**
HO! HO! HO!
JIM DAVIS 12-24
© 2020 PAWS, INC. All Rights Reserved.
Distributed by Andrews McMeel Syndication

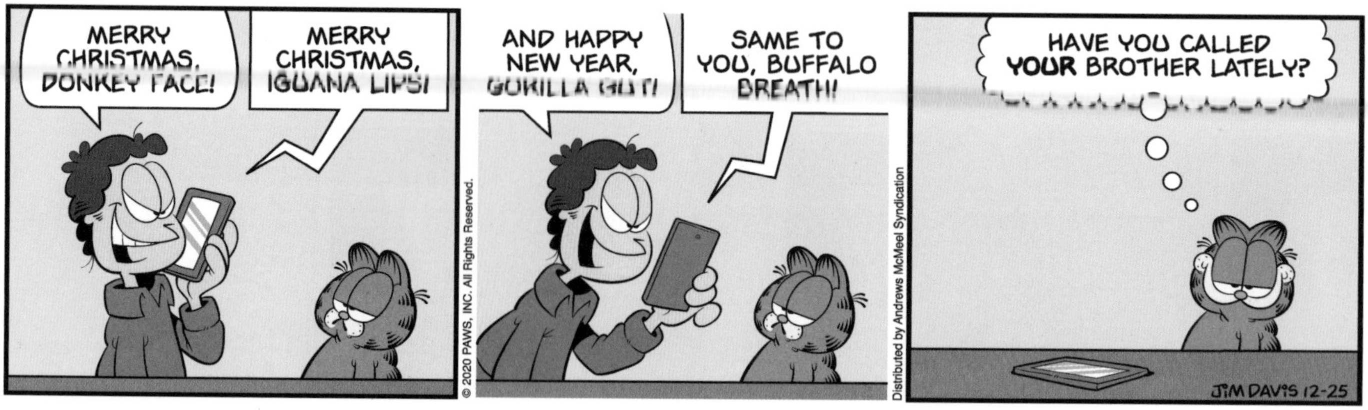
MERRY CHRISTMAS, DONKEY FACE!
MERRY CHRISTMAS, IGUANA LIPS!
AND HAPPY NEW YEAR, GORILLA GUT!
SAME TO YOU, BUFFALO BREATH!
HAVE YOU CALLED **YOUR** BROTHER LATELY?
JIM DAVIS 12-25
© 2020 PAWS, INC. All Rights Reserved.
Distributed by Andrews McMeel Syndication

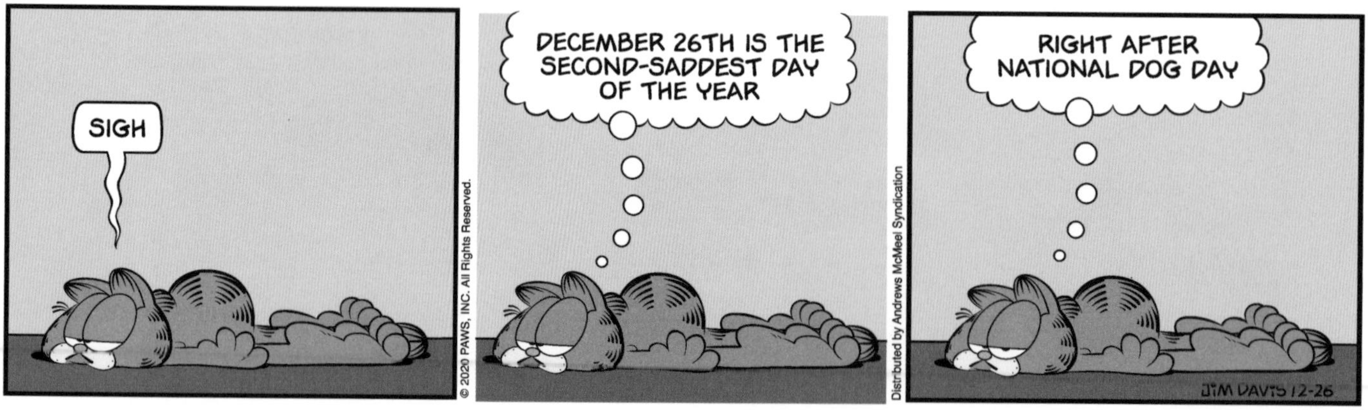
SIGH
DECEMBER 26TH IS THE SECOND-SADDEST DAY OF THE YEAR
RIGHT AFTER NATIONAL DOG DAY
JIM DAVIS 12-26
© 2020 PAWS, INC. All Rights Reserved.
Distributed by Andrews McMeel Syndication

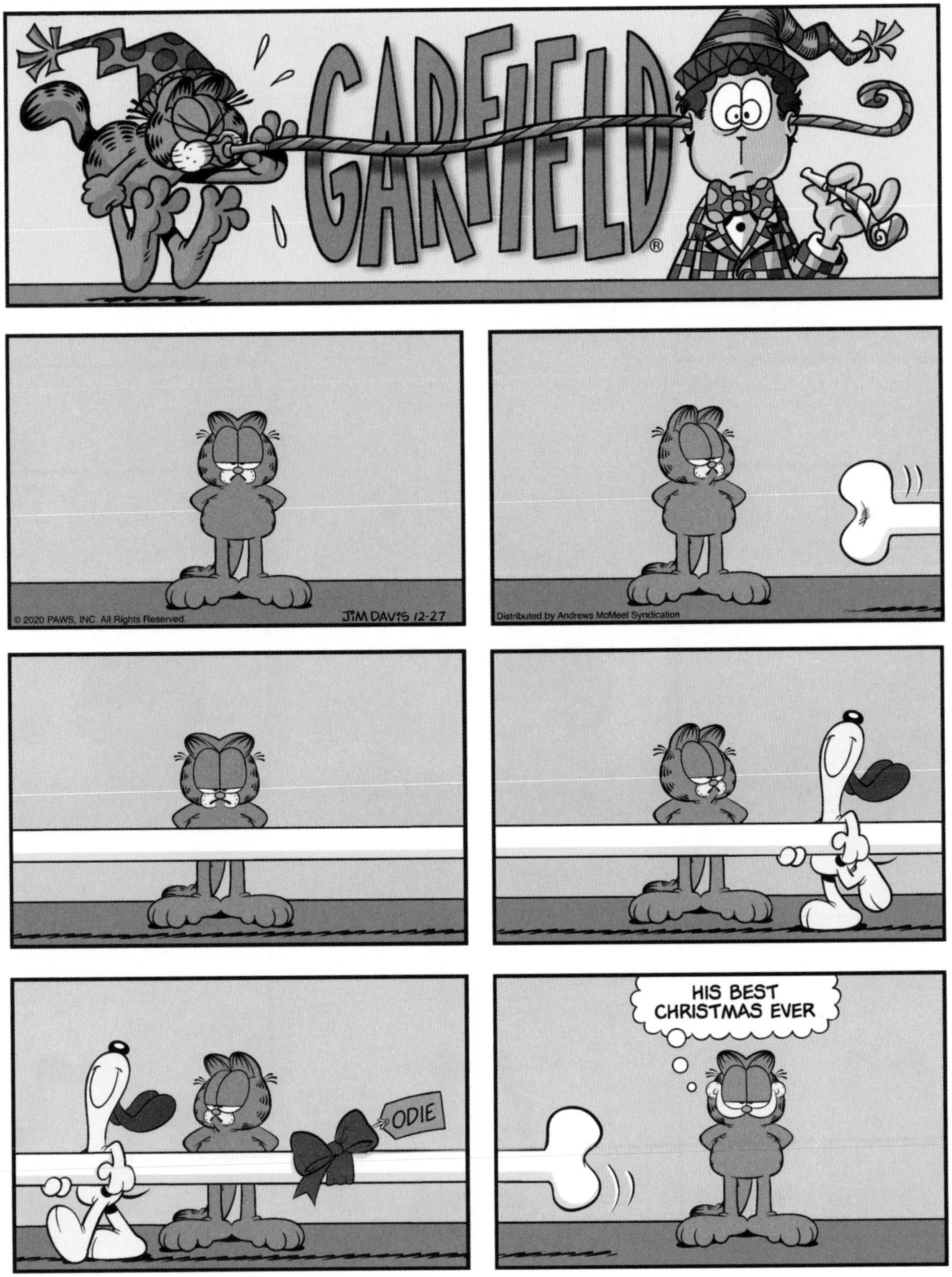
GARFIELD
© 2020 PAWS, INC. All Rights Reserved.
JIM DAVIS 12-27
Distributed by Andrews McMeel Syndication
ODIE
HIS BEST CHRISTMAS EVER

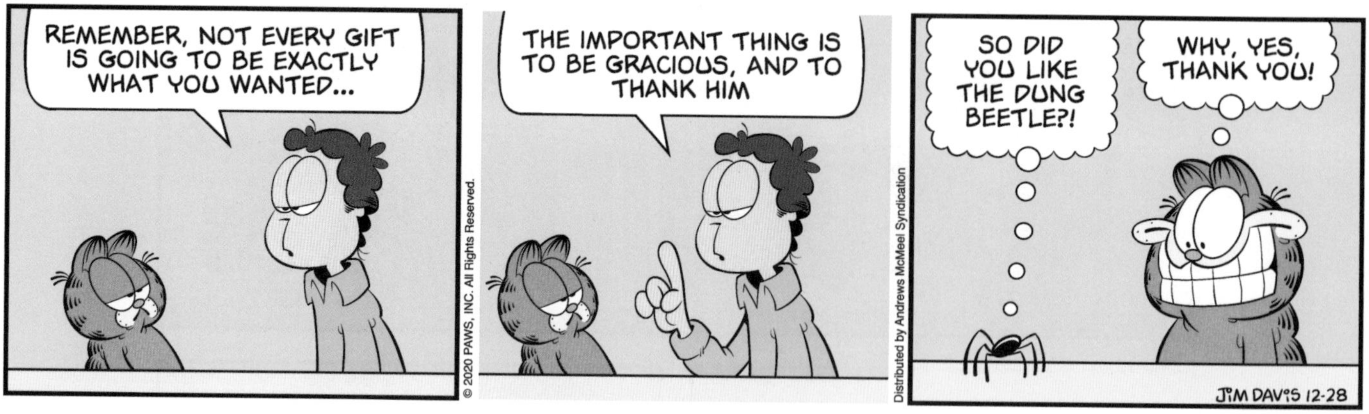
REMEMBER, NOT EVERY GIFT IS GOING TO BE EXACTLY WHAT YOU WANTED...
THE IMPORTANT THING IS TO BE GRACIOUS, AND TO THANK HIM
SO DID YOU LIKE THE DUNG BEETLE?!
WHY, YES, THANK YOU!
JIM DAVIS 12-28

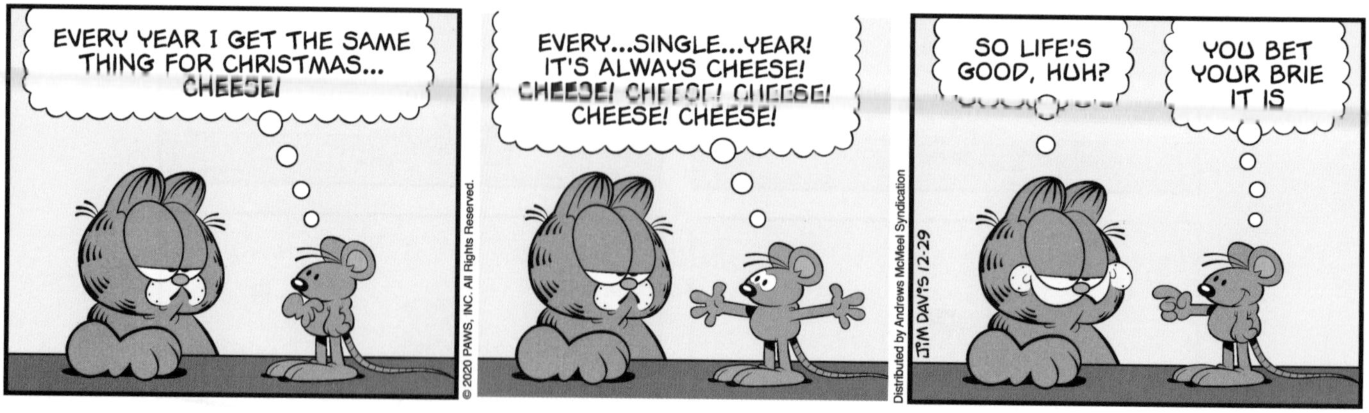
EVERY YEAR I GET THE SAME THING FOR CHRISTMAS... CHEESE!
EVERY...SINGLE...YEAR! IT'S ALWAYS CHEESE! CHEESE! CHEESE! CHEESE! CHEESE! CHEESE!
SO LIFE'S GOOD, HUH?
YOU BET YOUR BRIE IT IS
JIM DAVIS 12-29

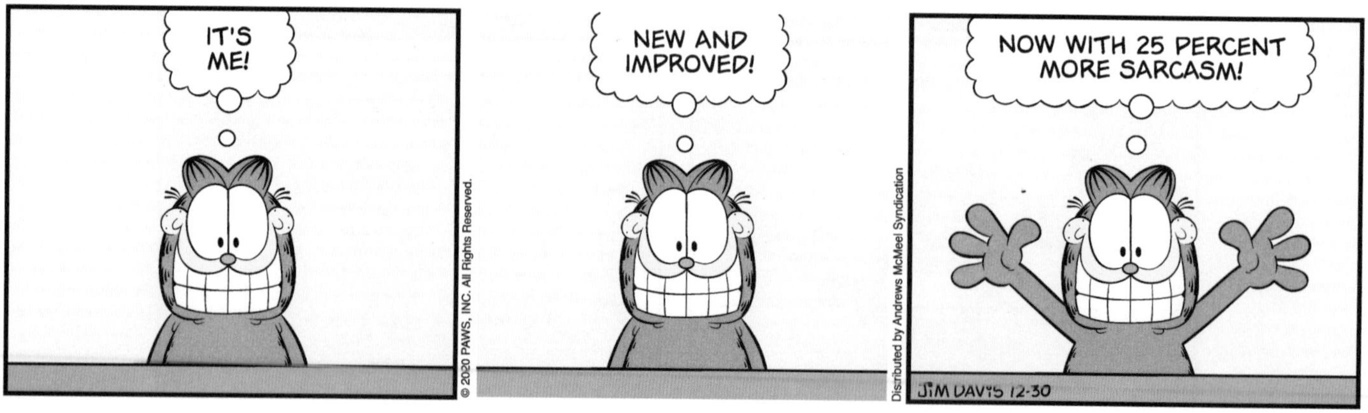
IT'S ME!
NEW AND IMPROVED!
NOW WITH 25 PERCENT MORE SARCASM!
JIM DAVIS 12-30

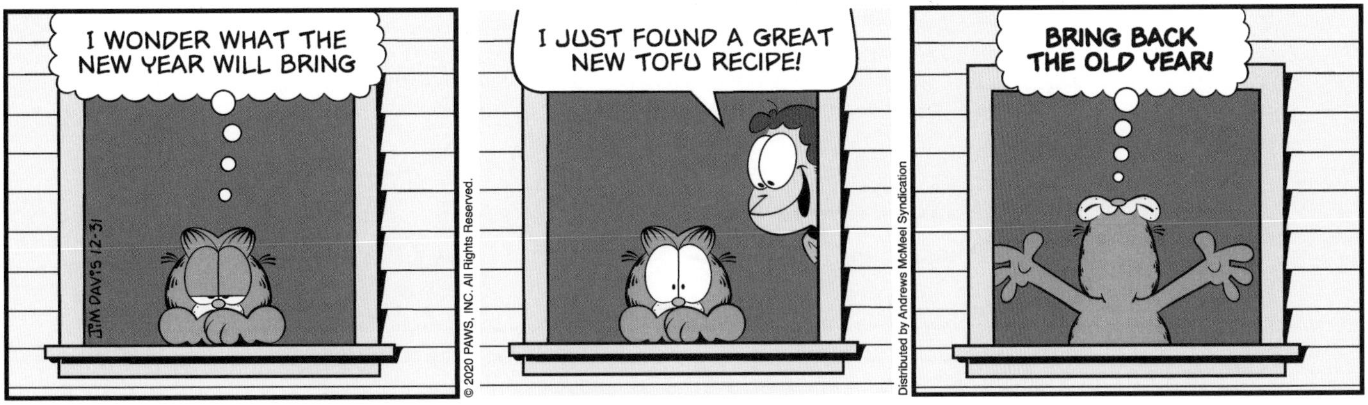
I WONDER WHAT THE NEW YEAR WILL BRING
I JUST FOUND A GREAT NEW TOFU RECIPE!
BRING BACK THE OLD YEAR!

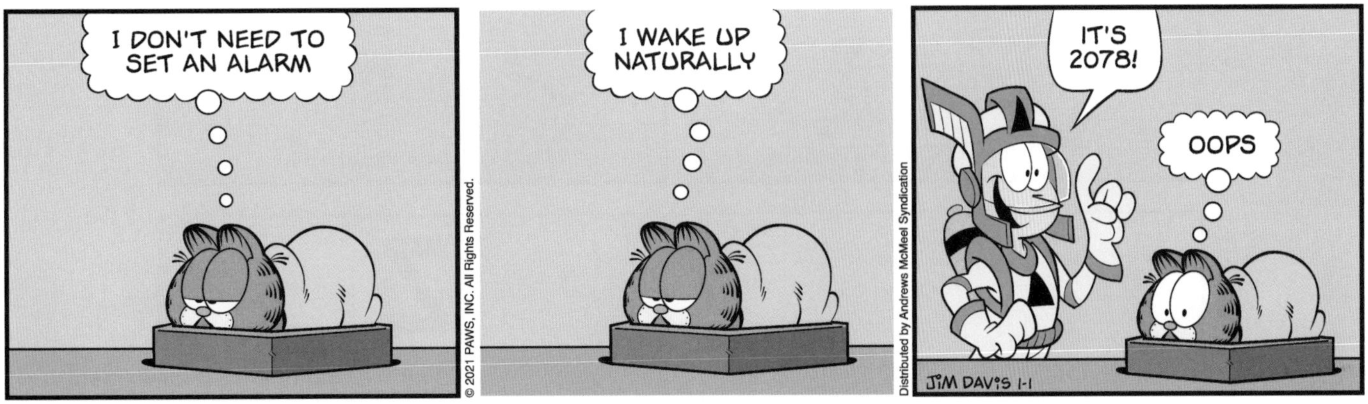
I DON'T NEED TO SET AN ALARM
I WAKE UP NATURALLY
IT'S 2078!
OOPS

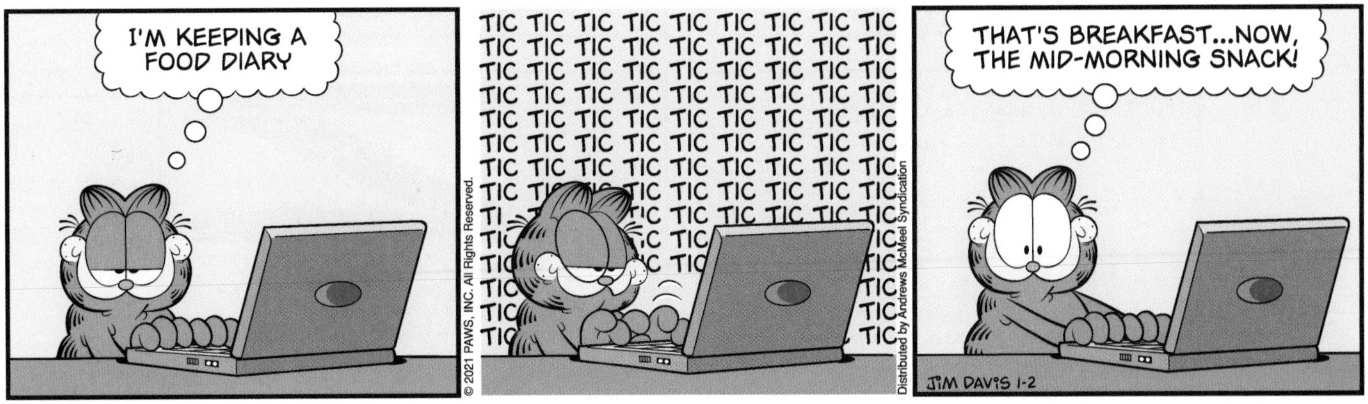
I'M KEEPING A FOOD DIARY
TIC TIC TIC TIC TIC TIC TIC TIC TIC
THAT'S BREAKFAST...NOW, THE MID-MORNING SNACK!

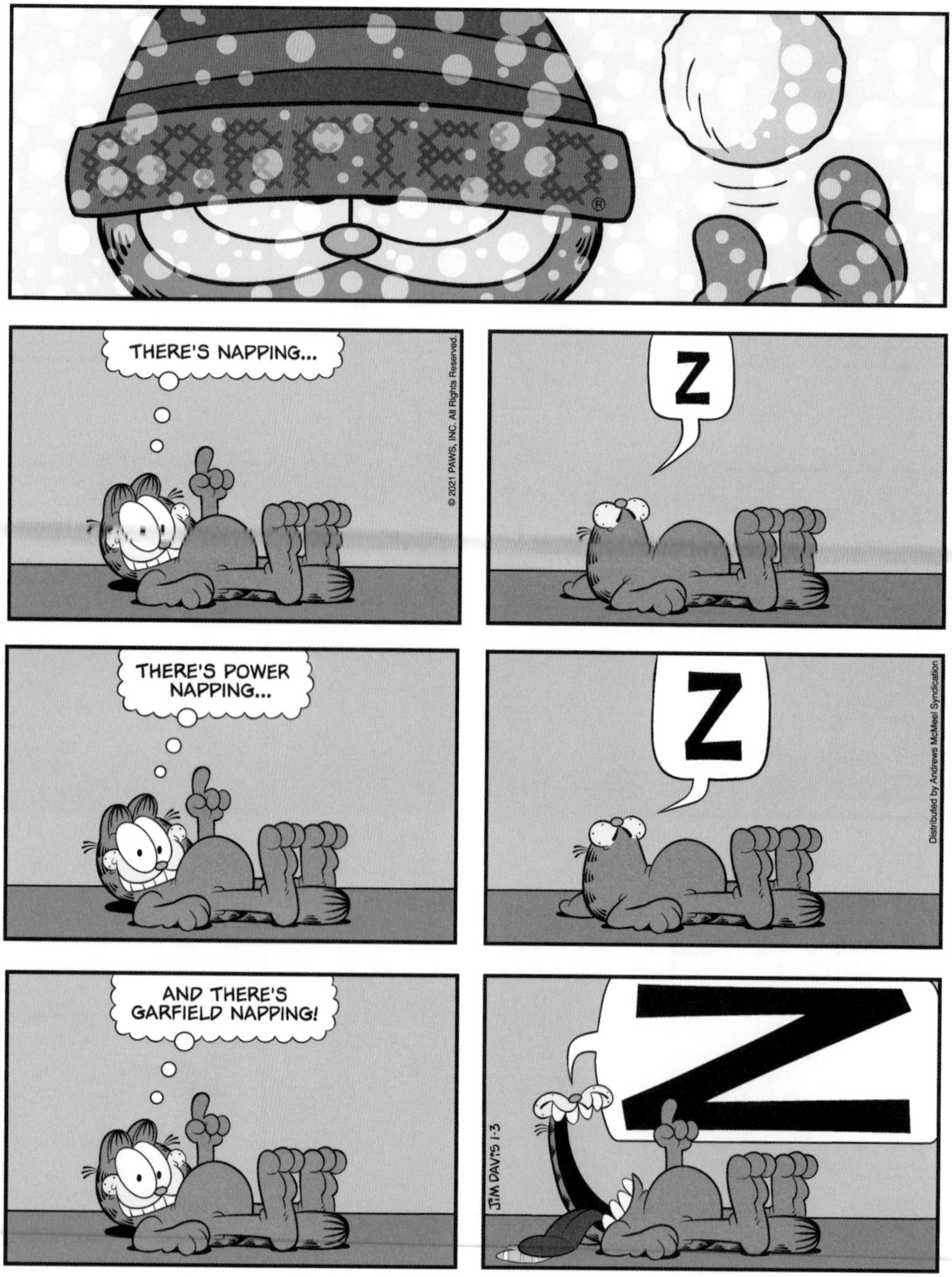
GARFIELD
THERE'S NAPPING...
Z
THERE'S POWER NAPPING...
Z
AND THERE'S GARFIELD NAPPING!
Z
JIM DAVIS 1-3
© 2021 PAWS, INC. All Rights Reserved.
Distributed by Andrews McMeel Syndication

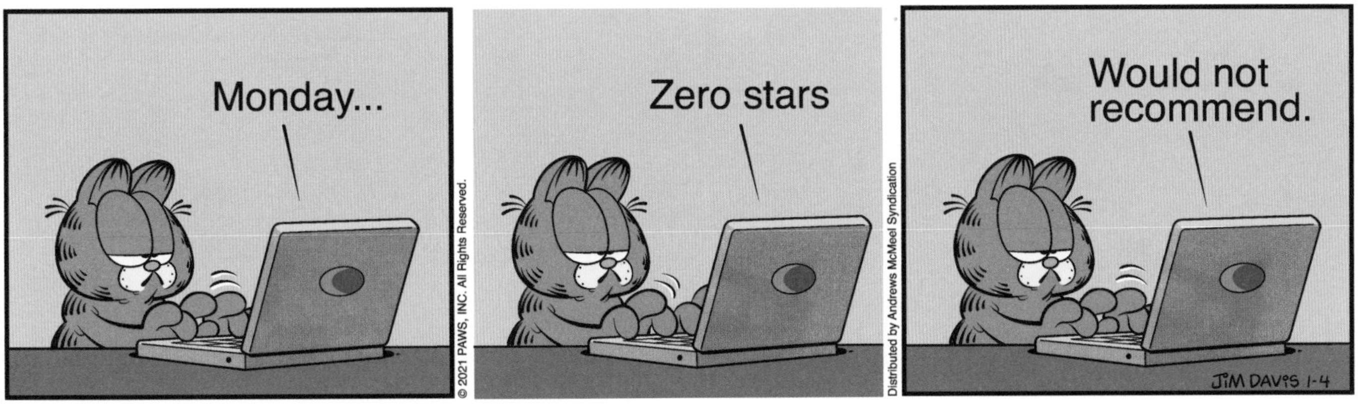
Monday...
Zero stars
Would not recommend.
JIM DAVIS 1-4
© 2021 PAWS, INC. All Rights Reserved.
Distributed by Andrews McMeel Syndication

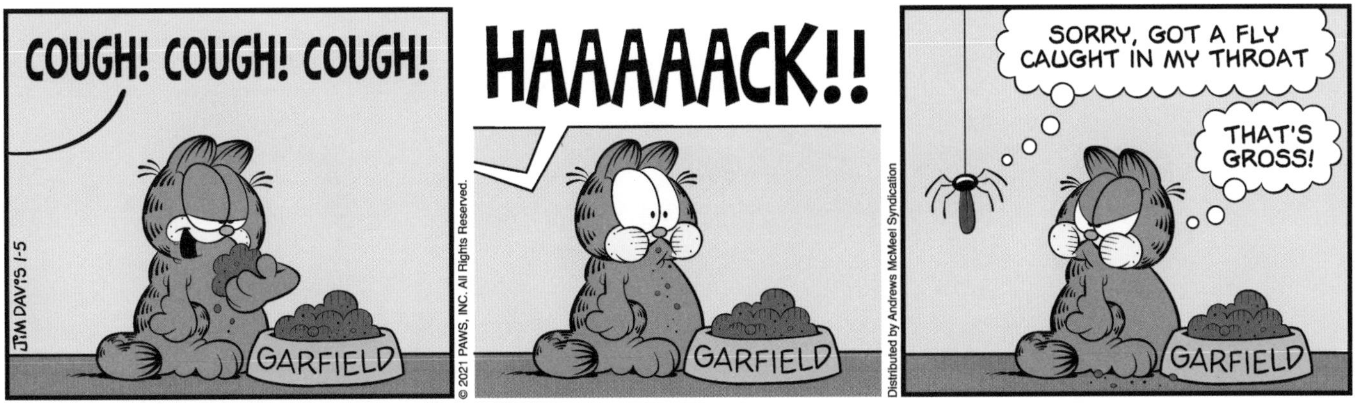
COUGH! COUGH! COUGH!
JIM DAVIS 1-5
GARFIELD
HAAAAACK!!
SORRY, GOT A FLY CAUGHT IN MY THROAT
THAT'S GROSS!
© 2021 PAWS, INC. All Rights Reserved.
Distributed by Andrews McMeel Syndication

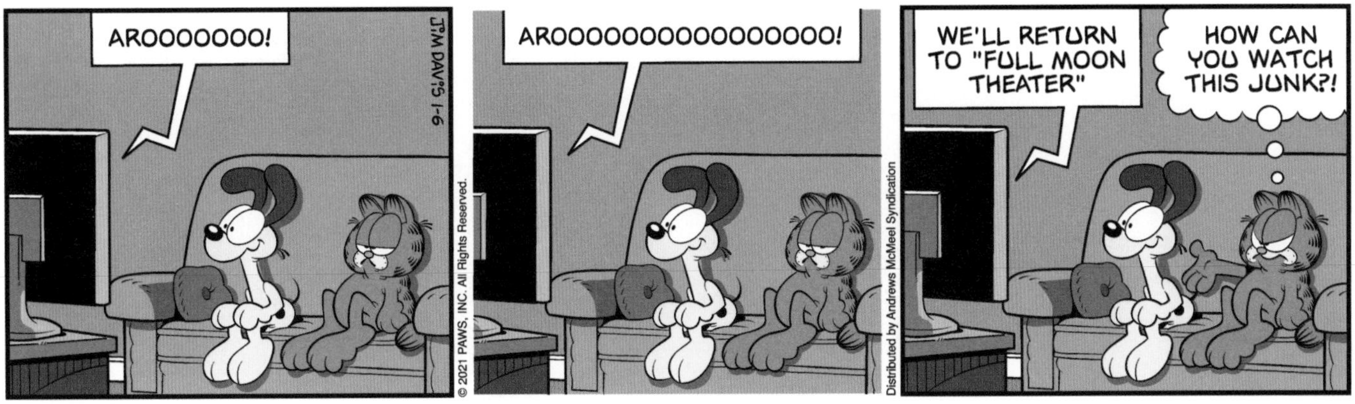
AROOOOOOO!
JIM DAVIS 1-6
AROOOOOOOOOOOOOOOO!
WE'LL RETURN TO "FULL MOON THEATER"
HOW CAN YOU WATCH THIS JUNK?!
© 2021 PAWS, INC. All Rights Reserved.
Distributed by Andrews McMeel Syndication

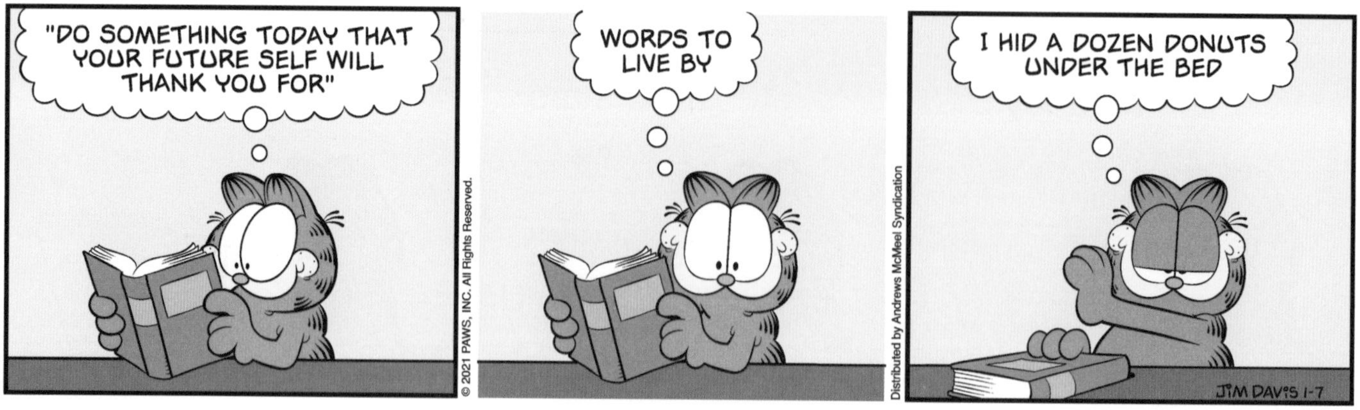
"DO SOMETHING TODAY THAT YOUR FUTURE SELF WILL THANK YOU FOR"
WORDS TO LIVE BY
I HID A DOZEN DONUTS UNDER THE BED
© 2021 PAWS, INC. All Rights Reserved.
Distributed by Andrews McMeel Syndication
JIM DAVIS 1-7

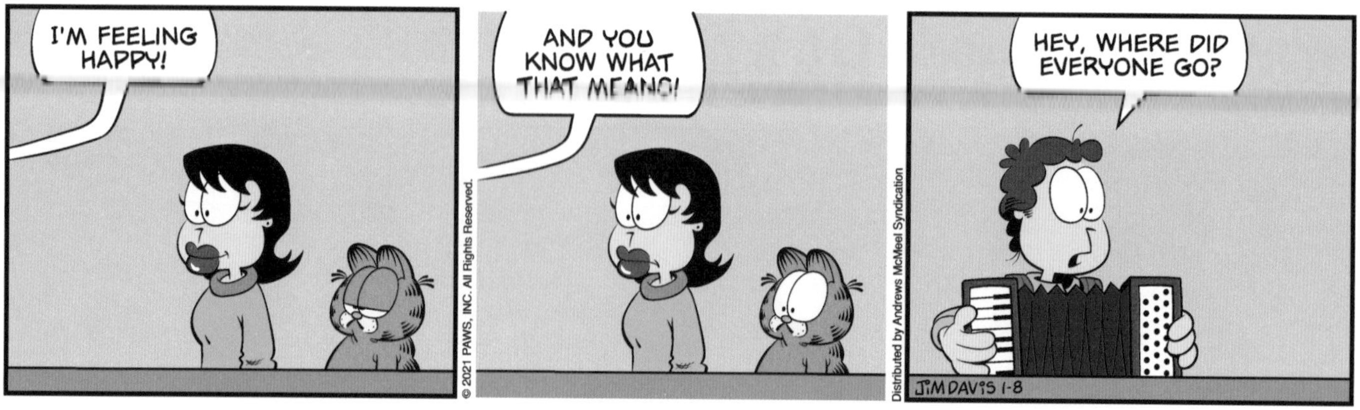
I'M FEELING HAPPY!
AND YOU KNOW WHAT THAT MEANS!
HEY, WHERE DID EVERYONE GO?
© 2021 PAWS, INC. All Rights Reserved.
Distributed by Andrews McMeel Syndication
JIM DAVIS 1-8

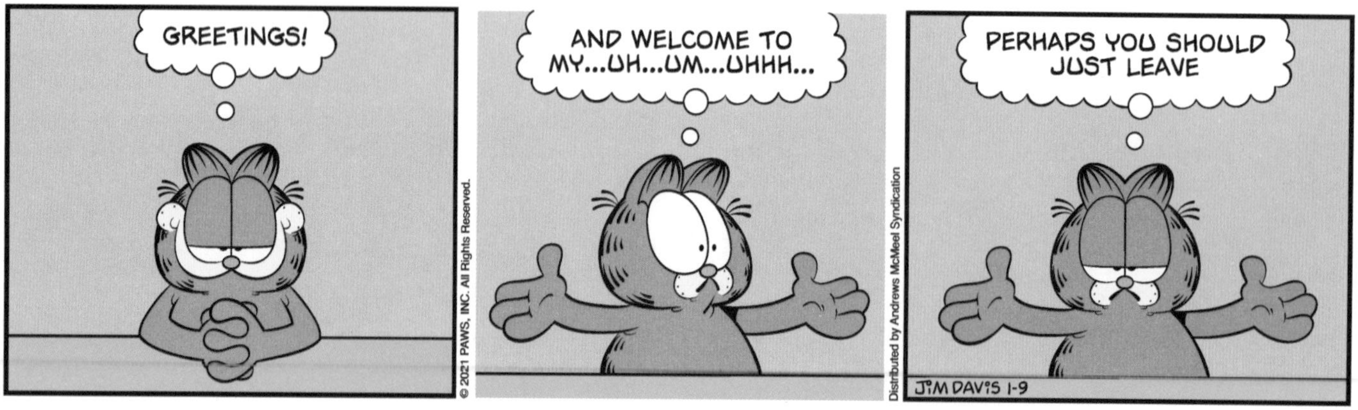
GREETINGS!
AND WELCOME TO MY...UH...UM...UHHH...
PERHAPS YOU SHOULD JUST LEAVE
© 2021 PAWS, INC. All Rights Reserved.
Distributed by Andrews McMeel Syndication
JIM DAVIS 1-9

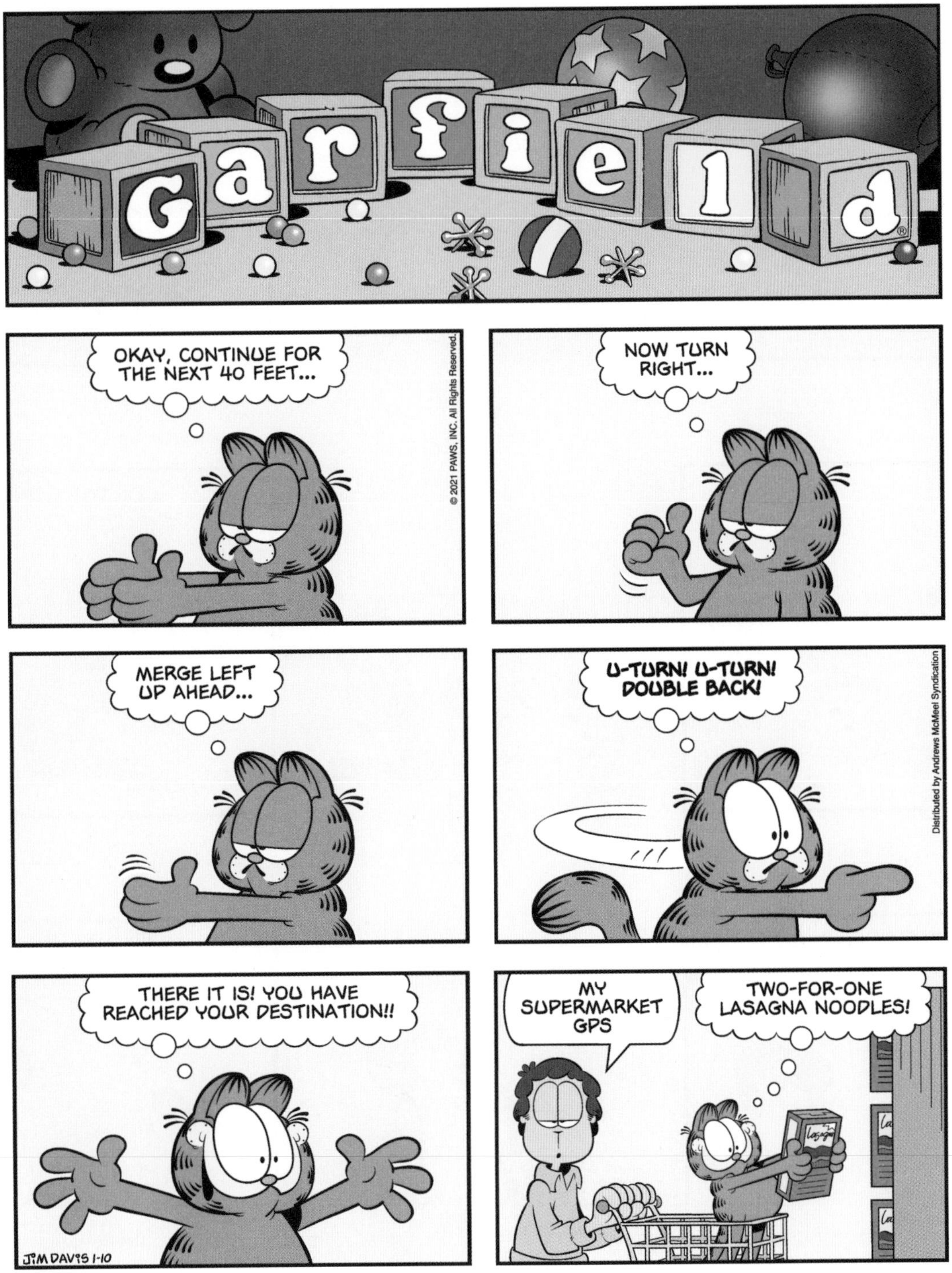
Garfield®
OKAY, CONTINUE FOR THE NEXT 40 FEET...
© 2021 PAWS, INC. All Rights Reserved.
NOW TURN RIGHT...
MERGE LEFT UP AHEAD...
U-TURN! U-TURN! DOUBLE BACK!
Distributed by Andrews McMeel Syndication
THERE IT IS! YOU HAVE REACHED YOUR DESTINATION!!
JIM DAVIS 1-10
MY SUPERMARKET GPS
TWO-FOR-ONE LASAGNA NOODLES!

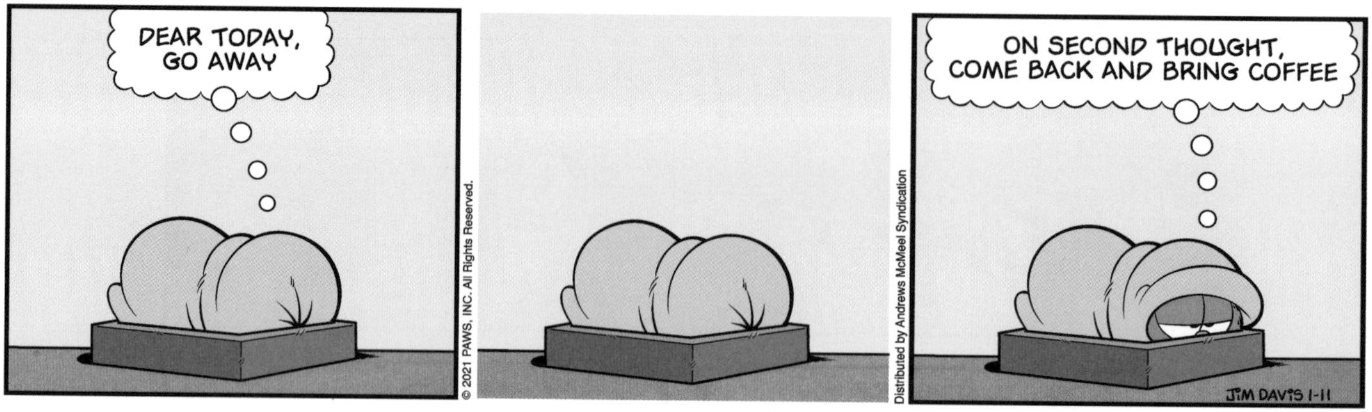
DEAR TODAY, GO AWAY
© 2021 PAWS, INC. All Rights Reserved.
Distributed by Andrews McMeel Syndication
ON SECOND THOUGHT, COME BACK AND BRING COFFEE
JIM DAVIS 1-11

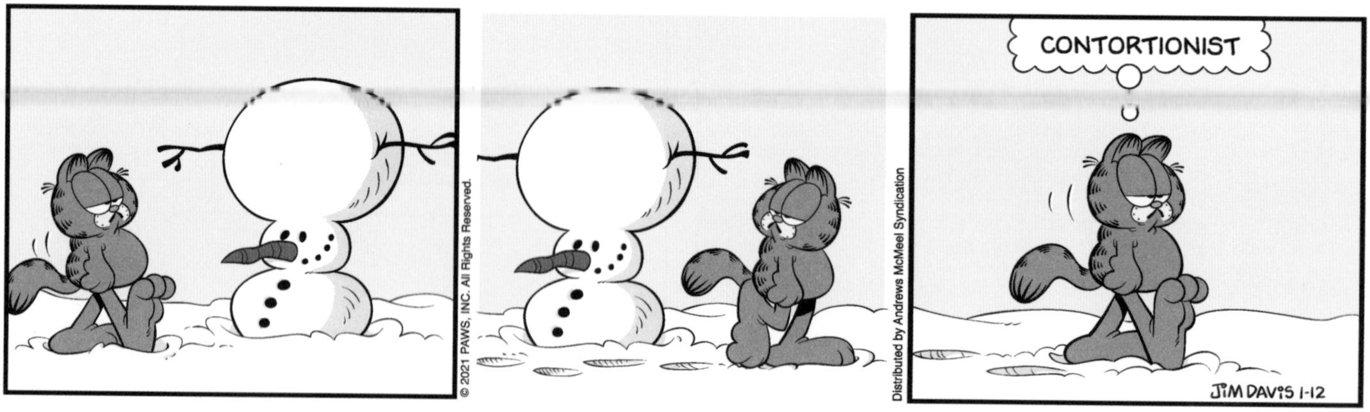
© 2021 PAWS, INC. All Rights Reserved.
Distributed by Andrews McMeel Syndication
CONTORTIONIST
JIM DAVIS 1-12

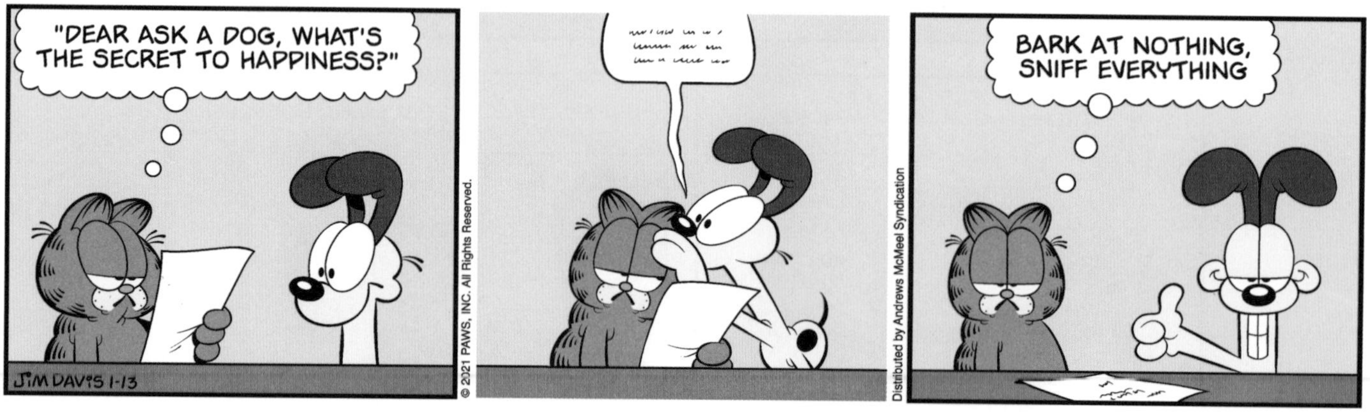
"DEAR ASK A DOG, WHAT'S THE SECRET TO HAPPINESS?"
JIM DAVIS 1-13
© 2021 PAWS, INC. All Rights Reserved.
Distributed by Andrews McMeel Syndication
BARK AT NOTHING, SNIFF EVERYTHING

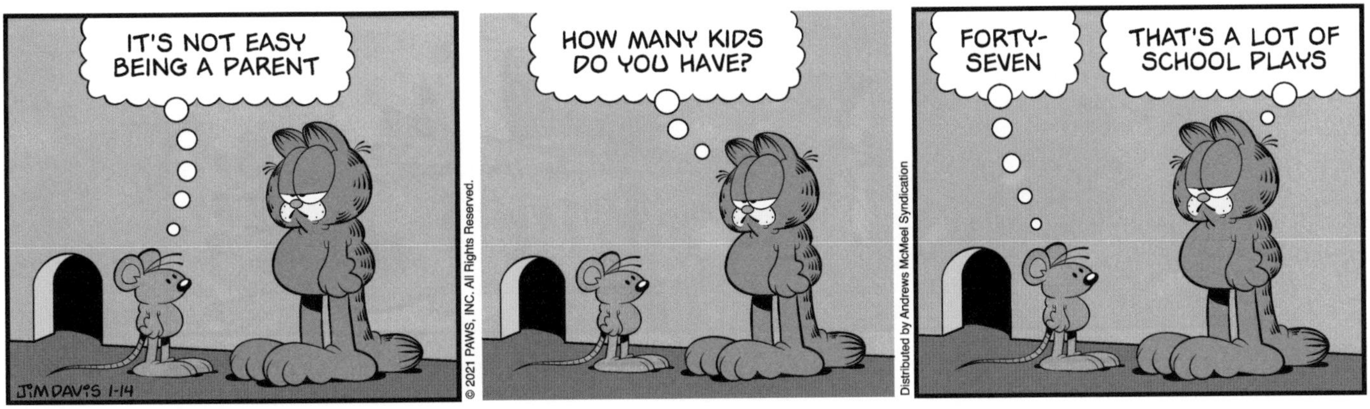
IT'S NOT EASY BEING A PARENT
JIM DAVIS 1-14
© 2021 PAWS, INC. All Rights Reserved.
HOW MANY KIDS DO YOU HAVE?
Distributed by Andrews McMeel Syndication
FORTY-SEVEN
THAT'S A LOT OF SCHOOL PLAYS

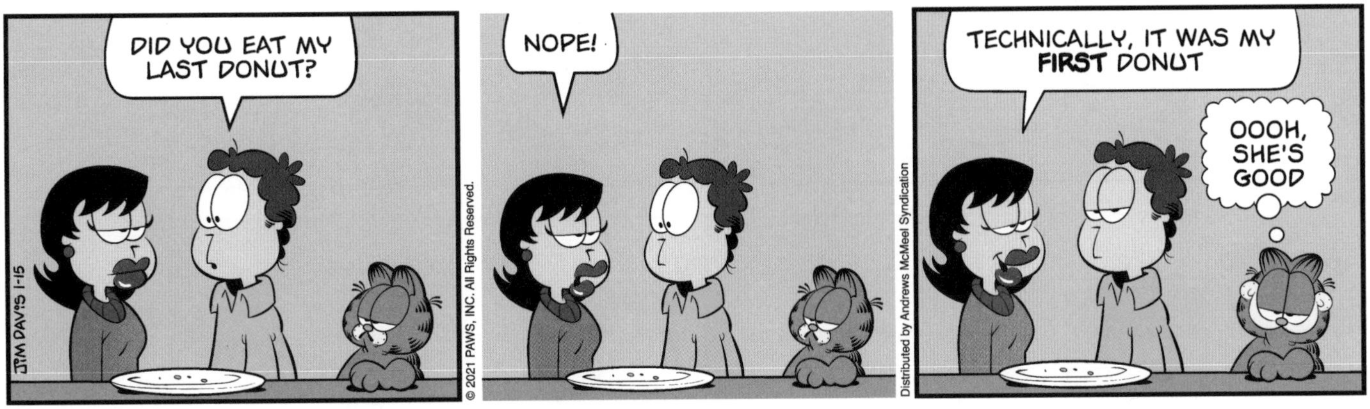
DID YOU EAT MY LAST DONUT?
JIM DAVIS 1-15
© 2021 PAWS, INC. All Rights Reserved.
NOPE!
Distributed by Andrews McMeel Syndication
TECHNICALLY, IT WAS MY **FIRST** DONUT
OOOH, SHE'S GOOD

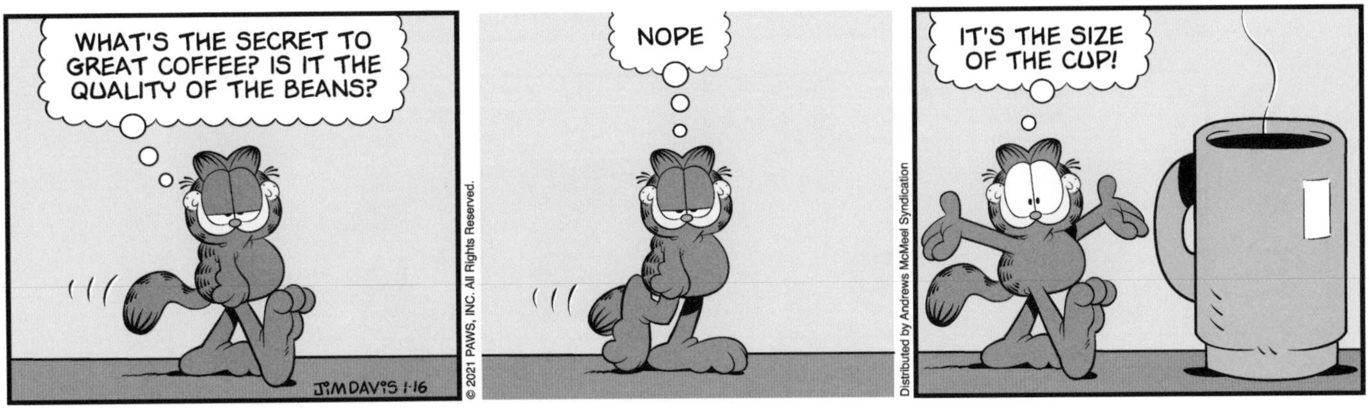
WHAT'S THE SECRET TO GREAT COFFEE? IS IT THE QUALITY OF THE BEANS?
JIM DAVIS 1-16
© 2021 PAWS, INC. All Rights Reserved.
NOPE
Distributed by Andrews McMeel Syndication
IT'S THE SIZE OF THE CUP!

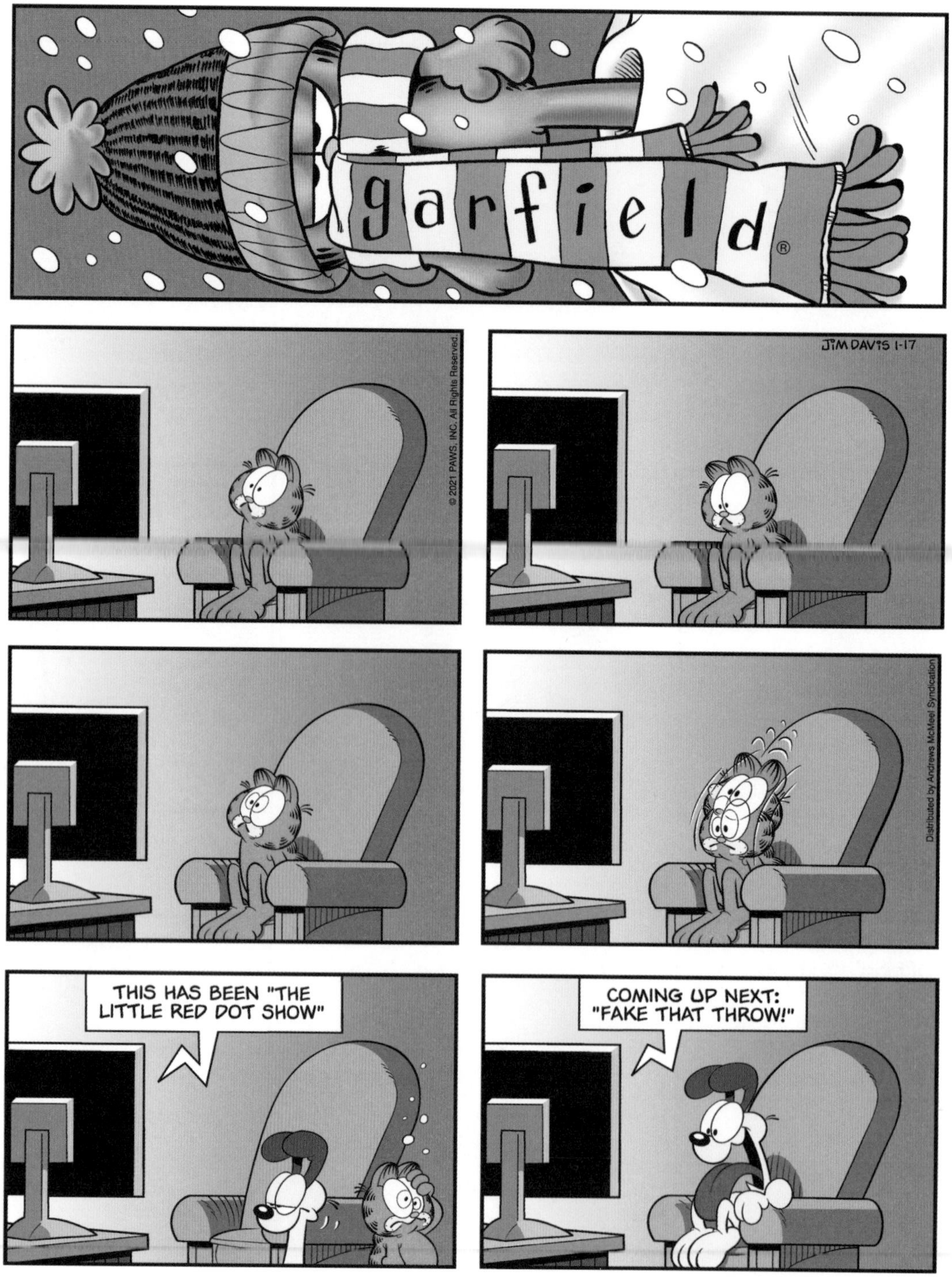
garfield®
JIM DAVIS 1-17
© 2021 PAWS, INC. All Rights Reserved.
Distributed by Andrews McMeel Syndication
THIS HAS BEEN "THE LITTLE RED DOT SHOW"
COMING UP NEXT: "FAKE THAT THROW!"

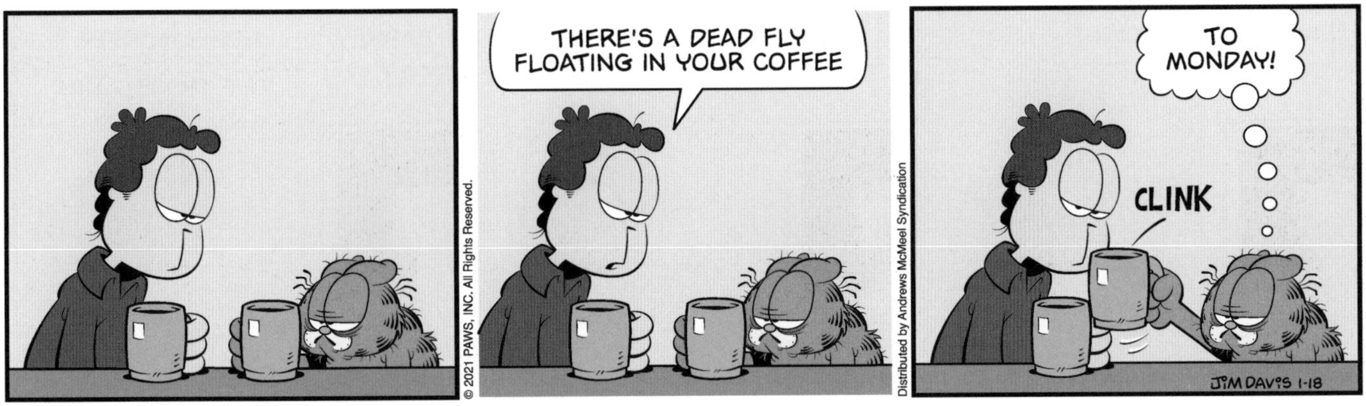
THERE'S A DEAD FLY FLOATING IN YOUR COFFEE
CLINK
TO MONDAY!
JIM DAVIS 1-18
© 2021 PAWS, INC. All Rights Reserved.
Distributed by Andrews McMeel Syndication

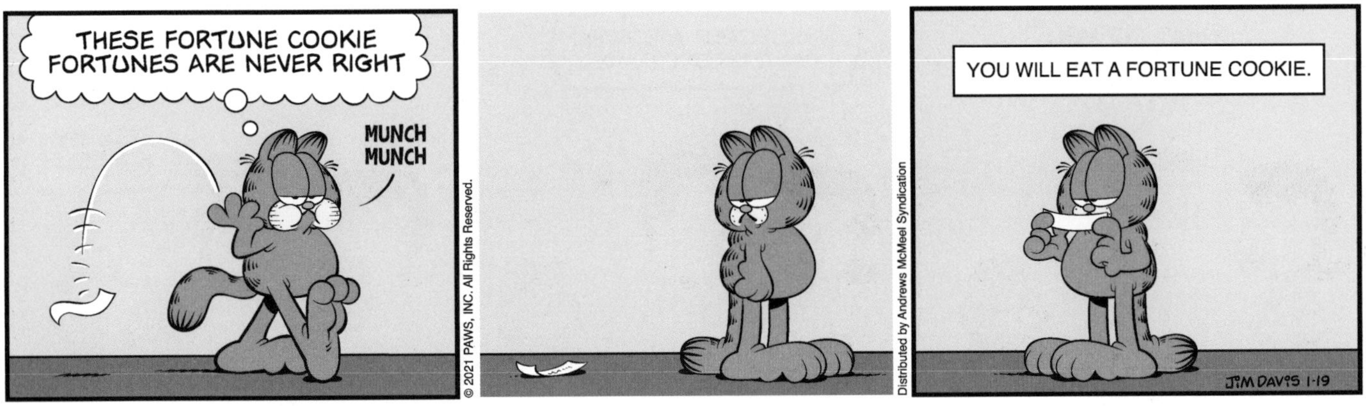
THESE FORTUNE COOKIE FORTUNES ARE NEVER RIGHT
MUNCH MUNCH
YOU WILL EAT A FORTUNE COOKIE.
JIM DAVIS 1-19
© 2021 PAWS, INC. All Rights Reserved.
Distributed by Andrews McMeel Syndication

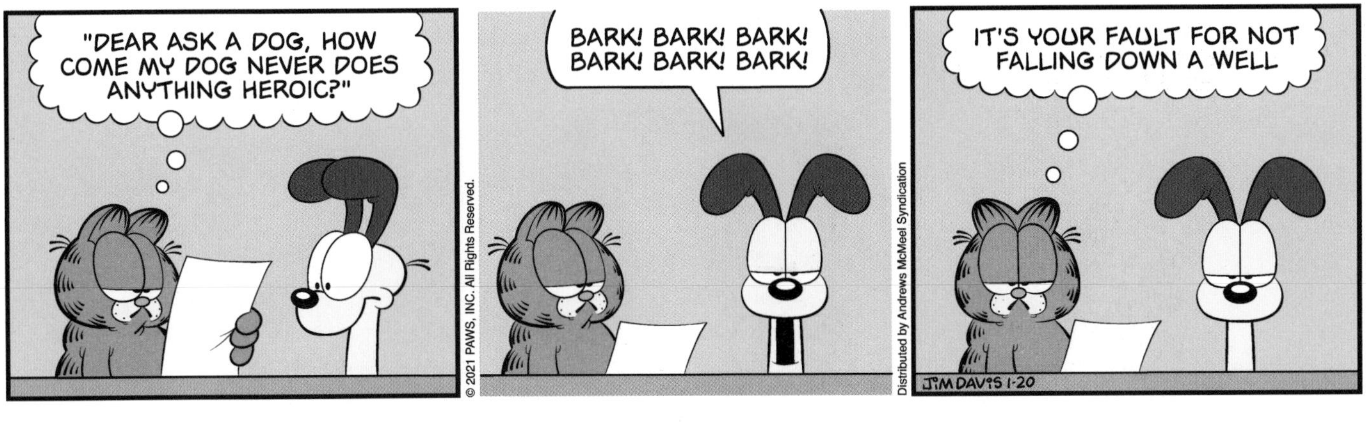
"DEAR ASK A DOG, HOW COME MY DOG NEVER DOES ANYTHING HEROIC?"
BARK! BARK! BARK! BARK! BARK! BARK!
IT'S YOUR FAULT FOR NOT FALLING DOWN A WELL
JIM DAVIS 1-20
© 2021 PAWS, INC. All Rights Reserved.
Distributed by Andrews McMeel Syndication

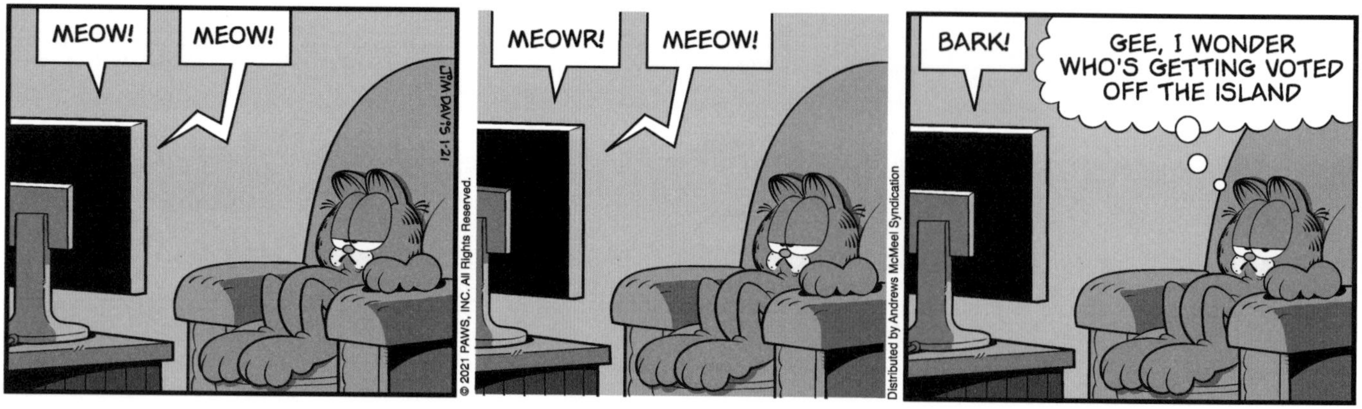
MEOW!
MEOW!
JIM DAVIS 1-21
© 2021 PAWS, INC. All Rights Reserved.
MEOWR!
MEEOW!
Distributed by Andrews McMeel Syndication
BARK!
GEE, I WONDER WHO'S GETTING VOTED OFF THE ISLAND

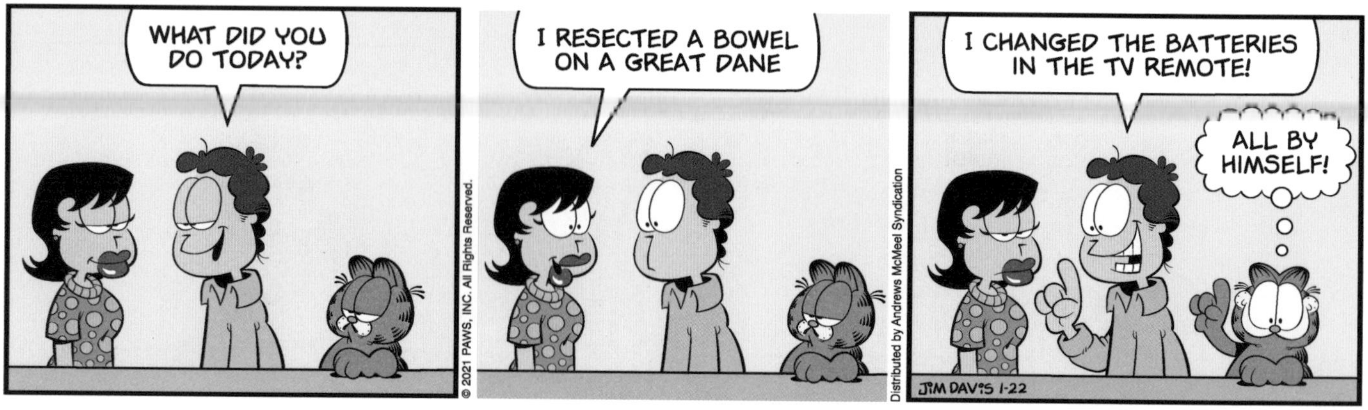
WHAT DID YOU DO TODAY?
© 2021 PAWS, INC. All Rights Reserved.
I RESECTED A BOWEL ON A GREAT DANE
Distributed by Andrews McMeel Syndication
I CHANGED THE BATTERIES IN THE TV REMOTE!
ALL BY HIMSELF!
JIM DAVIS 1-22

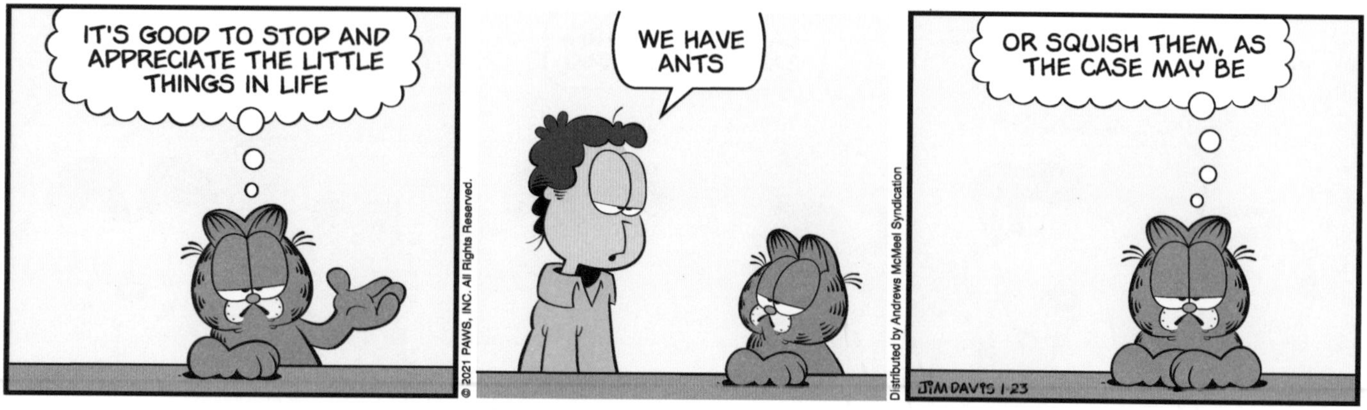
IT'S GOOD TO STOP AND APPRECIATE THE LITTLE THINGS IN LIFE
© 2021 PAWS, INC. All Rights Reserved.
WE HAVE ANTS
Distributed by Andrews McMeel Syndication
OR SQUISH THEM, AS THE CASE MAY BE
JIM DAVIS 1-23

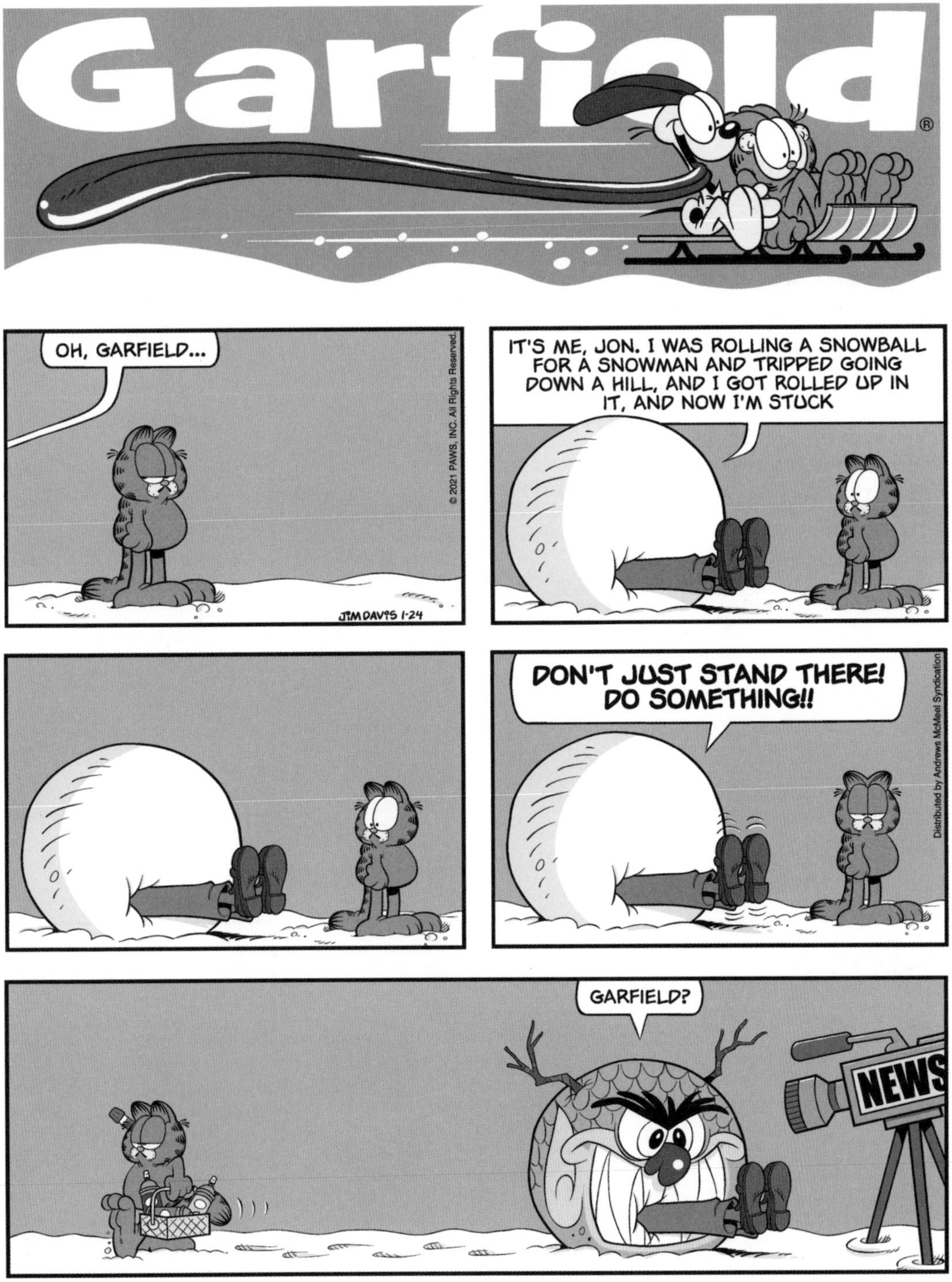
Garfield®
OH, GARFIELD...
© 2021 PAWS, INC. All Rights Reserved.
JIM DAVIS 1-24
IT'S ME, JON. I WAS ROLLING A SNOWBALL FOR A SNOWMAN AND TRIPPED GOING DOWN A HILL, AND I GOT ROLLED UP IN IT, AND NOW I'M STUCK
DON'T JUST STAND THERE! DO SOMETHING!!
Distributed by Andrews McMeel Syndication
GARFIELD?
NEWS

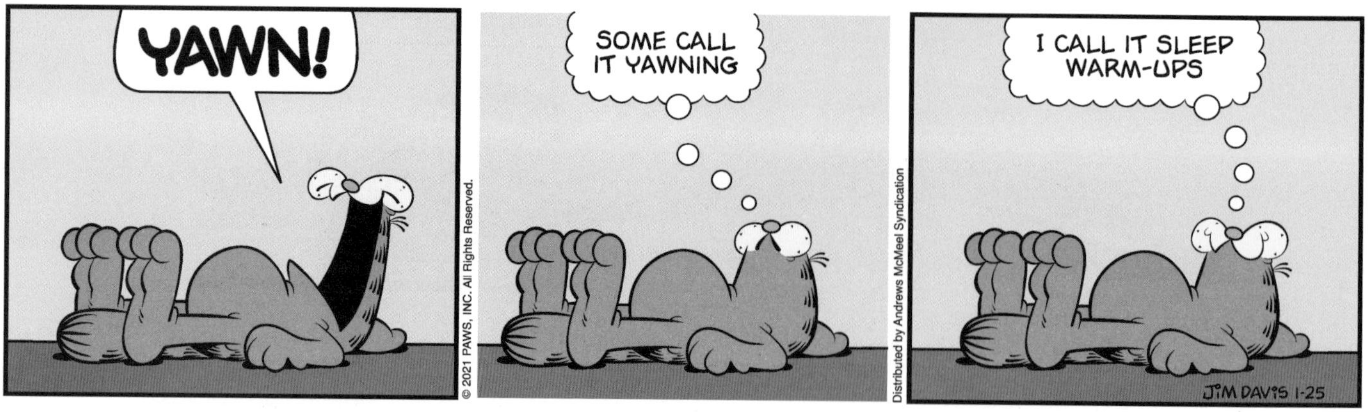
YAWN!
SOME CALL IT YAWNING
I CALL IT SLEEP WARM-UPS
© 2021 PAWS, INC. All Rights Reserved.
Distributed by Andrews McMeel Syndication
JIM DAVIS 1-25

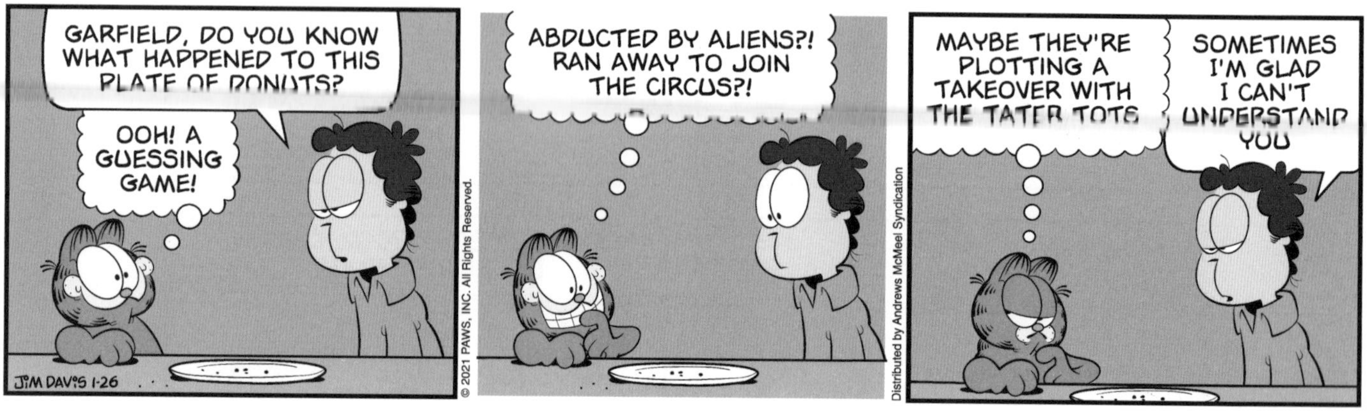
GARFIELD, DO YOU KNOW WHAT HAPPENED TO THIS PLATE OF DONUTS?
OOH! A GUESSING GAME!
ABDUCTED BY ALIENS?! RAN AWAY TO JOIN THE CIRCUS?!
MAYBE THEY'RE PLOTTING A TAKEOVER WITH THE TATER TOTS
SOMETIMES I'M GLAD I CAN'T UNDERSTAND YOU
JIM DAVIS 1-26
© 2021 PAWS, INC. All Rights Reserved.
Distributed by Andrews McMeel Syndication

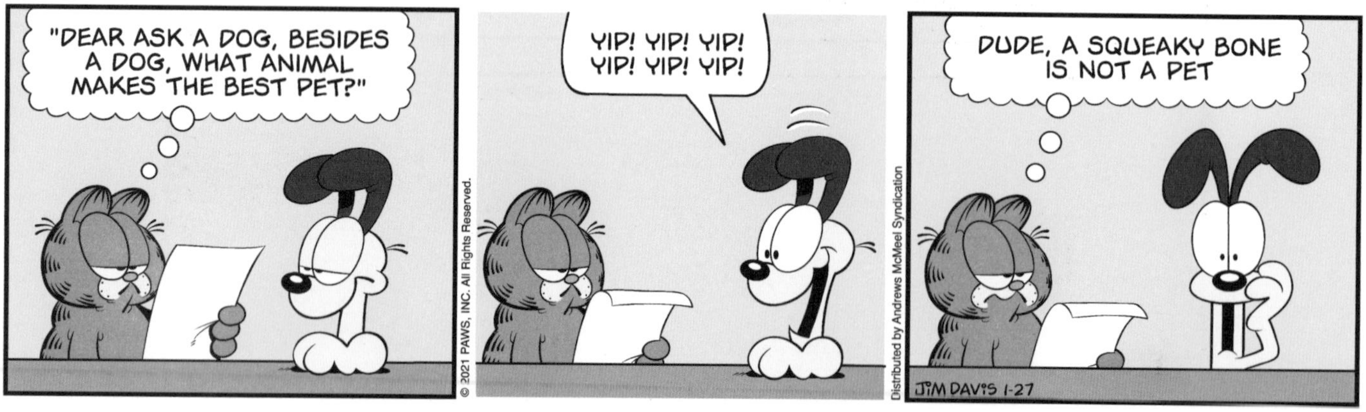
"DEAR ASK A DOG, BESIDES A DOG, WHAT ANIMAL MAKES THE BEST PET?"
YIP! YIP! YIP! YIP! YIP! YIP!
DUDE, A SQUEAKY BONE IS NOT A PET
© 2021 PAWS, INC. All Rights Reserved.
Distributed by Andrews McMeel Syndication
JIM DAVIS 1-27

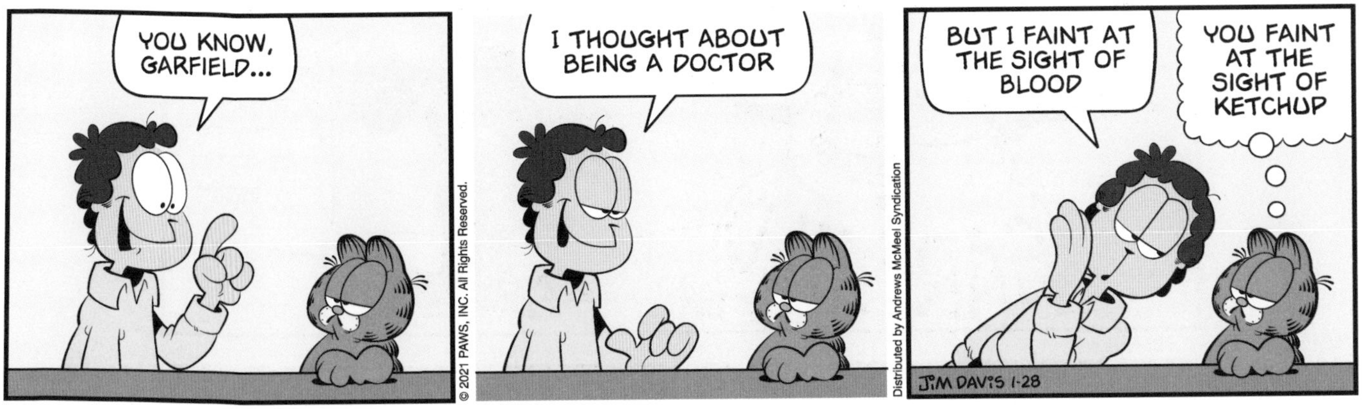
YOU KNOW, GARFIELD...
I THOUGHT ABOUT BEING A DOCTOR
BUT I FAINT AT THE SIGHT OF BLOOD
YOU FAINT AT THE SIGHT OF KETCHUP
© 2021 PAWS, INC. All Rights Reserved.
Distributed by Andrews McMeel Syndication
JIM DAVIS 1-28

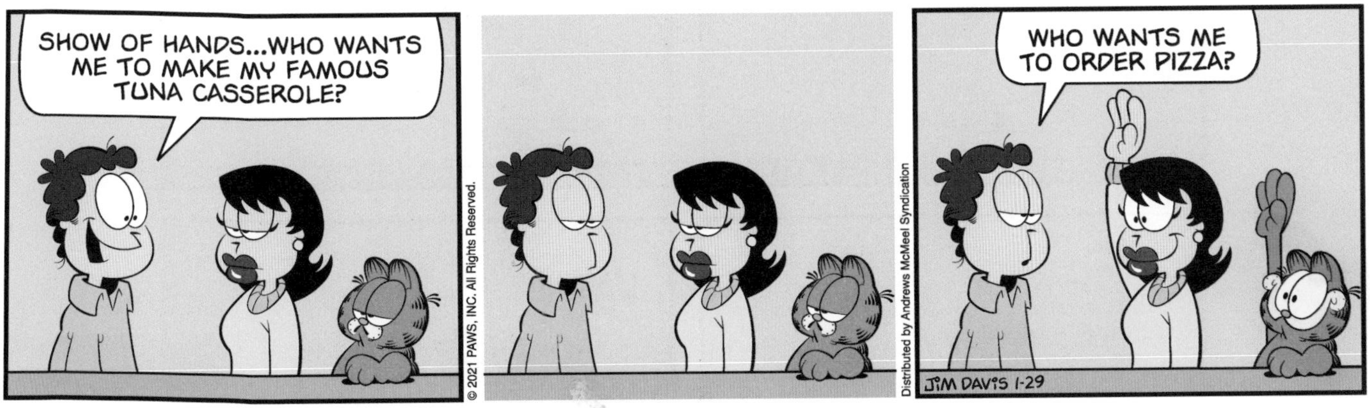
SHOW OF HANDS...WHO WANTS ME TO MAKE MY FAMOUS TUNA CASSEROLE?
WHO WANTS ME TO ORDER PIZZA?
© 2021 PAWS, INC. All Rights Reserved.
Distributed by Andrews McMeel Syndication
JIM DAVIS 1-29

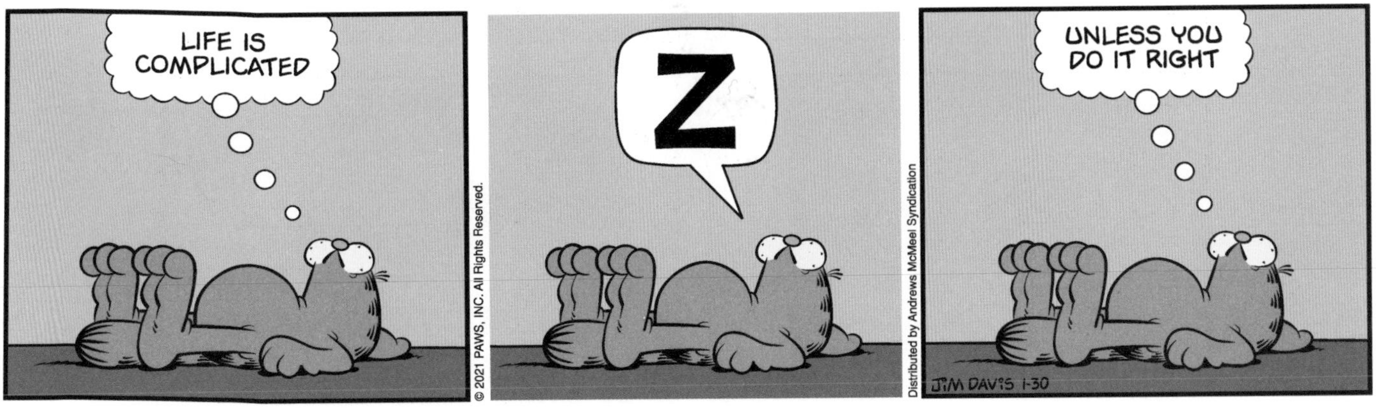
LIFE IS COMPLICATED
Z
UNLESS YOU DO IT RIGHT
© 2021 PAWS, INC. All Rights Reserved.
Distributed by Andrews McMeel Syndication
JIM DAVIS 1-30

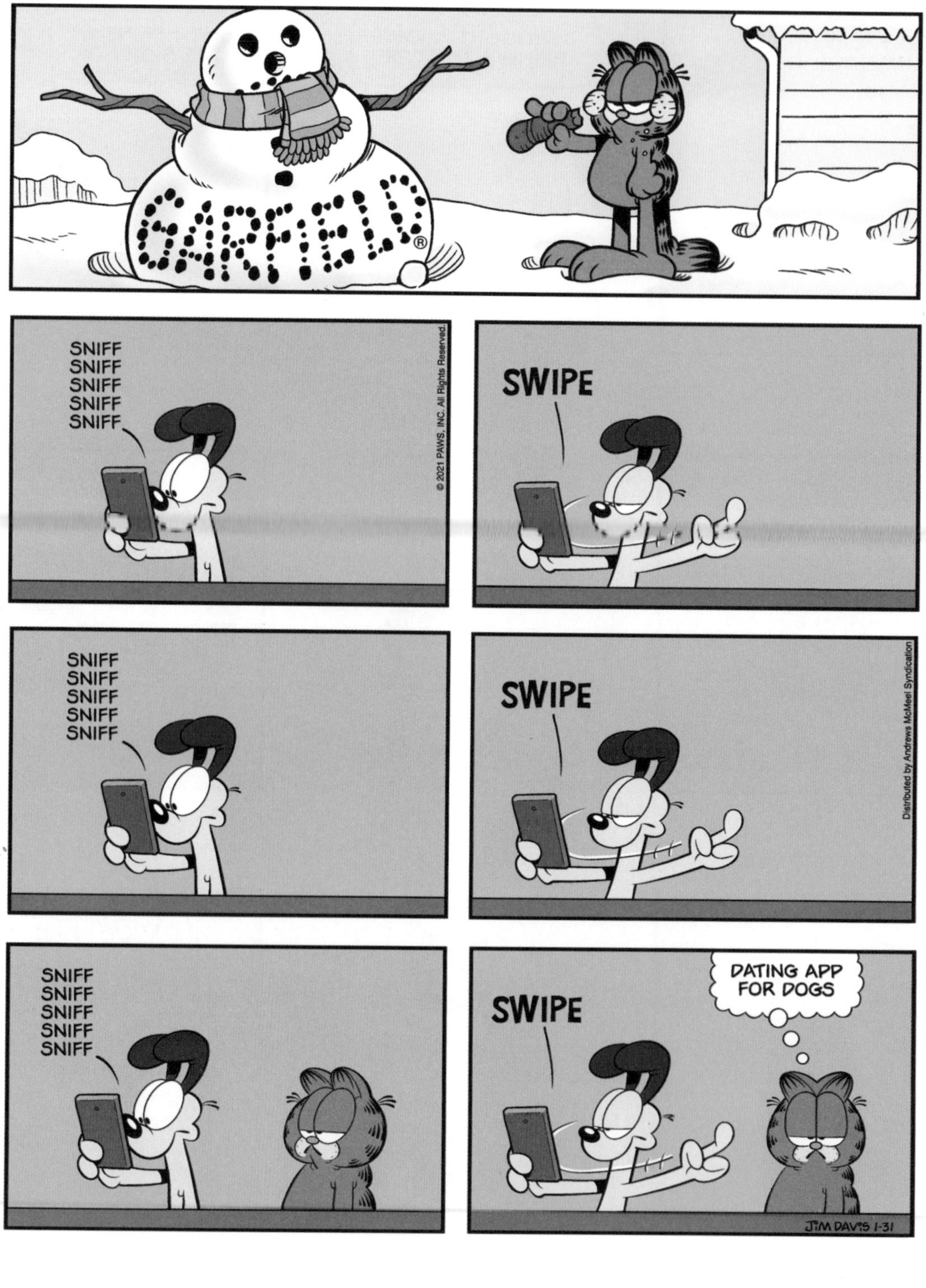
GARFIELD®
© 2021 PAWS, INC. All Rights Reserved.
SNIFF
SNIFF
SNIFF
SNIFF
SNIFF
SWIPE
SNIFF
SNIFF
SNIFF
SNIFF
SNIFF
SWIPE
Distributed by Andrews McMeel Syndication
SNIFF
SNIFF
SNIFF
SNIFF
SNIFF
SWIPE
DATING APP
FOR DOGS
JIM DAVIS 1-31

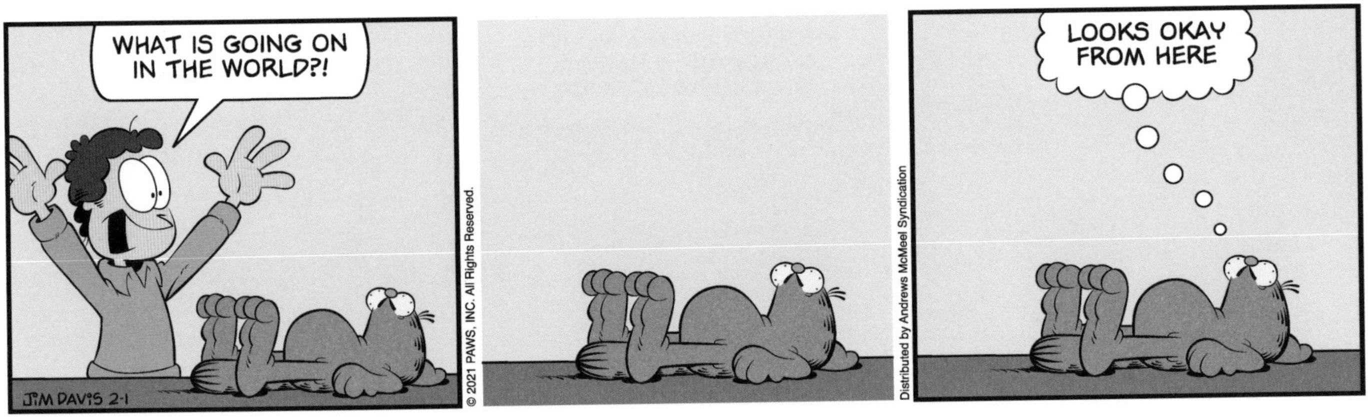
WHAT IS GOING ON IN THE WORLD?!
LOOKS OKAY FROM HERE
JIM DAVIS 2-1
© 2021 PAWS, INC. All Rights Reserved.
Distributed by Andrews McMeel Syndication

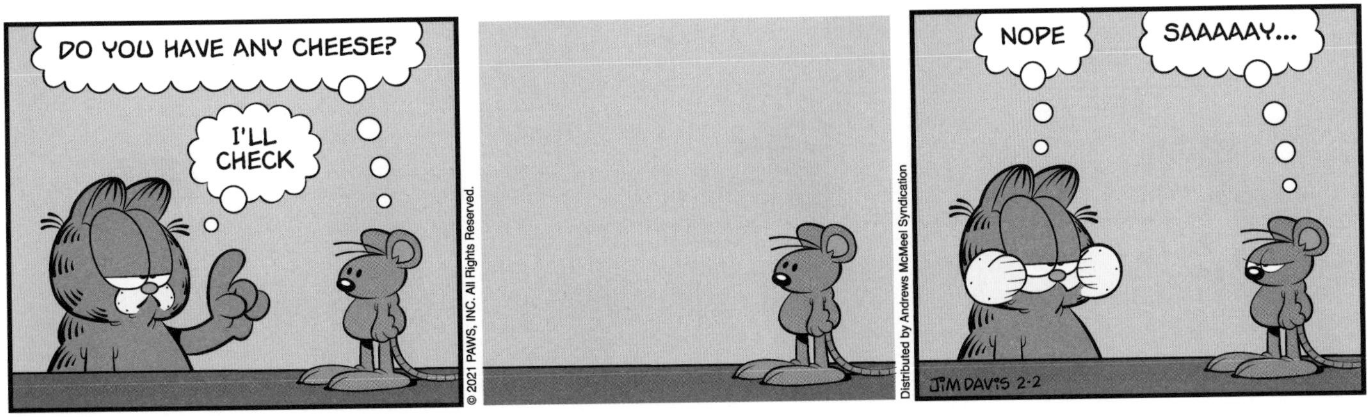
DO YOU HAVE ANY CHEESE?
I'LL CHECK
NOPE
SAAAAAY...
JIM DAVIS 2-2
© 2021 PAWS, INC. All Rights Reserved.
Distributed by Andrews McMeel Syndication

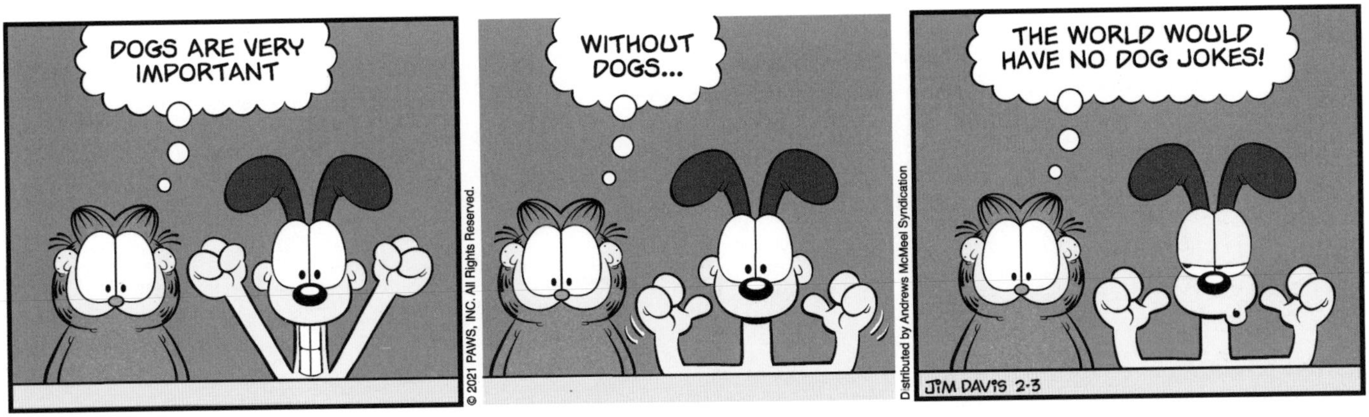
DOGS ARE VERY IMPORTANT
WITHOUT DOGS...
THE WORLD WOULD HAVE NO DOG JOKES!
JIM DAVIS 2-3
© 2021 PAWS, INC. All Rights Reserved.
Distributed by Andrews McMeel Syndication

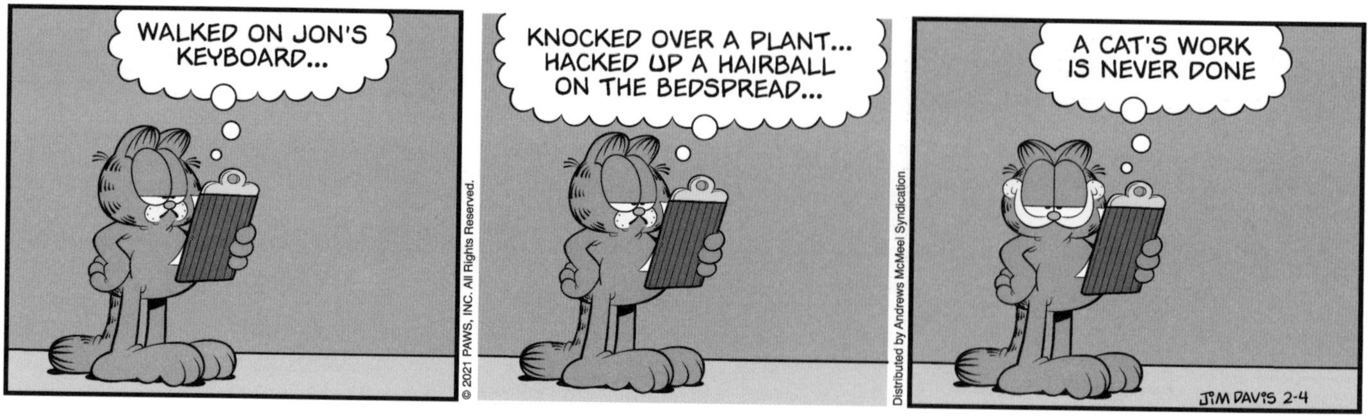
WALKED ON JON'S KEYBOARD...
KNOCKED OVER A PLANT... HACKED UP A HAIRBALL ON THE BEDSPREAD...
A CAT'S WORK IS NEVER DONE
© 2021 PAWS, INC. All Rights Reserved.
Distributed by Andrews McMeel Syndication
JIM DAVIS 2-4

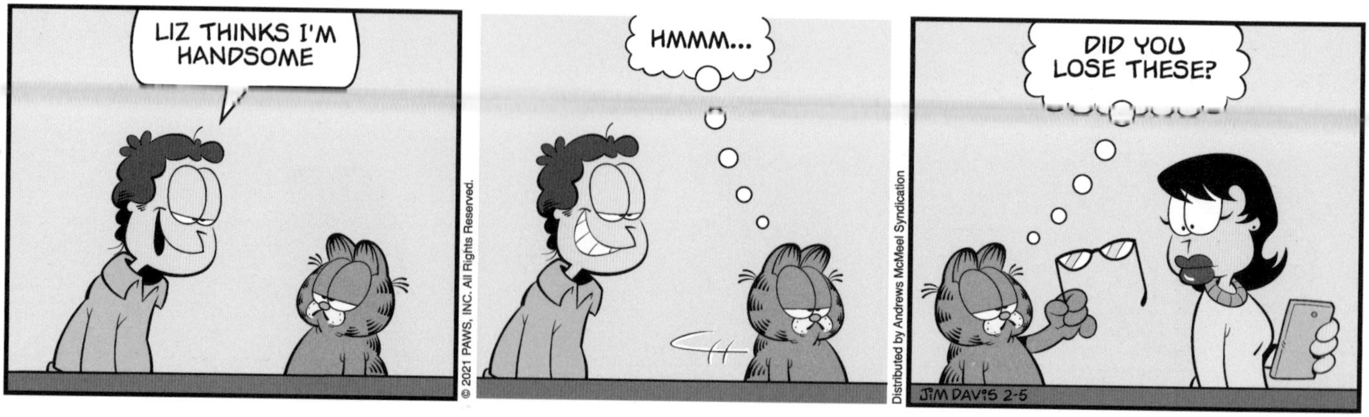
LIZ THINKS I'M HANDSOME
HMMM...
DID YOU LOSE THESE?
© 2021 PAWS, INC. All Rights Reserved.
Distributed by Andrews McMeel Syndication
JIM DAVIS 2-5

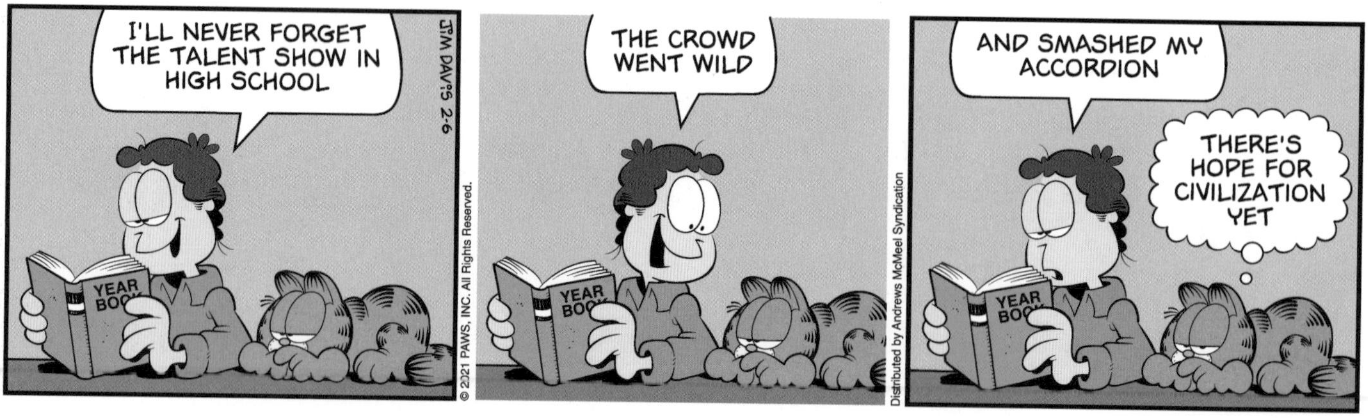
I'LL NEVER FORGET THE TALENT SHOW IN HIGH SCHOOL
YEAR BOOK
THE CROWD WENT WILD
AND SMASHED MY ACCORDION
THERE'S HOPE FOR CIVILIZATION YET
JIM DAVIS 2-6
© 2021 PAWS, INC. All Rights Reserved.
Distributed by Andrews McMeel Syndication

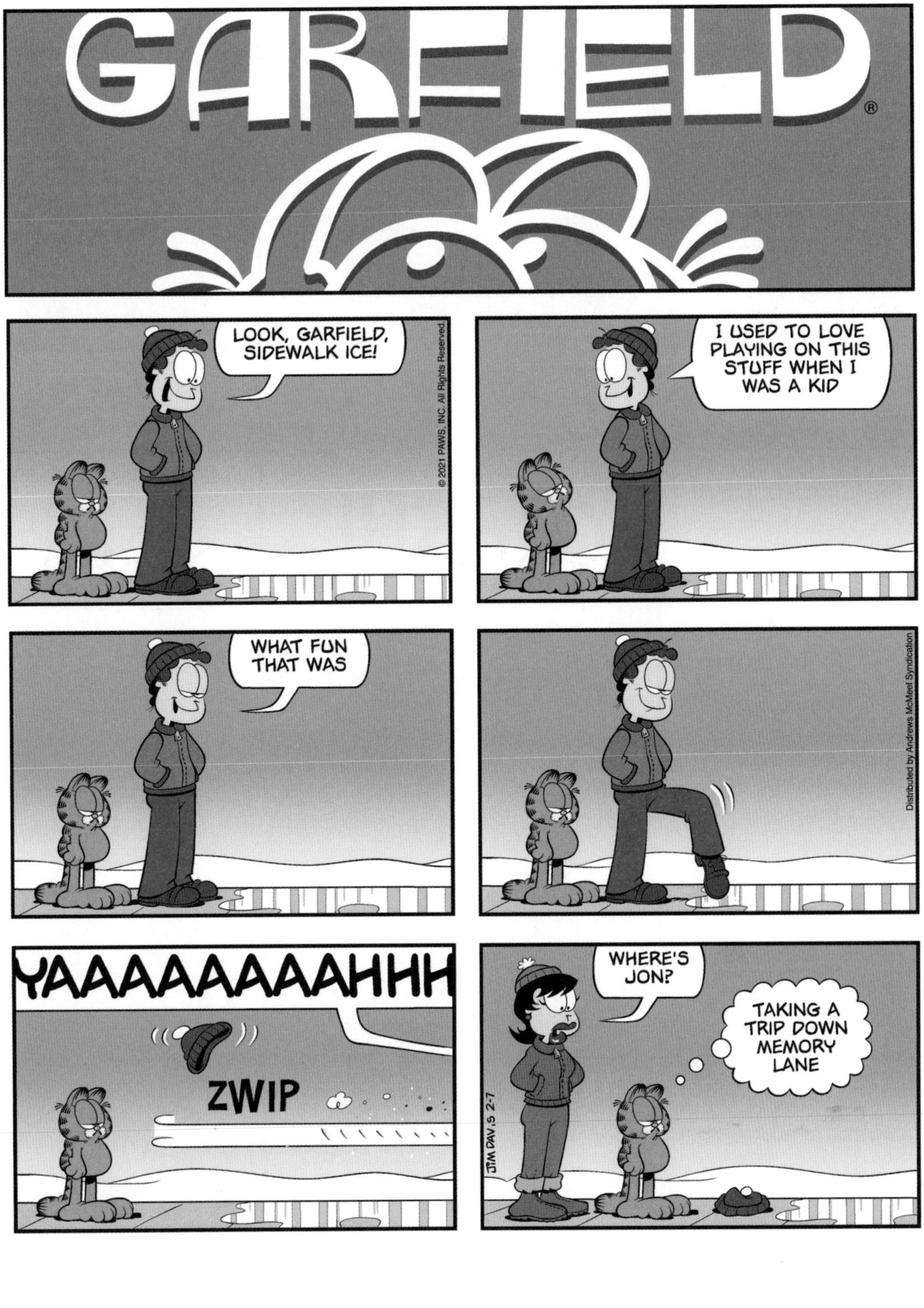
GARFIELD®
LOOK, GARFIELD, SIDEWALK ICE!
© 2021 PAWS, INC. All Rights Reserved.
I USED TO LOVE PLAYING ON THIS STUFF WHEN I WAS A KID
WHAT FUN THAT WAS
Distributed by Andrews McMeel Syndication
YAAAAAAAAHHH
ZWIP
JIM DAVIS 2-7
WHERE'S JON?
TAKING A TRIP DOWN MEMORY LANE

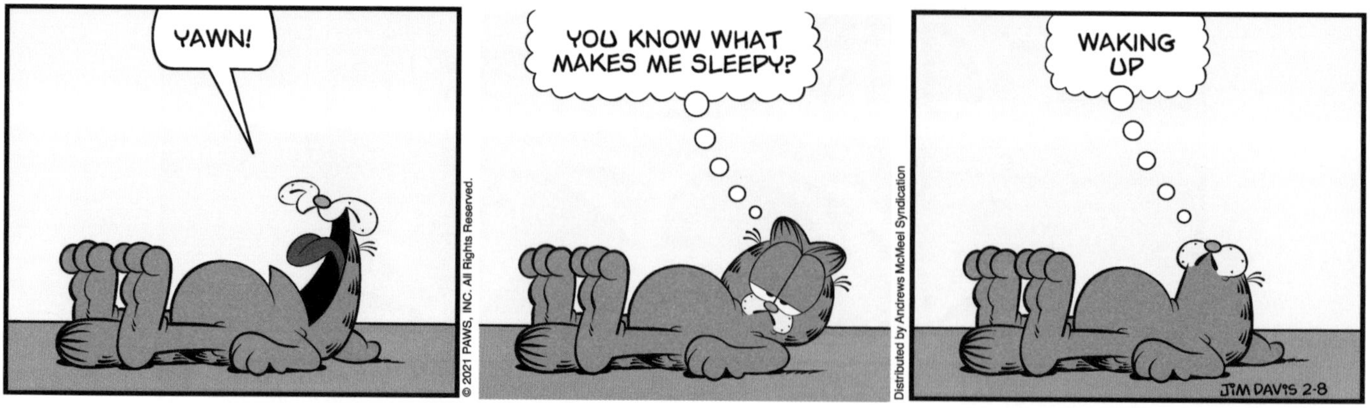
YAWN!
YOU KNOW WHAT MAKES ME SLEEPY?
WAKING UP
JIM DAVIS 2-8

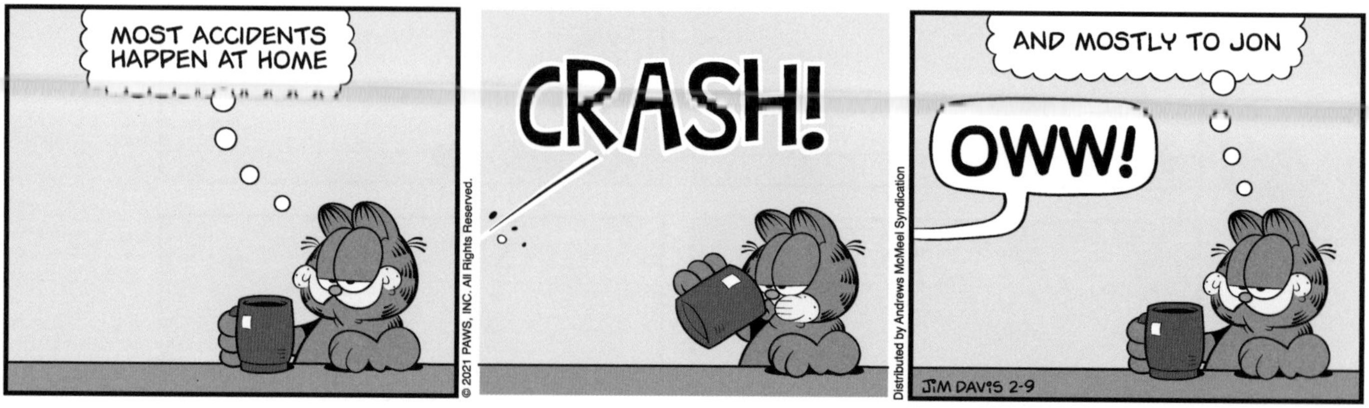
MOST ACCIDENTS HAPPEN AT HOME
CRASH!
AND MOSTLY TO JON
OWW!
JIM DAVIS 2-9

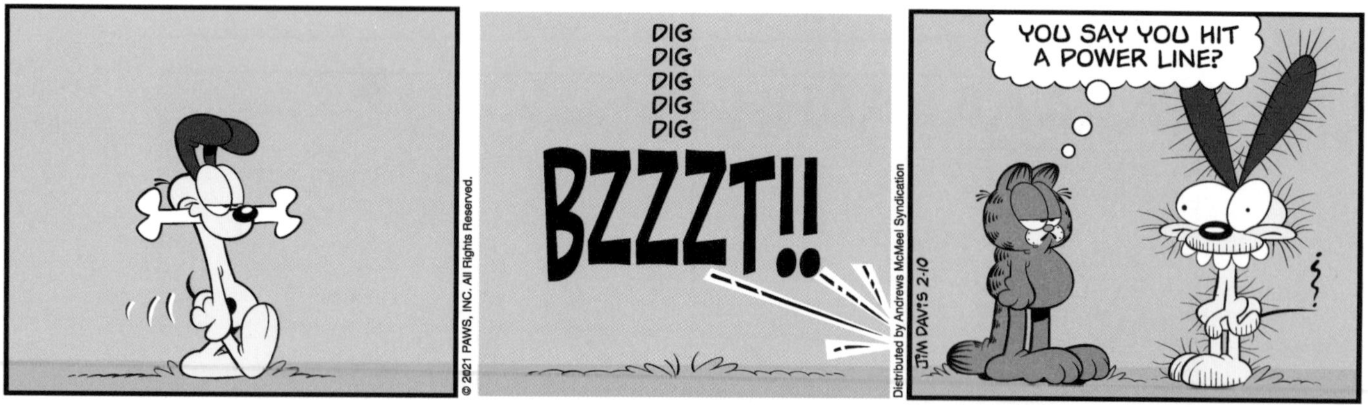
DIG
DIG
DIG
DIG
DIG
BZZZT!!
YOU SAY YOU HIT A POWER LINE?
JIM DAVIS 2-10

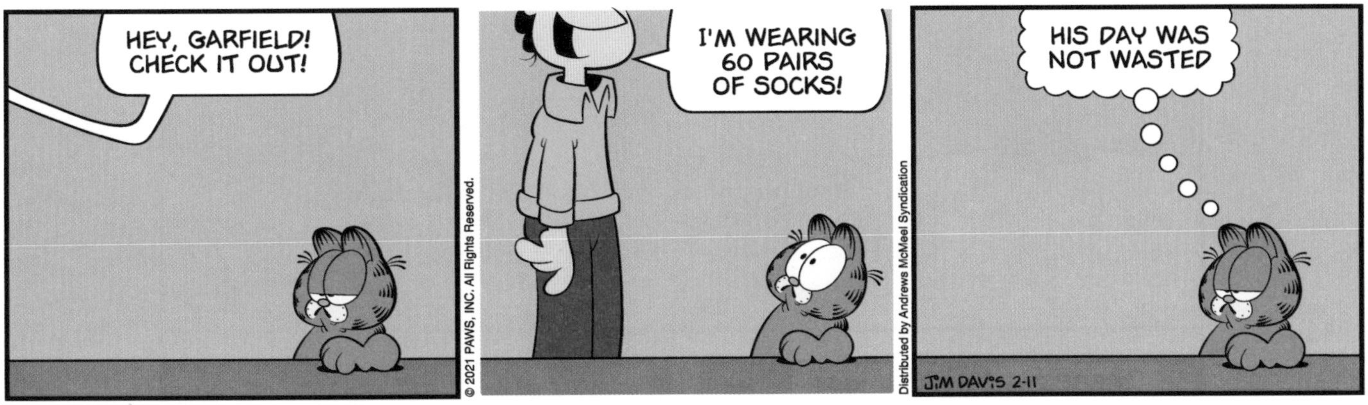

HEY, GARFIELD! CHECK IT OUT!
I'M WEARING 60 PAIRS OF SOCKS!
HIS DAY WAS NOT WASTED
© 2021 PAWS, INC. All Rights Reserved.
Distributed by Andrews McMeel Syndication
JIM DAVIS 2-11

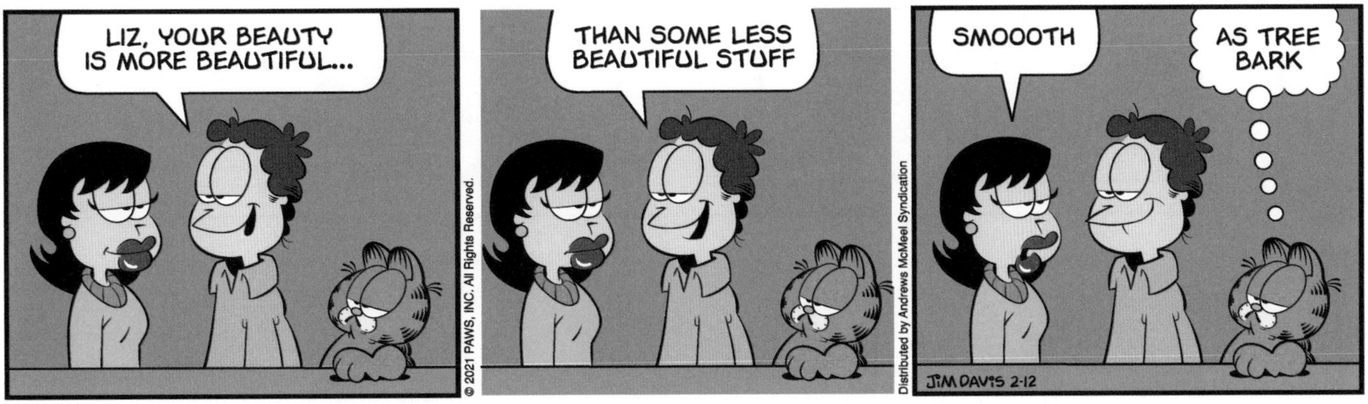

LIZ, YOUR BEAUTY IS MORE BEAUTIFUL...
THAN SOME LESS BEAUTIFUL STUFF
SMOOOTH
AS TREE BARK
© 2021 PAWS, INC. All Rights Reserved.
Distributed by Andrews McMeel Syndication
JIM DAVIS 2-12

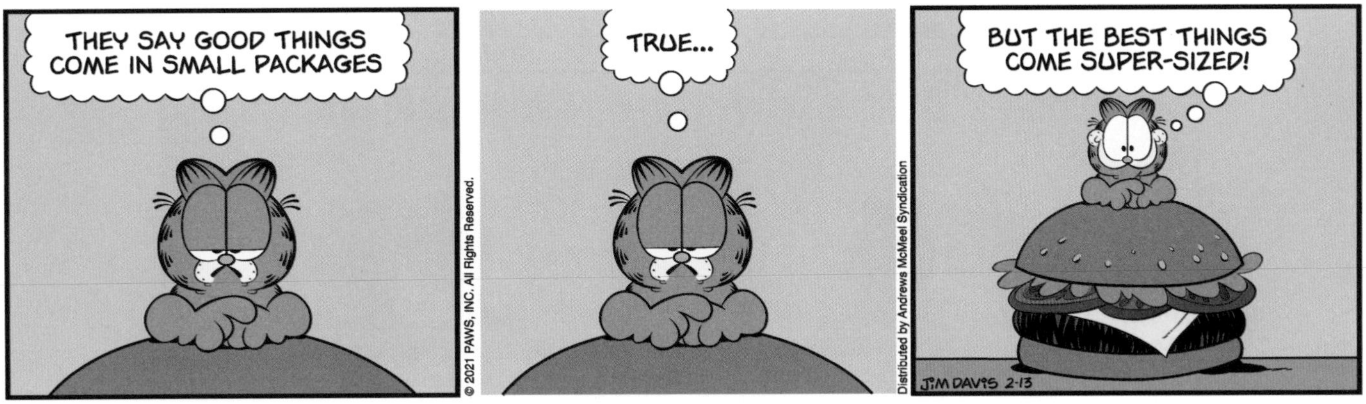

THEY SAY GOOD THINGS COME IN SMALL PACKAGES
TRUE...
BUT THE BEST THINGS COME SUPER-SIZED!
© 2021 PAWS, INC. All Rights Reserved.
Distributed by Andrews McMeel Syndication
JIM DAVIS 2-13

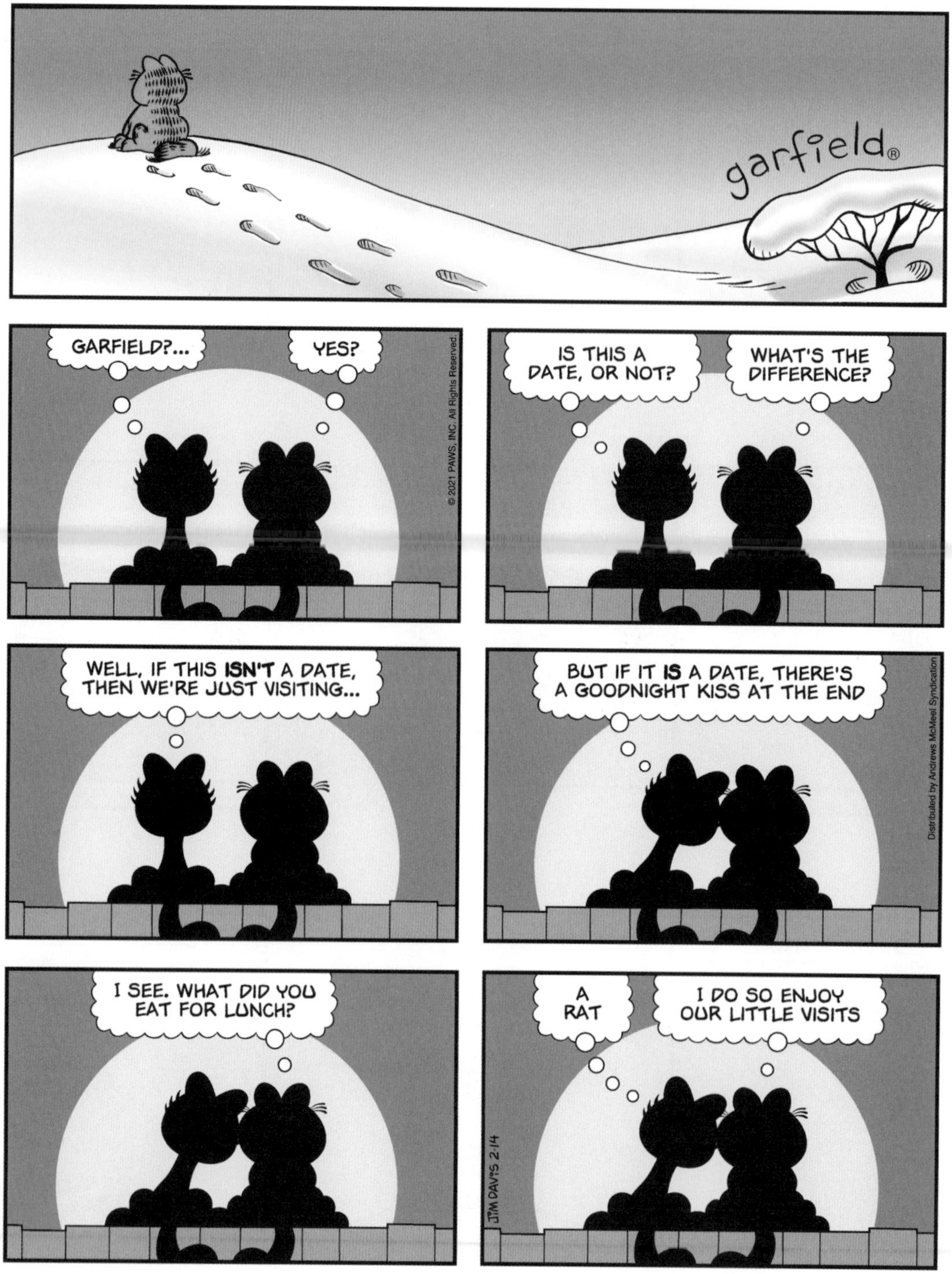
garfield®
GARFIELD?...
YES?
© 2021 PAWS, INC. All Rights Reserved.
IS THIS A DATE, OR NOT?
WHAT'S THE DIFFERENCE?
WELL, IF THIS **ISN'T** A DATE, THEN WE'RE JUST VISITING...
BUT IF IT **IS** A DATE, THERE'S A GOODNIGHT KISS AT THE END
Distributed by Andrews McMeel Syndication
I SEE. WHAT DID YOU EAT FOR LUNCH?
JIM DAVIS 2-14
A RAT
I DO SO ENJOY OUR LITTLE VISITS

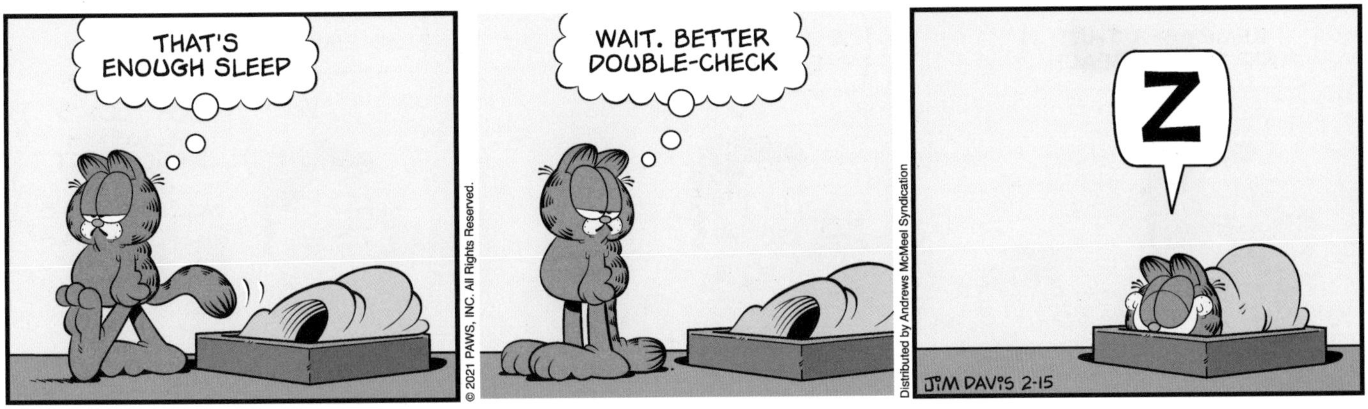
THAT'S ENOUGH SLEEP
© 2021 PAWS, INC. All Rights Reserved.
WAIT. BETTER DOUBLE-CHECK
Distributed by Andrews McMeel Syndication
Z
JIM DAVIS 2-15

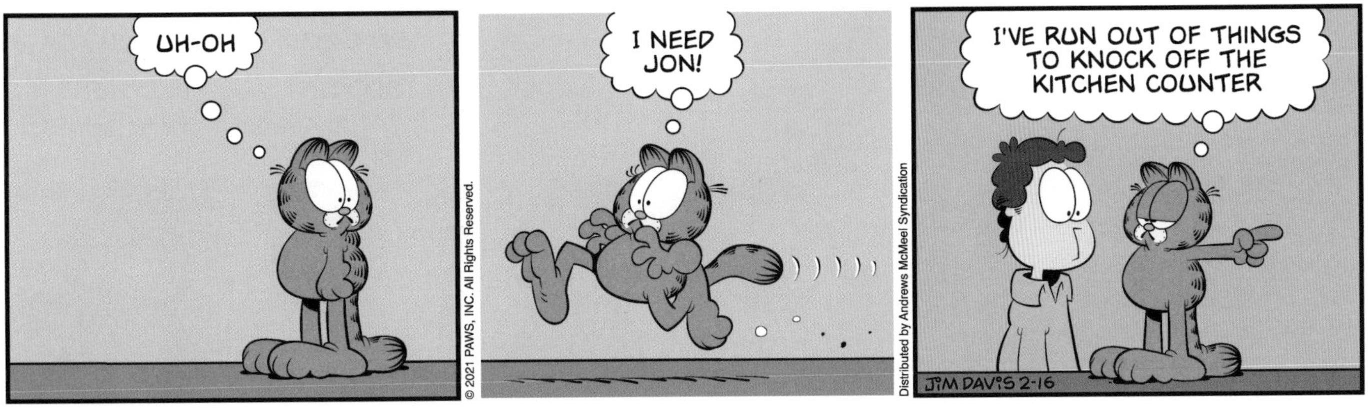
UH-OH
© 2021 PAWS, INC. All Rights Reserved.
I NEED JON!
Distributed by Andrews McMeel Syndication
I'VE RUN OUT OF THINGS TO KNOCK OFF THE KITCHEN COUNTER
JIM DAVIS 2-16

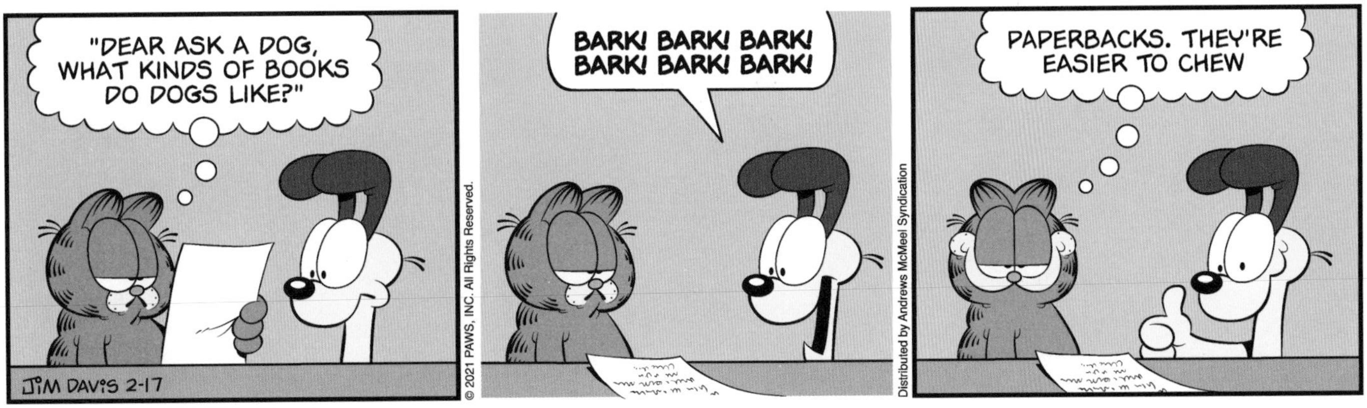
"DEAR ASK A DOG, WHAT KINDS OF BOOKS DO DOGS LIKE?"
JIM DAVIS 2-17
© 2021 PAWS, INC. All Rights Reserved.
BARK! BARK! BARK! BARK! BARK! BARK!
Distributed by Andrews McMeel Syndication
PAPERBACKS. THEY'RE EASIER TO CHEW

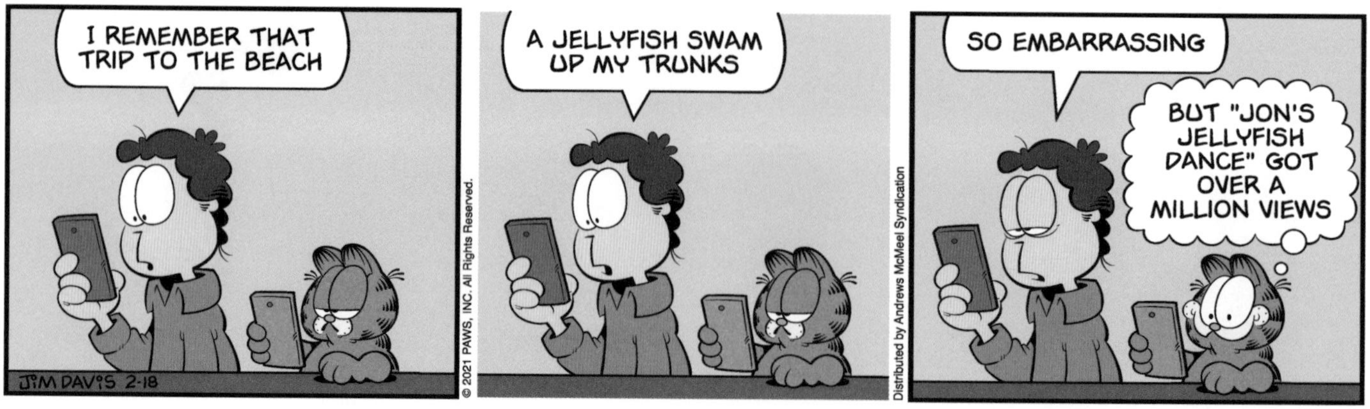
I REMEMBER THAT TRIP TO THE BEACH
JIM DAVIS 2-18
A JELLYFISH SWAM UP MY TRUNKS
SO EMBARRASSING
BUT "JON'S JELLYFISH DANCE" GOT OVER A MILLION VIEWS

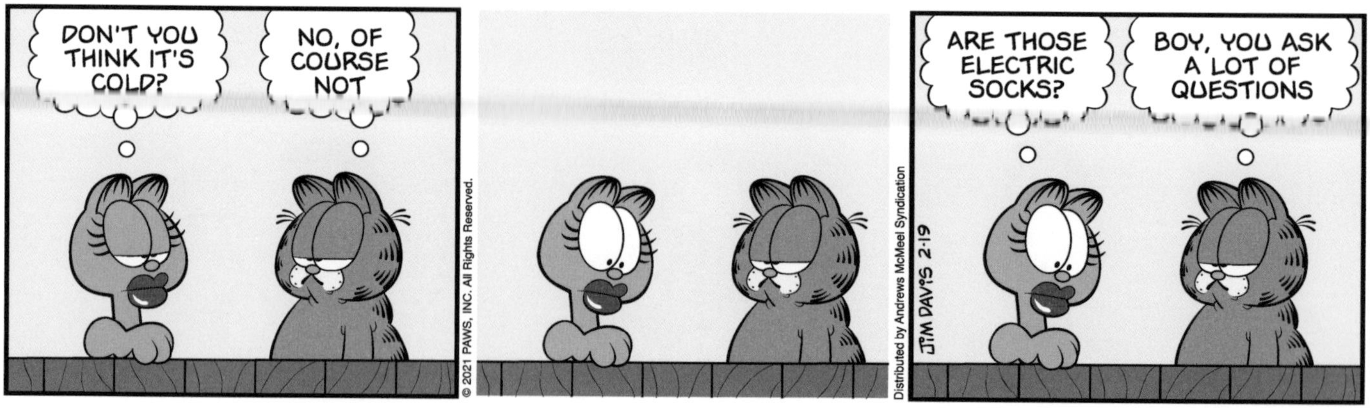
DON'T YOU THINK IT'S COLD?
NO, OF COURSE NOT
JIM DAVIS 2-19
ARE THOSE ELECTRIC SOCKS?
BOY, YOU ASK A LOT OF QUESTIONS

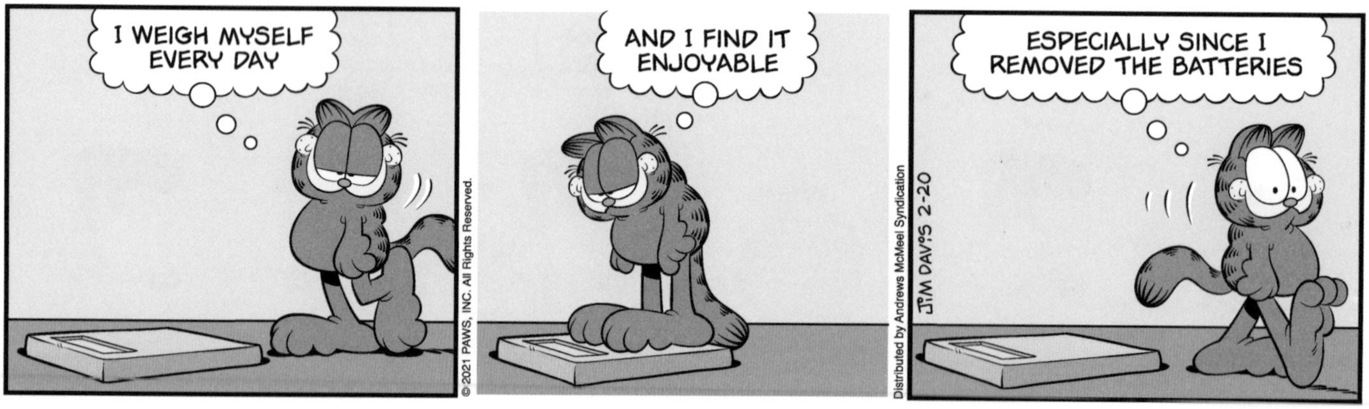
I WEIGH MYSELF EVERY DAY
AND I FIND IT ENJOYABLE
JIM DAVIS 2-20
ESPECIALLY SINCE I REMOVED THE BATTERIES

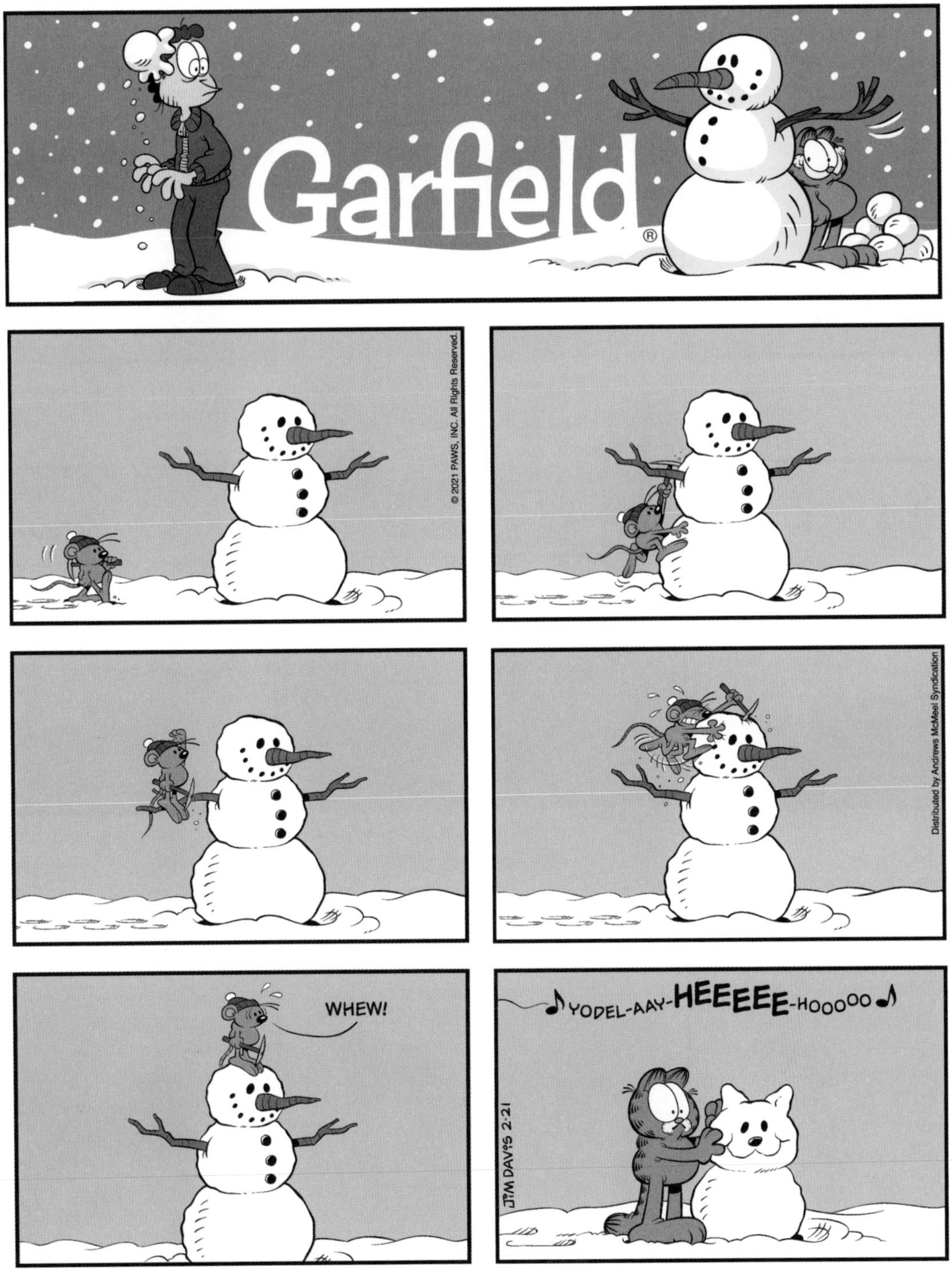
Garfield®
© 2021 PAWS, INC. All Rights Reserved.
Distributed by Andrews McMeel Syndication
WHEW!
♪YODEL-AAY-HEEEEE-HOOOOO♪
JIM DAVIS 2·21

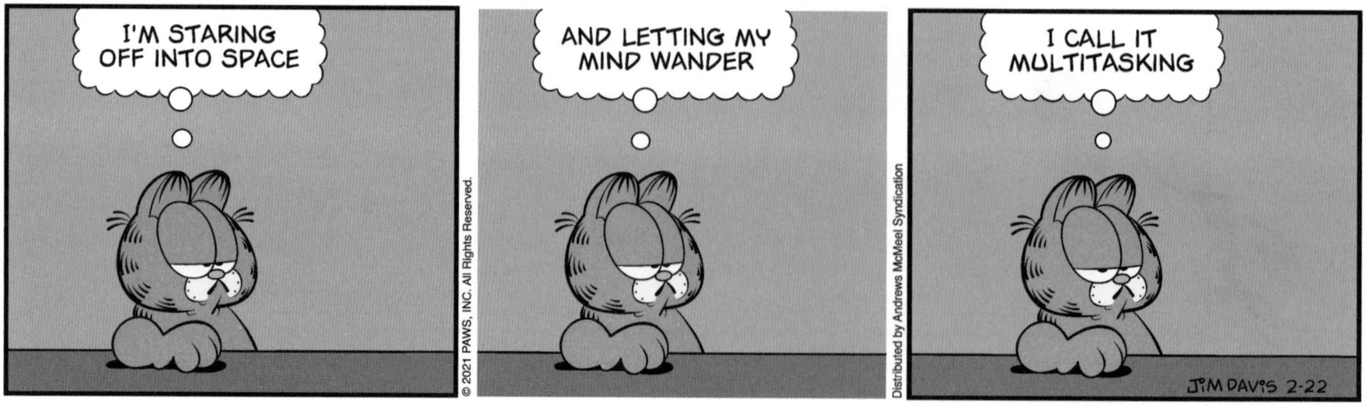
I'M STARING OFF INTO SPACE
© 2021 PAWS, INC. All Rights Reserved.
AND LETTING MY MIND WANDER
Distributed by Andrews McMeel Syndication
I CALL IT MULTITASKING
JIM DAVIS 2-22

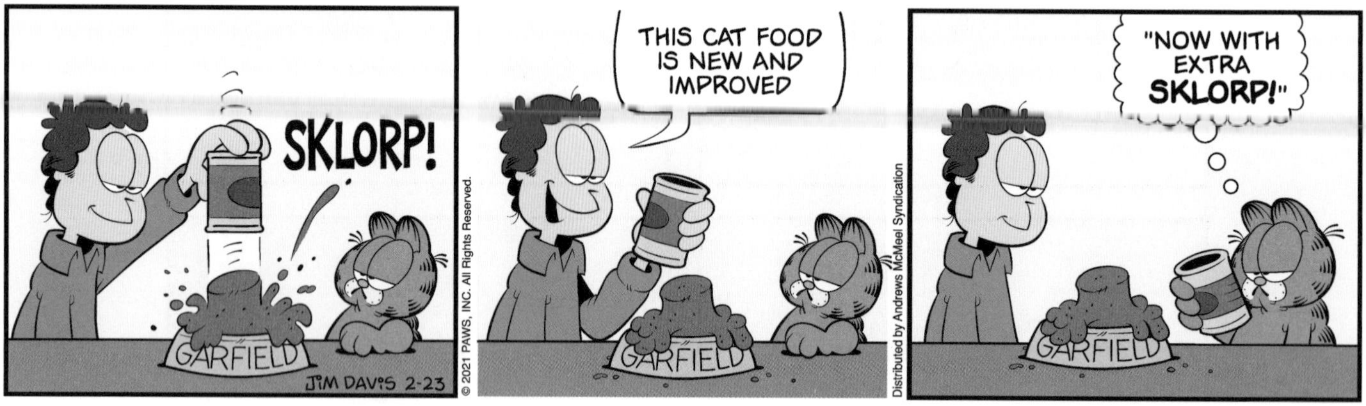
SKLORP!
GARFIELD
JIM DAVIS 2-23
© 2021 PAWS, INC. All Rights Reserved.
THIS CAT FOOD IS NEW AND IMPROVED
GARFIELD
Distributed by Andrews McMeel Syndication
"NOW WITH EXTRA SKLORP!"
GARFIELD

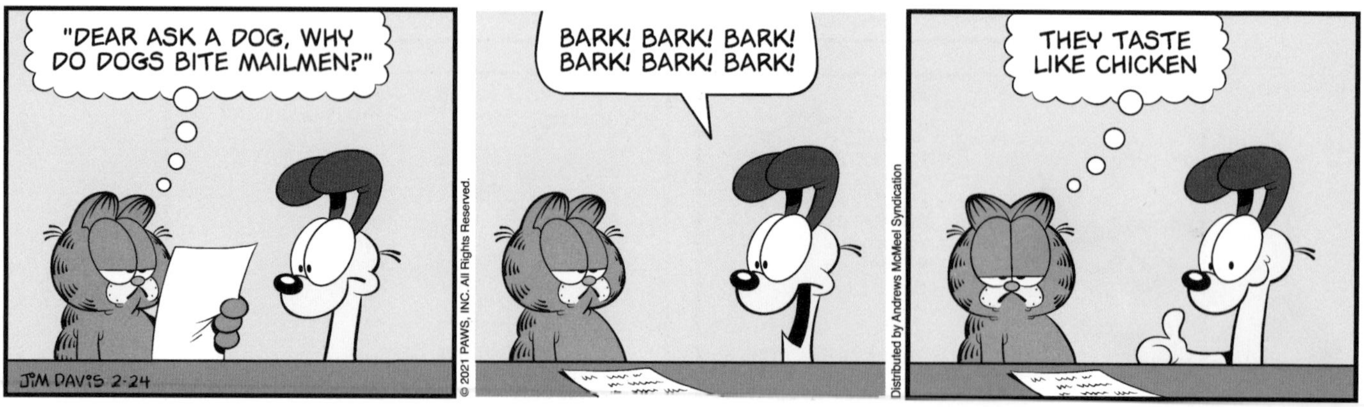
"DEAR ASK A DOG, WHY DO DOGS BITE MAILMEN?"
JIM DAVIS 2-24
© 2021 PAWS, INC. All Rights Reserved.
BARK! BARK! BARK! BARK! BARK! BARK!
Distributed by Andrews McMeel Syndication
THEY TASTE LIKE CHICKEN

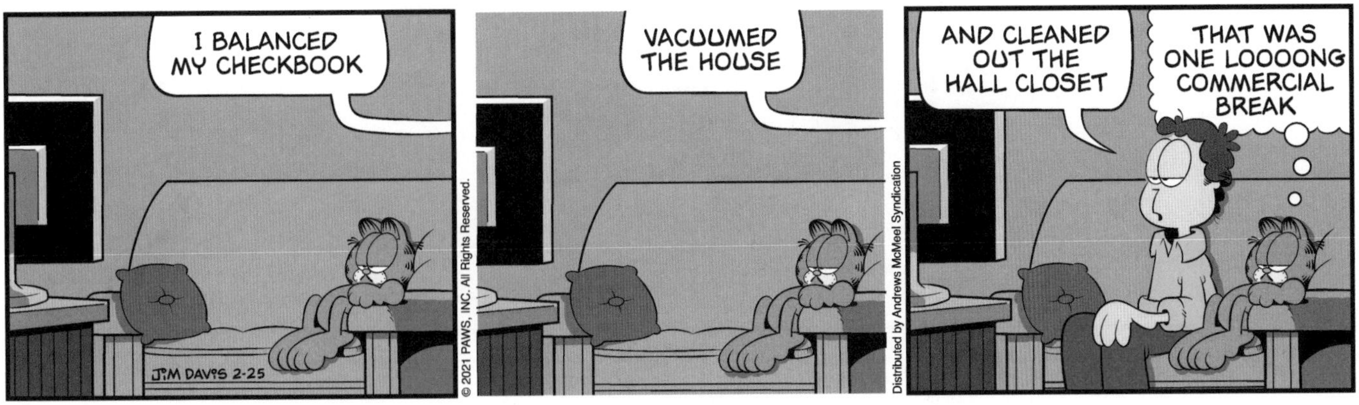
I BALANCED MY CHECKBOOK
JIM DAVIS 2-25
© 2021 PAWS, INC. All Rights Reserved.
VACUUMED THE HOUSE
Distributed by Andrews McMeel Syndication
AND CLEANED OUT THE HALL CLOSET
THAT WAS ONE LOOOONG COMMERCIAL BREAK

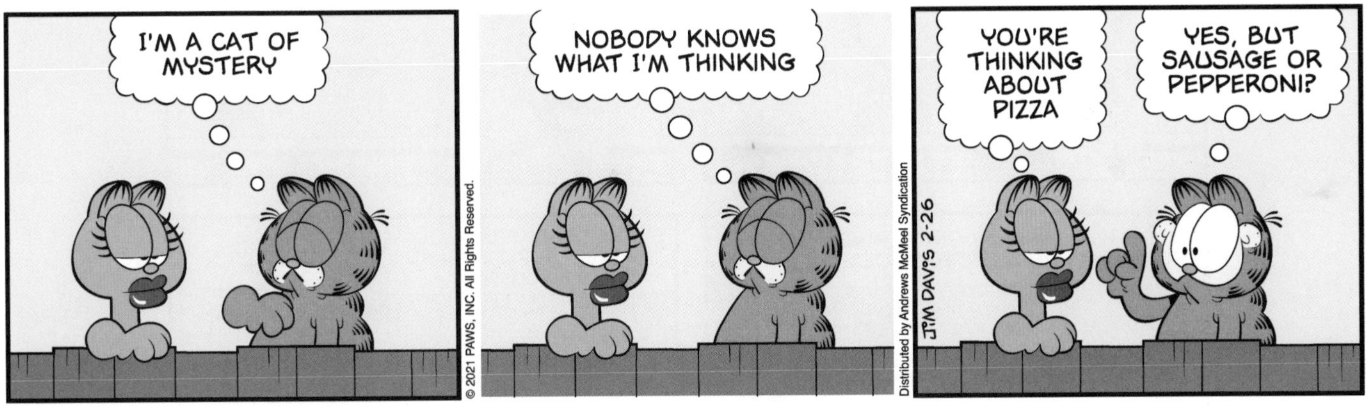
I'M A CAT OF MYSTERY
© 2021 PAWS, INC. All Rights Reserved.
NOBODY KNOWS WHAT I'M THINKING
Distributed by Andrews McMeel Syndication
JIM DAVIS 2-26
YOU'RE THINKING ABOUT PIZZA
YES, BUT SAUSAGE OR PEPPERONI?

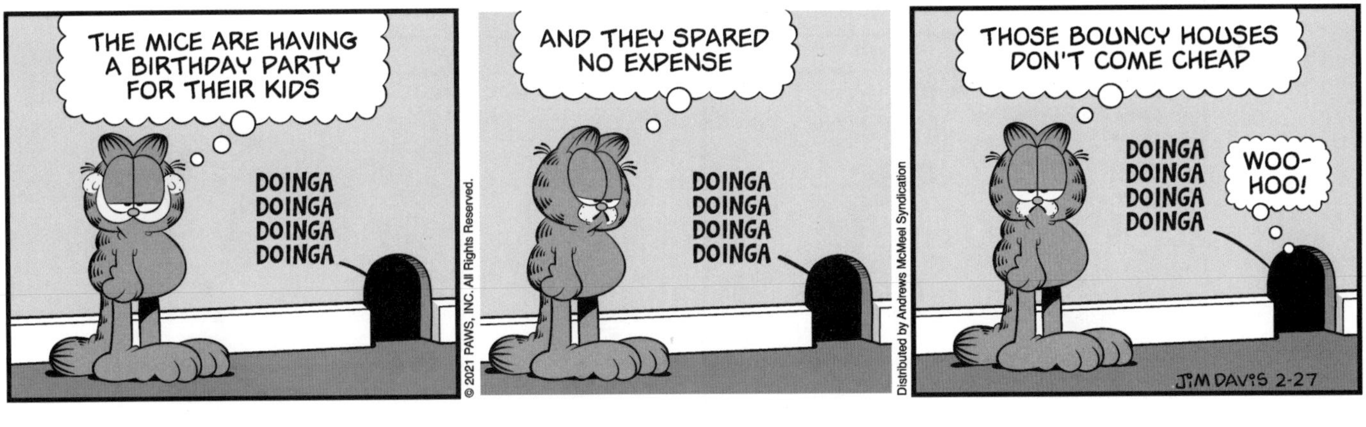
THE MICE ARE HAVING A BIRTHDAY PARTY FOR THEIR KIDS
DOINGA DOINGA DOINGA DOINGA
© 2021 PAWS, INC. All Rights Reserved.
AND THEY SPARED NO EXPENSE
DOINGA DOINGA DOINGA DOINGA
Distributed by Andrews McMeel Syndication
THOSE BOUNCY HOUSES DON'T COME CHEAP
DOINGA DOINGA DOINGA DOINGA
WOO-HOO!
JIM DAVIS 2-27

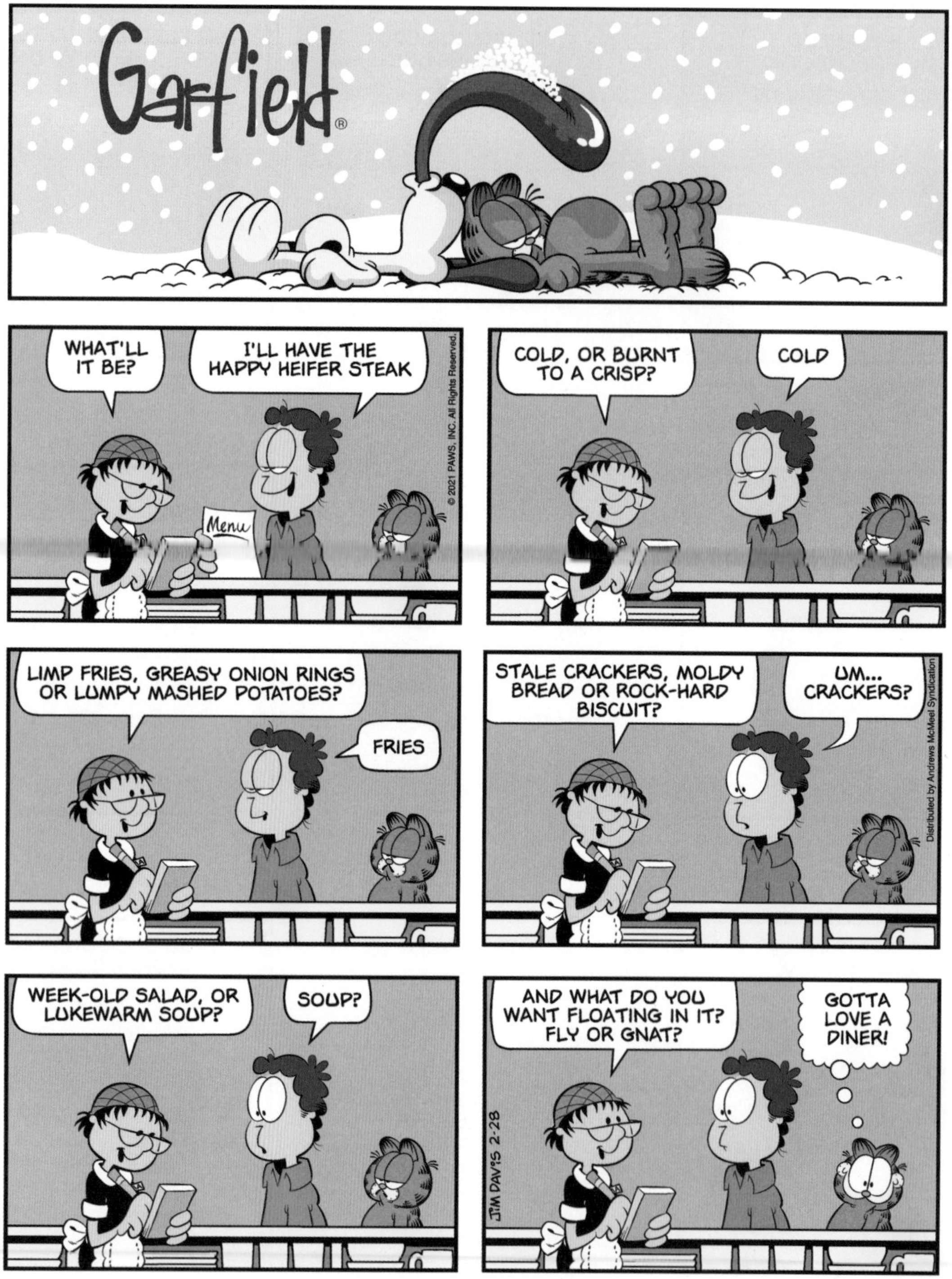
Garfield®
© 2021 PAWS, INC. All Rights Reserved.
WHAT'LL IT BE?
I'LL HAVE THE HAPPY HEIFER STEAK
Menu
COLD, OR BURNT TO A CRISP?
COLD
LIMP FRIES, GREASY ONION RINGS OR LUMPY MASHED POTATOES?
FRIES
STALE CRACKERS, MOLDY BREAD OR ROCK-HARD BISCUIT?
UM... CRACKERS?
Distributed by Andrews McMeel Syndication
WEEK-OLD SALAD, OR LUKEWARM SOUP?
SOUP?
JIM DAVIS 2-28
AND WHAT DO YOU WANT FLOATING IN IT? FLY OR GNAT?
GOTTA LOVE A DINER!

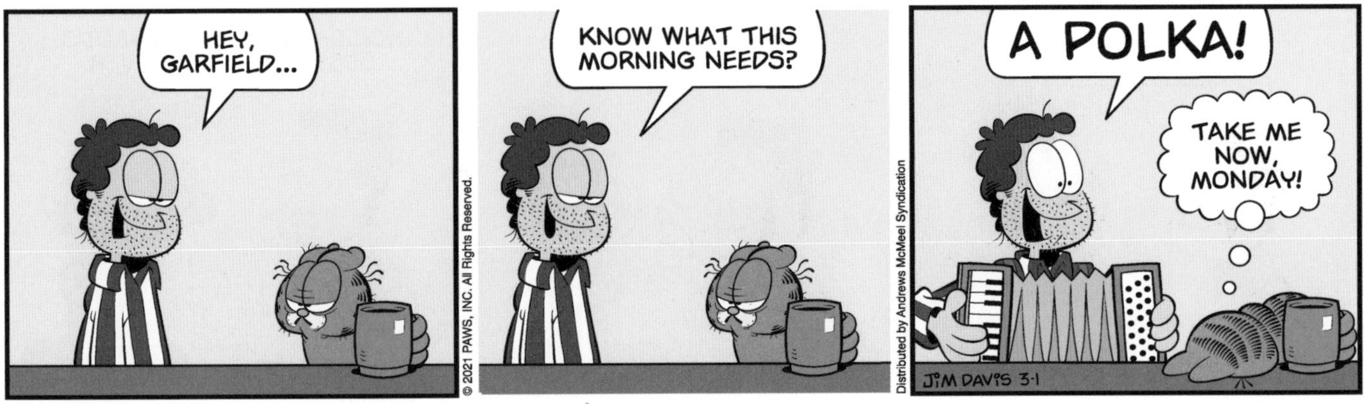
HEY, GARFIELD...
KNOW WHAT THIS MORNING NEEDS?
A POLKA!
TAKE ME NOW, MONDAY!
© 2021 PAWS, INC. All Rights Reserved.
Distributed by Andrews McMeel Syndication
JiM DAVIS 3-1

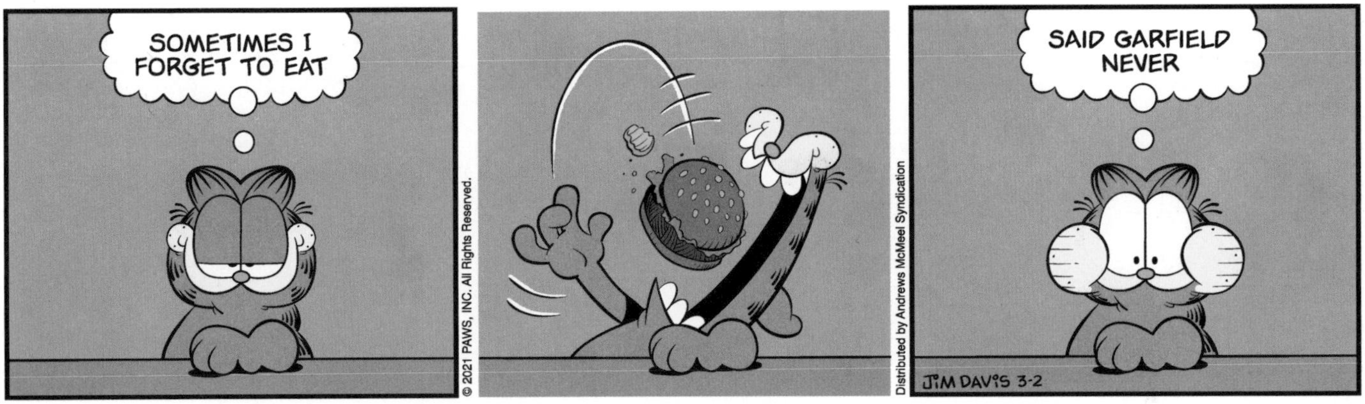
SOMETIMES I FORGET TO EAT
SAID GARFIELD NEVER
© 2021 PAWS, INC. All Rights Reserved.
Distributed by Andrews McMeel Syndication
JiM DAVIS 3-2

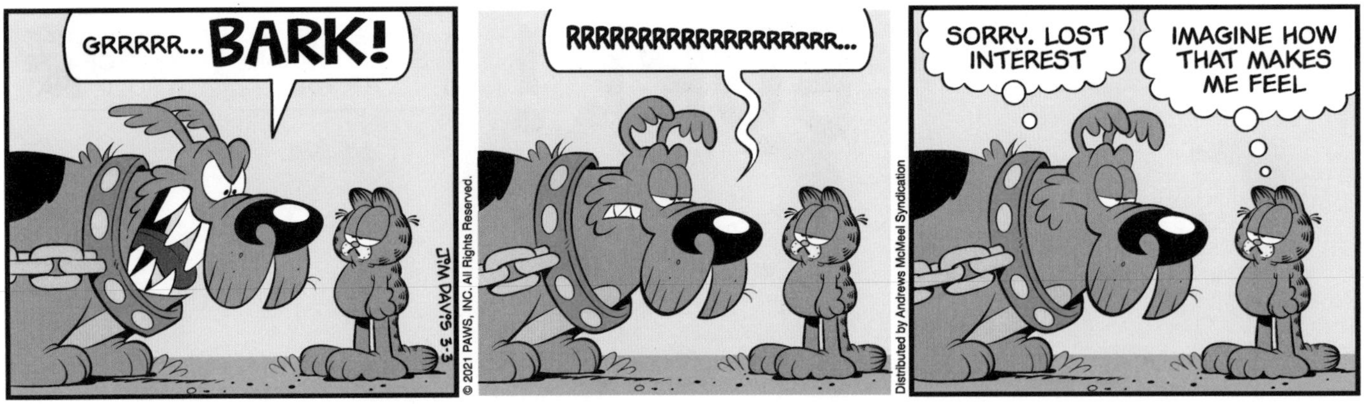
GRRRRR... BARK!
RRRRRRRRRRRRRRRRRRRR...
SORRY. LOST INTEREST
IMAGINE HOW THAT MAKES ME FEEL
© 2021 PAWS, INC. All Rights Reserved.
Distributed by Andrews McMeel Syndication
JiM DAVIS 3-3

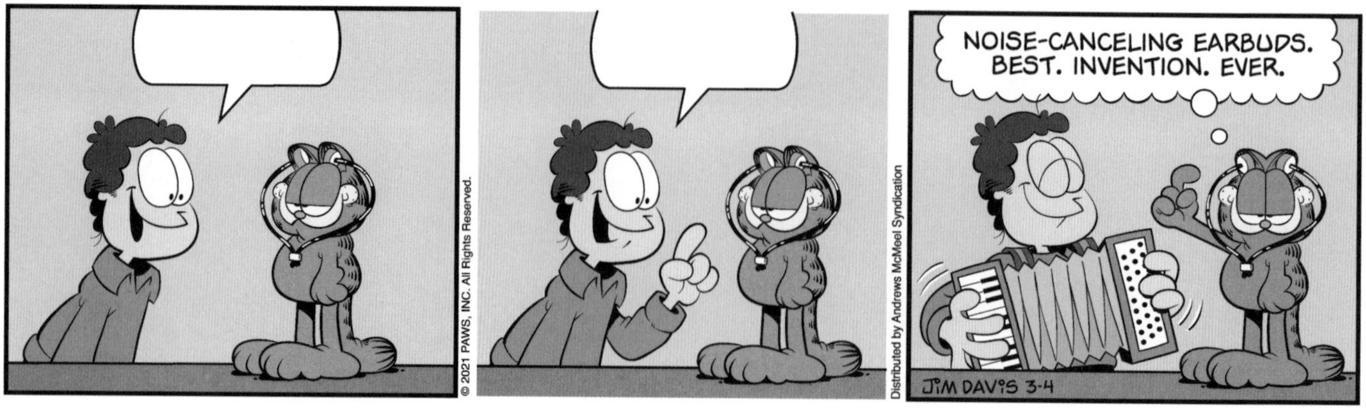
NOISE-CANCELING EARBUDS. BEST. INVENTION. EVER.
© 2021 PAWS, INC. All Rights Reserved.
Distributed by Andrews McMeel Syndication
JIM DAVIS 3-4

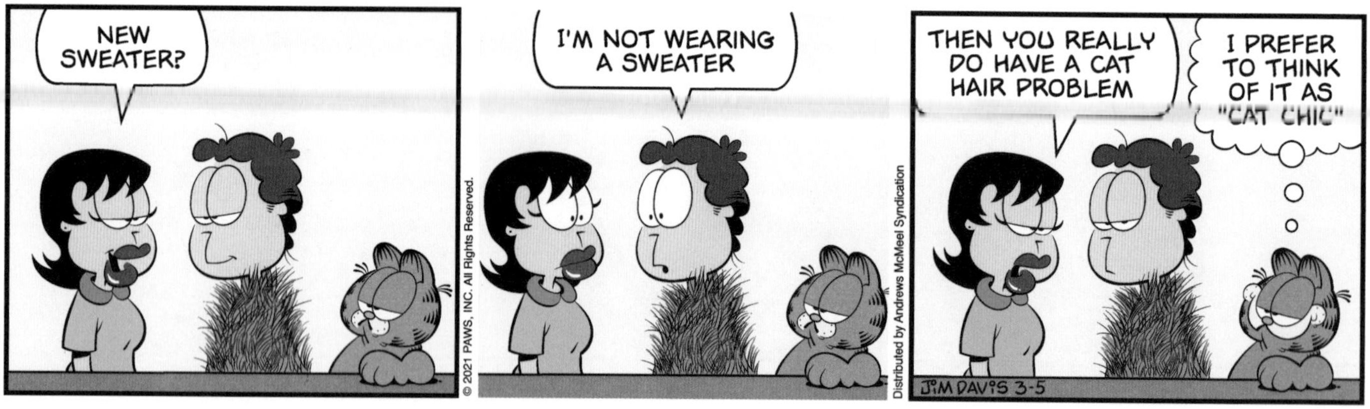
NEW SWEATER?
I'M NOT WEARING A SWEATER
THEN YOU REALLY DO HAVE A CAT HAIR PROBLEM
I PREFER TO THINK OF IT AS "CAT CHIC"
© 2021 PAWS, INC. All Rights Reserved.
Distributed by Andrews McMeel Syndication
JIM DAVIS 3-5

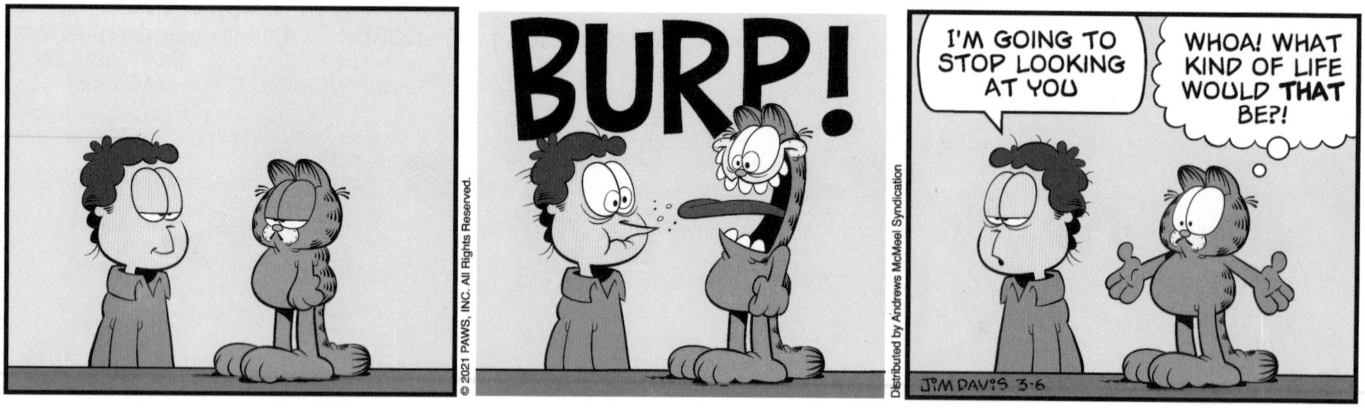
BURP!
I'M GOING TO STOP LOOKING AT YOU
WHOA! WHAT KIND OF LIFE WOULD **THAT** BE?!
© 2021 PAWS, INC. All Rights Reserved.
Distributed by Andrews McMeel Syndication
JIM DAVIS 3-6

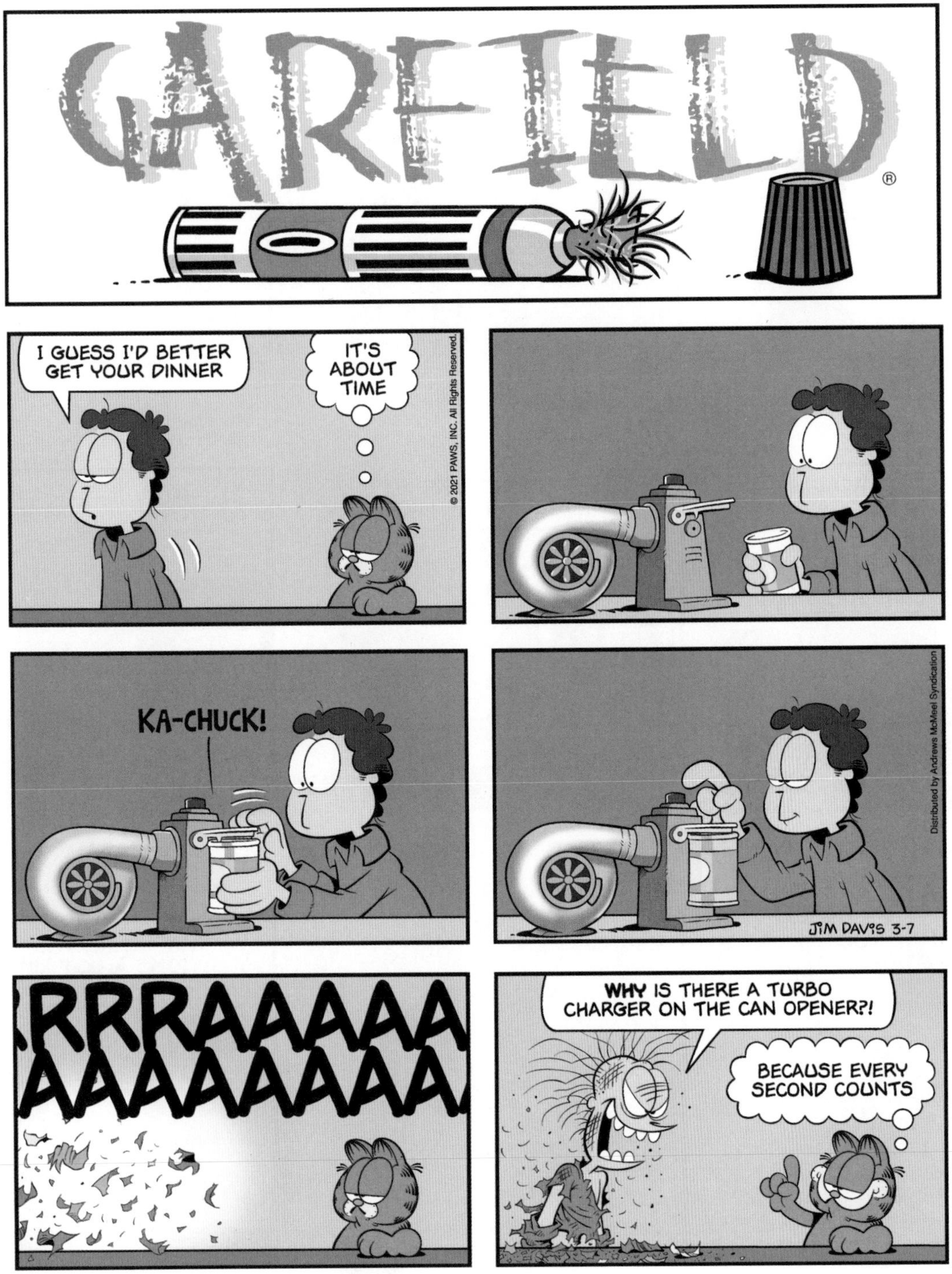
GARFIELD®
I GUESS I'D BETTER GET YOUR DINNER
IT'S ABOUT TIME
© 2021 PAWS, INC. All Rights Reserved.
KA-CHUCK!
Distributed by Andrews McMeel Syndication
JIM DAVIS 3-7
RRRAAAAA AAAAAAAA
WHY IS THERE A TURBO CHARGER ON THE CAN OPENER?!
BECAUSE EVERY SECOND COUNTS

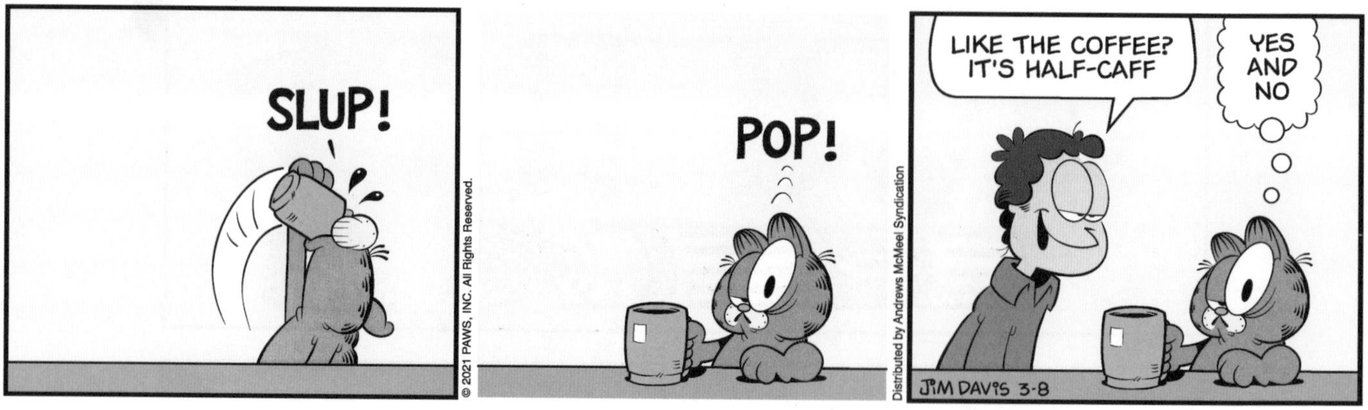
SLUP!
POP!
© 2021 PAWS, INC. All Rights Reserved.
Distributed by Andrews McMeel Syndication
LIKE THE COFFEE? IT'S HALF-CAFF
YES AND NO
JIM DAVIS 3-8

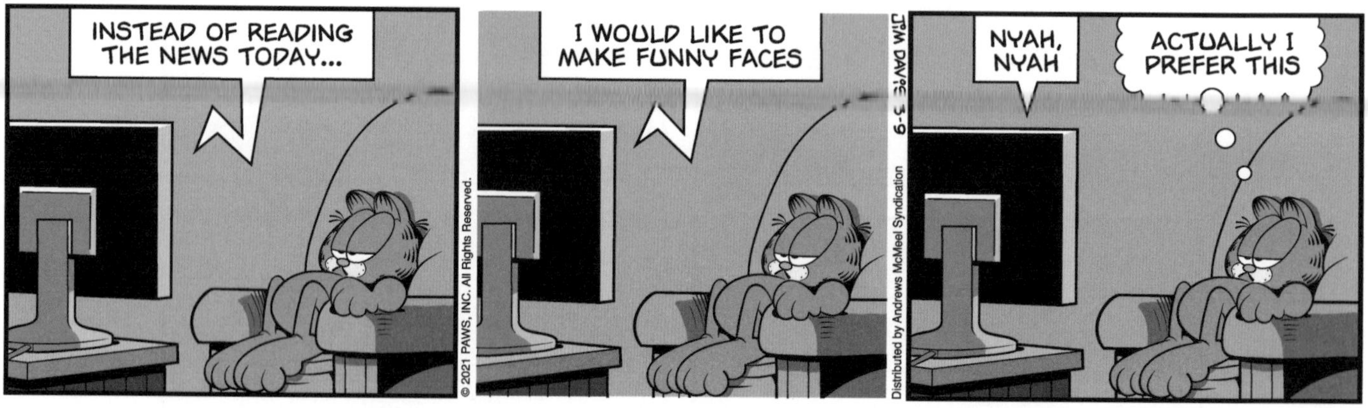
INSTEAD OF READING THE NEWS TODAY...
© 2021 PAWS, INC. All Rights Reserved.
I WOULD LIKE TO MAKE FUNNY FACES
JIM DAVIS 3-9
Distributed by Andrews McMeel Syndication
NYAH, NYAH
ACTUALLY I PREFER THIS

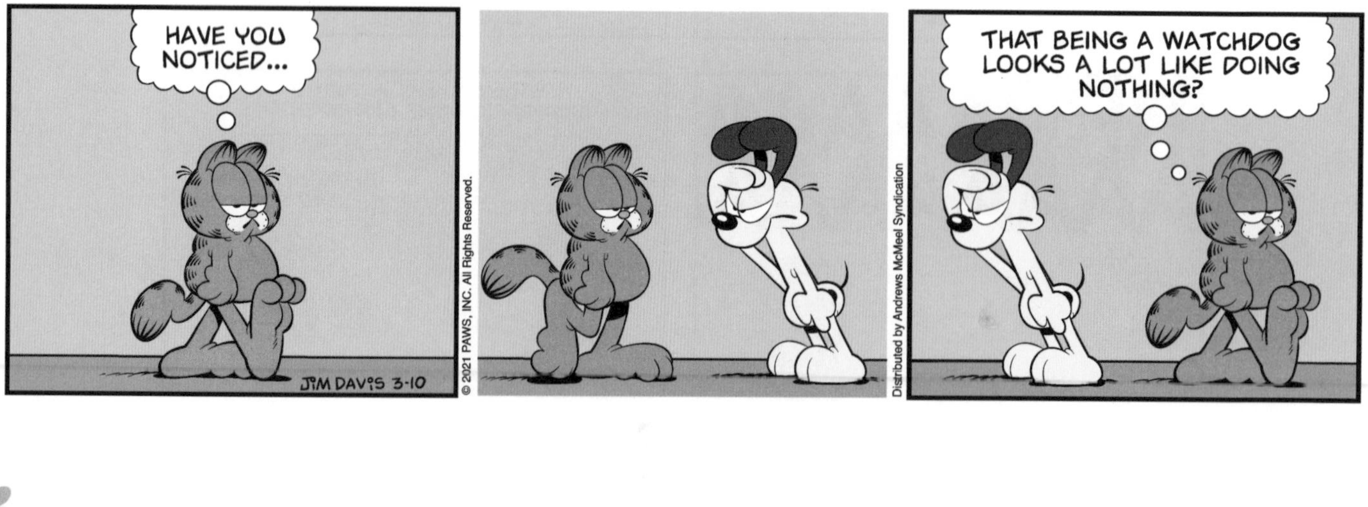
HAVE YOU NOTICED...
JIM DAVIS 3-10
© 2021 PAWS, INC. All Rights Reserved.
Distributed by Andrews McMeel Syndication
THAT BEING A WATCHDOG LOOKS A LOT LIKE DOING NOTHING?

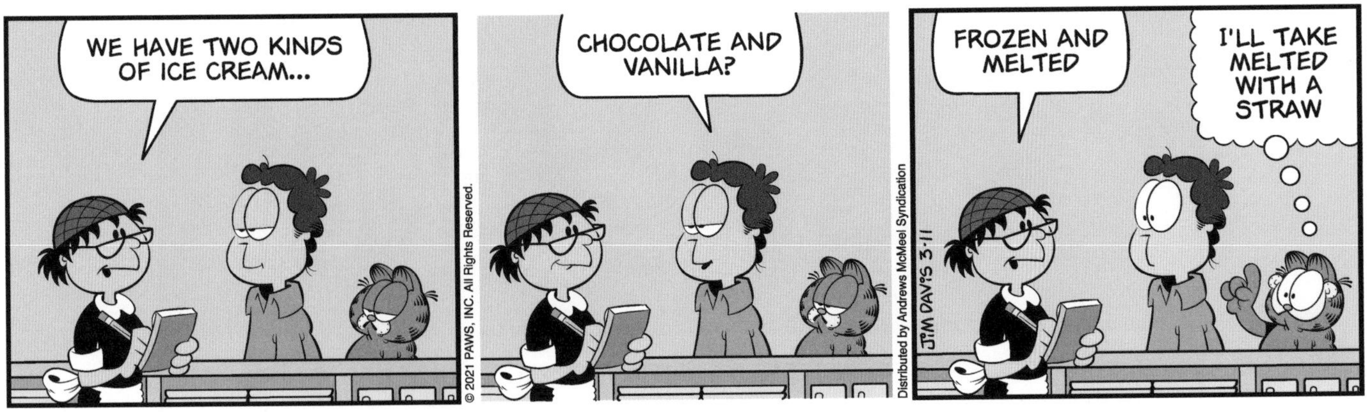
WE HAVE TWO KINDS OF ICE CREAM...
CHOCOLATE AND VANILLA?
FROZEN AND MELTED
I'LL TAKE MELTED WITH A STRAW
© 2021 PAWS, INC. All Rights Reserved.
Distributed by Andrews McMeel Syndication
JIM DAVIS 3-11

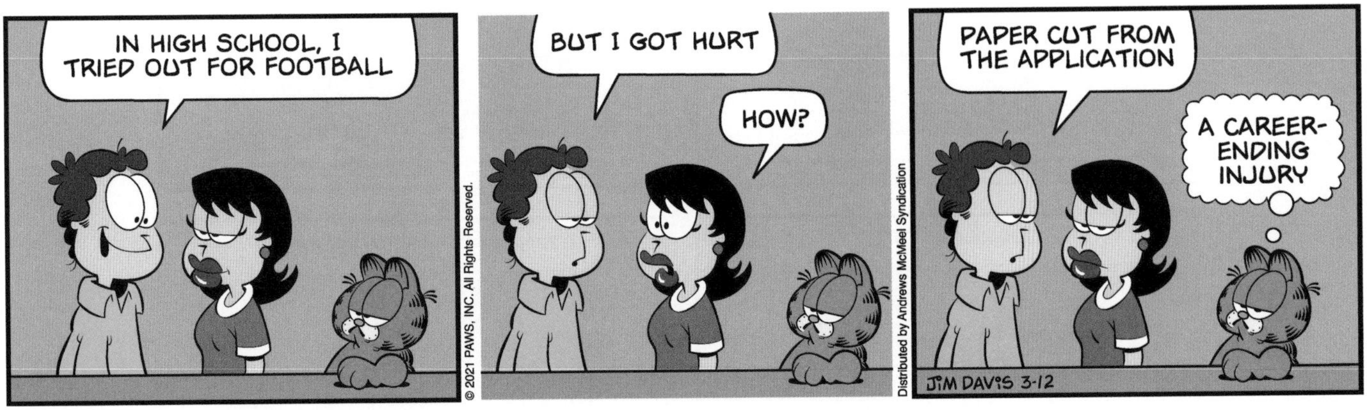
IN HIGH SCHOOL, I TRIED OUT FOR FOOTBALL
BUT I GOT HURT
HOW?
PAPER CUT FROM THE APPLICATION
A CAREER-ENDING INJURY
© 2021 PAWS, INC. All Rights Reserved.
Distributed by Andrews McMeel Syndication
JIM DAVIS 3-12

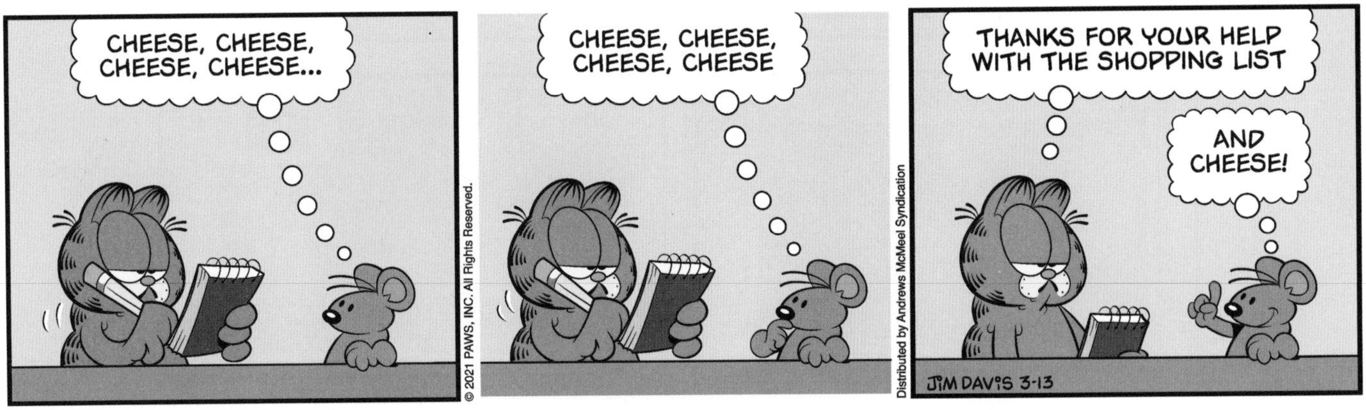
CHEESE, CHEESE, CHEESE, CHEESE...
CHEESE, CHEESE, CHEESE, CHEESE
THANKS FOR YOUR HELP WITH THE SHOPPING LIST
AND CHEESE!
© 2021 PAWS, INC. All Rights Reserved.
Distributed by Andrews McMeel Syndication
JIM DAVIS 3-13

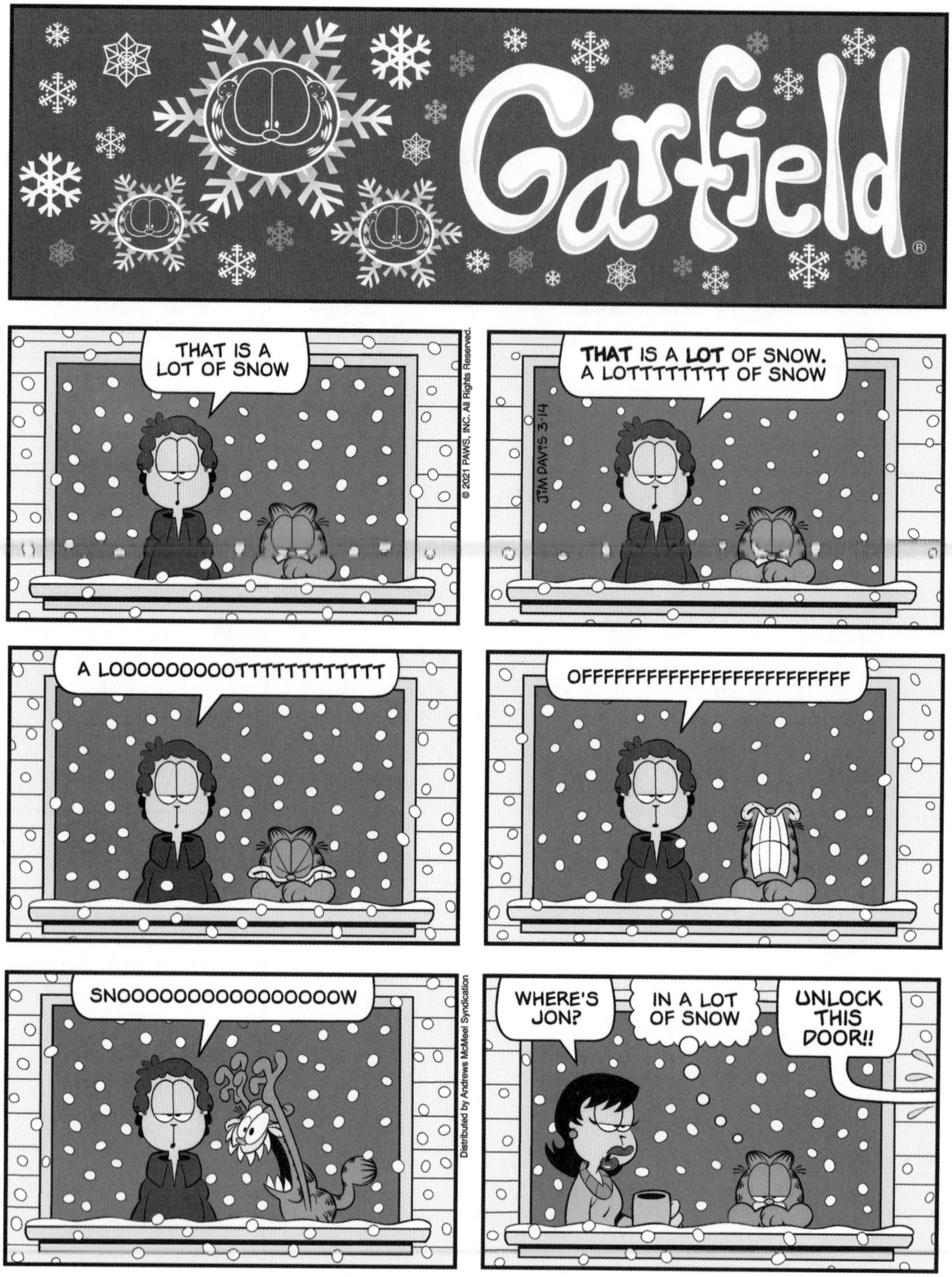
Garfield
THAT IS A LOT OF SNOW
THAT IS A LOT OF SNOW. A LOTTTTTTTT OF SNOW
A LOOOOOOOOOTTTTTTTTTTTT
OFFFFFFFFFFFFFFFFFFFFFFFF
SNOOOOOOOOOOOOOOOOW
WHERE'S JON?
IN A LOT OF SNOW
UNLOCK THIS DOOR!!
JIM DAVIS 3-14
© 2021 PAWS, INC. All Rights Reserved.
Distributed by Andrews McMeel Syndication

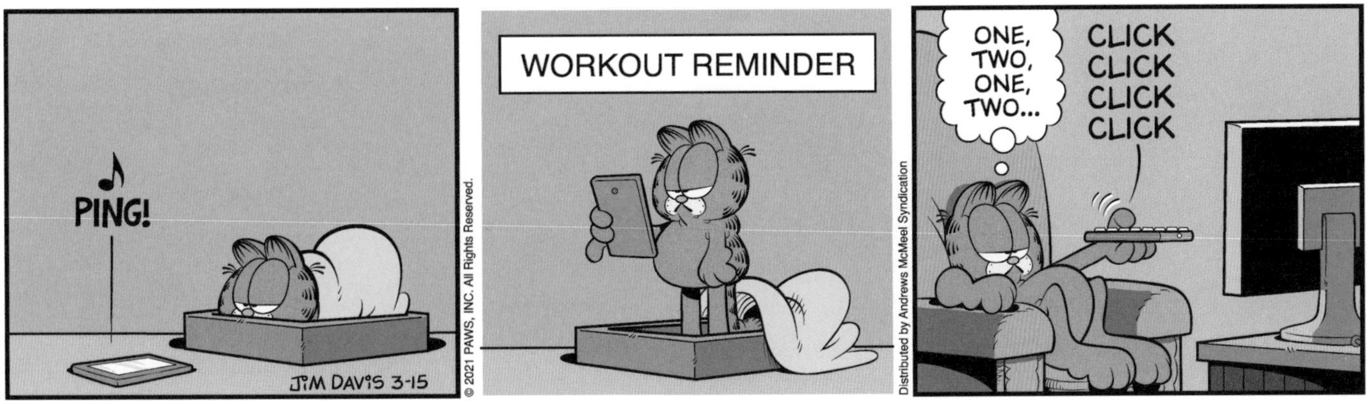
PING!
JIM DAVIS 3-15
© 2021 PAWS, INC. All Rights Reserved.
WORKOUT REMINDER
Distributed by Andrews McMeel Syndication
ONE, TWO, ONE, TWO...
CLICK CLICK CLICK CLICK

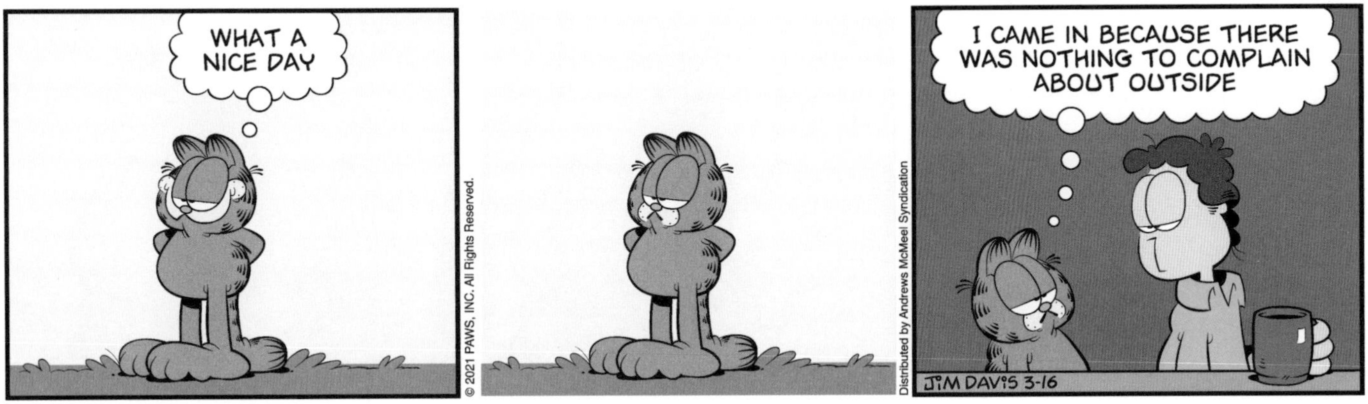
WHAT A NICE DAY
© 2021 PAWS, INC. All Rights Reserved.
Distributed by Andrews McMeel Syndication
I CAME IN BECAUSE THERE WAS NOTHING TO COMPLAIN ABOUT OUTSIDE
JIM DAVIS 3-16

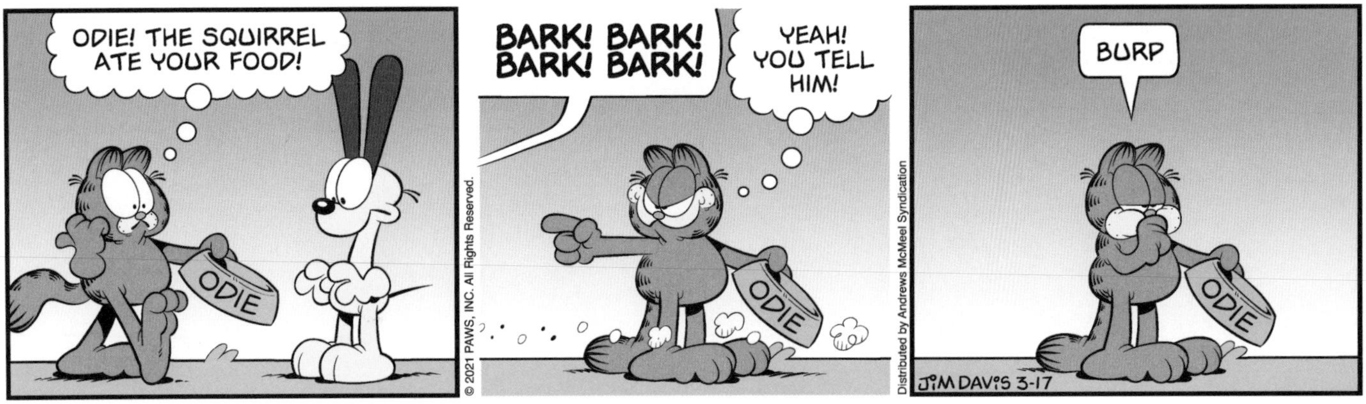
ODIE! THE SQUIRREL ATE YOUR FOOD!
ODIE
© 2021 PAWS, INC. All Rights Reserved.
BARK! BARK! BARK! BARK!
YEAH! YOU TELL HIM!
ODIE
Distributed by Andrews McMeel Syndication
BURP
ODIE
JIM DAVIS 3-17

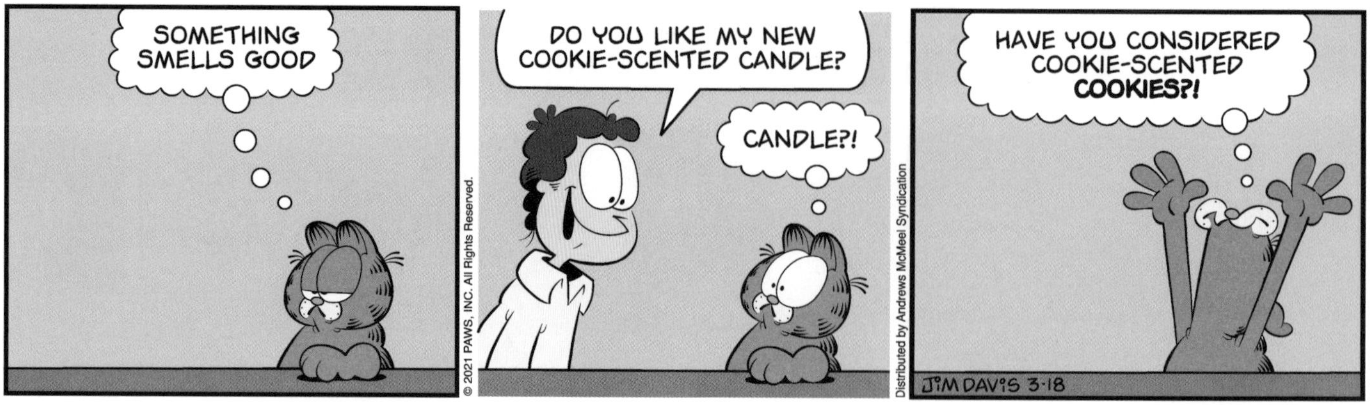
SOMETHING SMELLS GOOD
DO YOU LIKE MY NEW COOKIE-SCENTED CANDLE?
CANDLE?!
HAVE YOU CONSIDERED COOKIE-SCENTED **COOKIES?!**
© 2021 PAWS, INC. All Rights Reserved.
Distributed by Andrews McMeel Syndication
JIM DAVIS 3-18

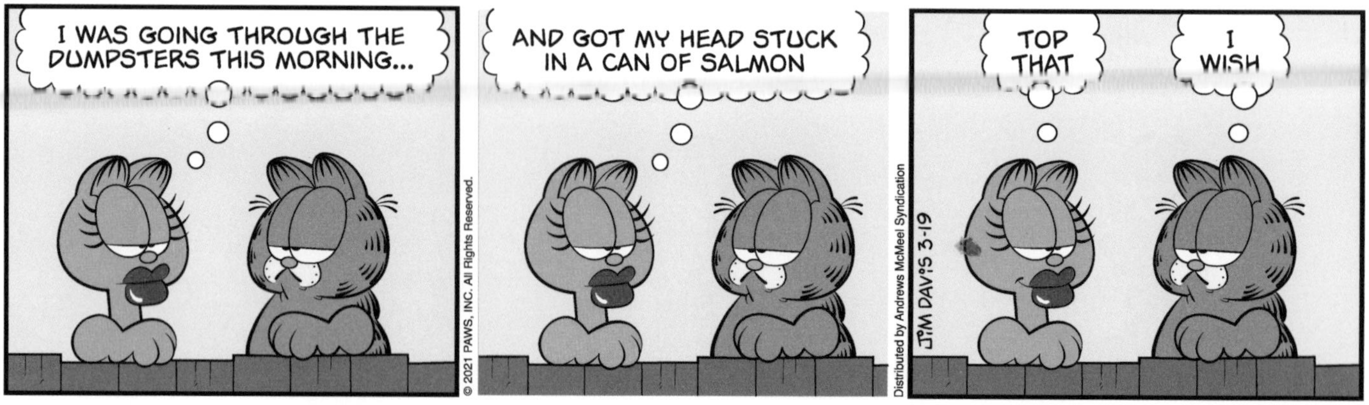
I WAS GOING THROUGH THE DUMPSTERS THIS MORNING...
AND GOT MY HEAD STUCK IN A CAN OF SALMON
TOP THAT
I WISH
© 2021 PAWS, INC. All Rights Reserved.
Distributed by Andrews McMeel Syndication
JIM DAVIS 3-19

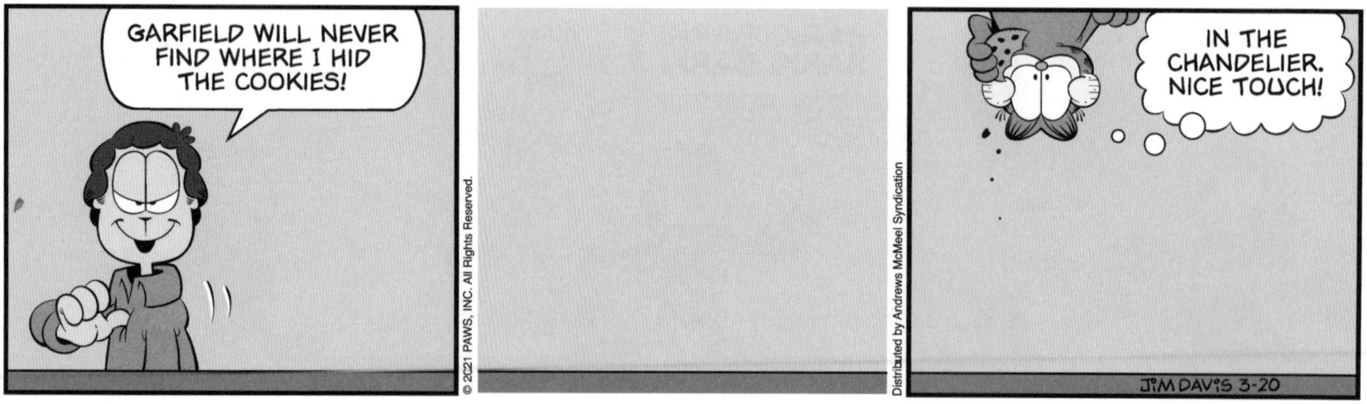
GARFIELD WILL NEVER FIND WHERE I HID THE COOKIES!
IN THE CHANDELIER. NICE TOUCH!
© 2021 PAWS, INC. All Rights Reserved.
Distributed by Andrews McMeel Syndication
JIM DAVIS 3-20

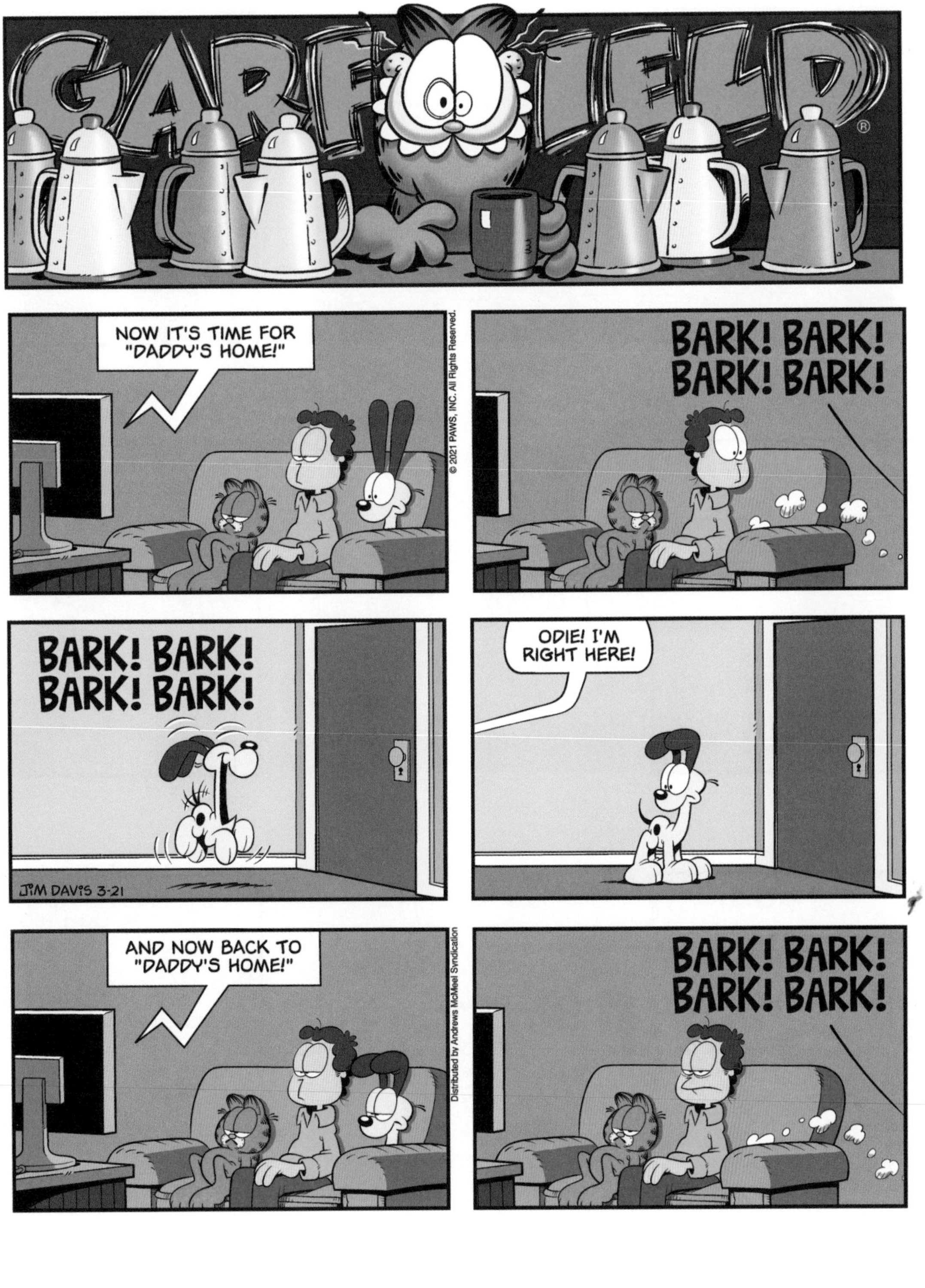
GARFIELD®
NOW IT'S TIME FOR "DADDY'S HOME!"
© 2021 PAWS, INC. All Rights Reserved.
BARK! BARK! BARK! BARK!
BARK! BARK! BARK! BARK!
JIM DAVIS 3-21
ODIE! I'M RIGHT HERE!
AND NOW BACK TO "DADDY'S HOME!"
Distributed by Andrews McMeel Syndication
BARK! BARK! BARK! BARK!

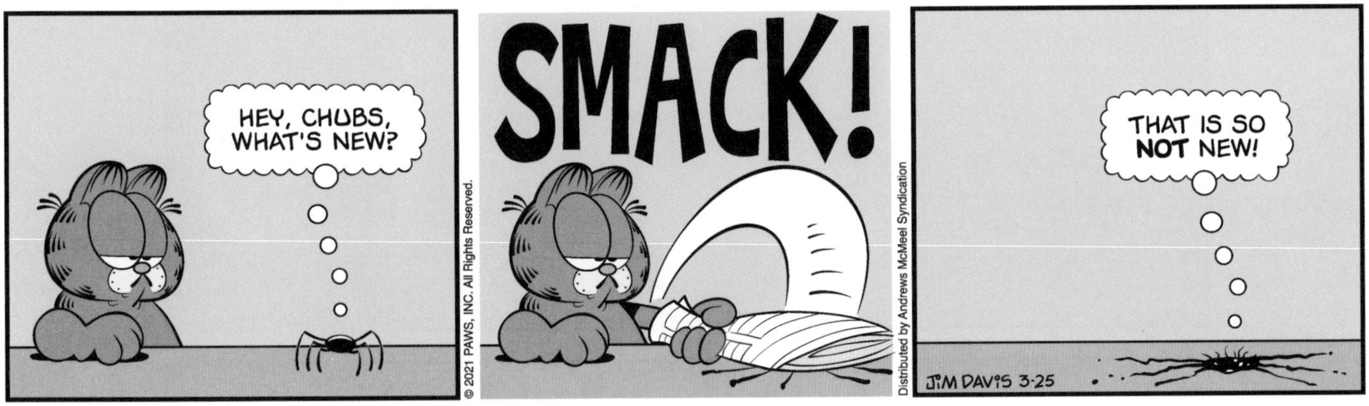
HEY, CHUBS, WHAT'S NEW?
SMACK!
© 2021 PAWS, INC. All Rights Reserved.
Distributed by Andrews McMeel Syndication
THAT IS SO **NOT** NEW!
JIM DAVIS 3-25

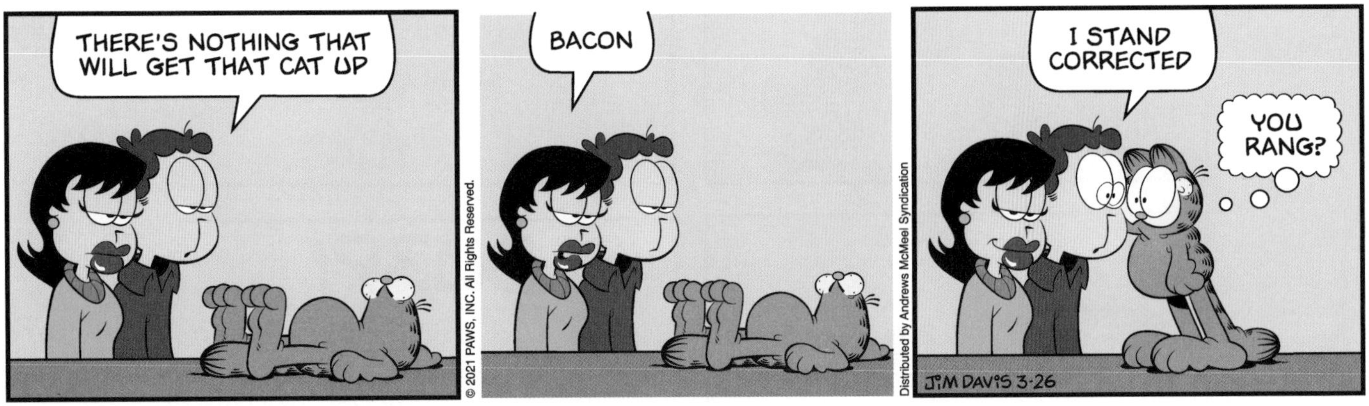
THERE'S NOTHING THAT WILL GET THAT CAT UP
© 2021 PAWS, INC. All Rights Reserved.
BACON
Distributed by Andrews McMeel Syndication
I STAND CORRECTED
YOU RANG?
JIM DAVIS 3-26

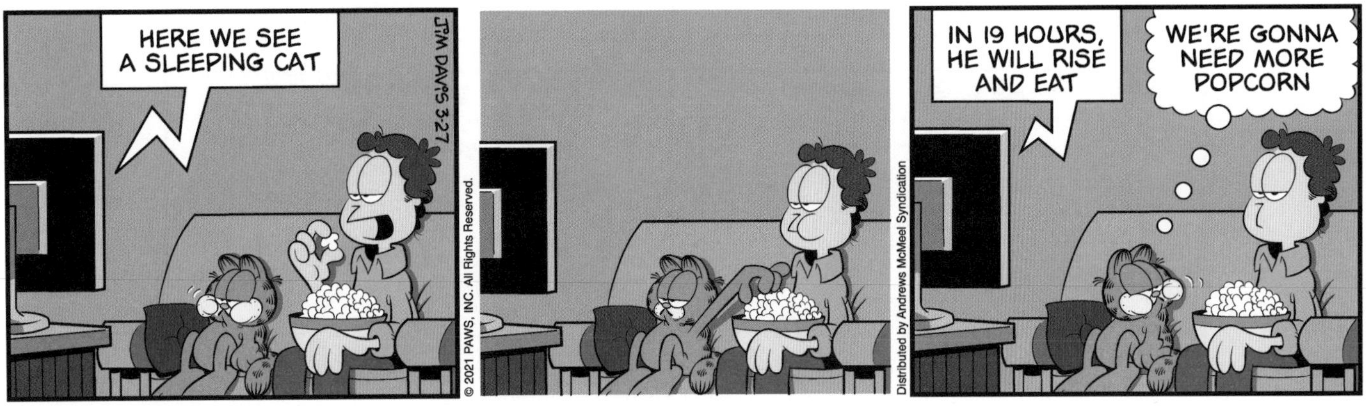
HERE WE SEE A SLEEPING CAT
JIM DAVIS 3-27
© 2021 PAWS, INC. All Rights Reserved.
Distributed by Andrews McMeel Syndication
IN 19 HOURS, HE WILL RISE AND EAT
WE'RE GONNA NEED MORE POPCORN

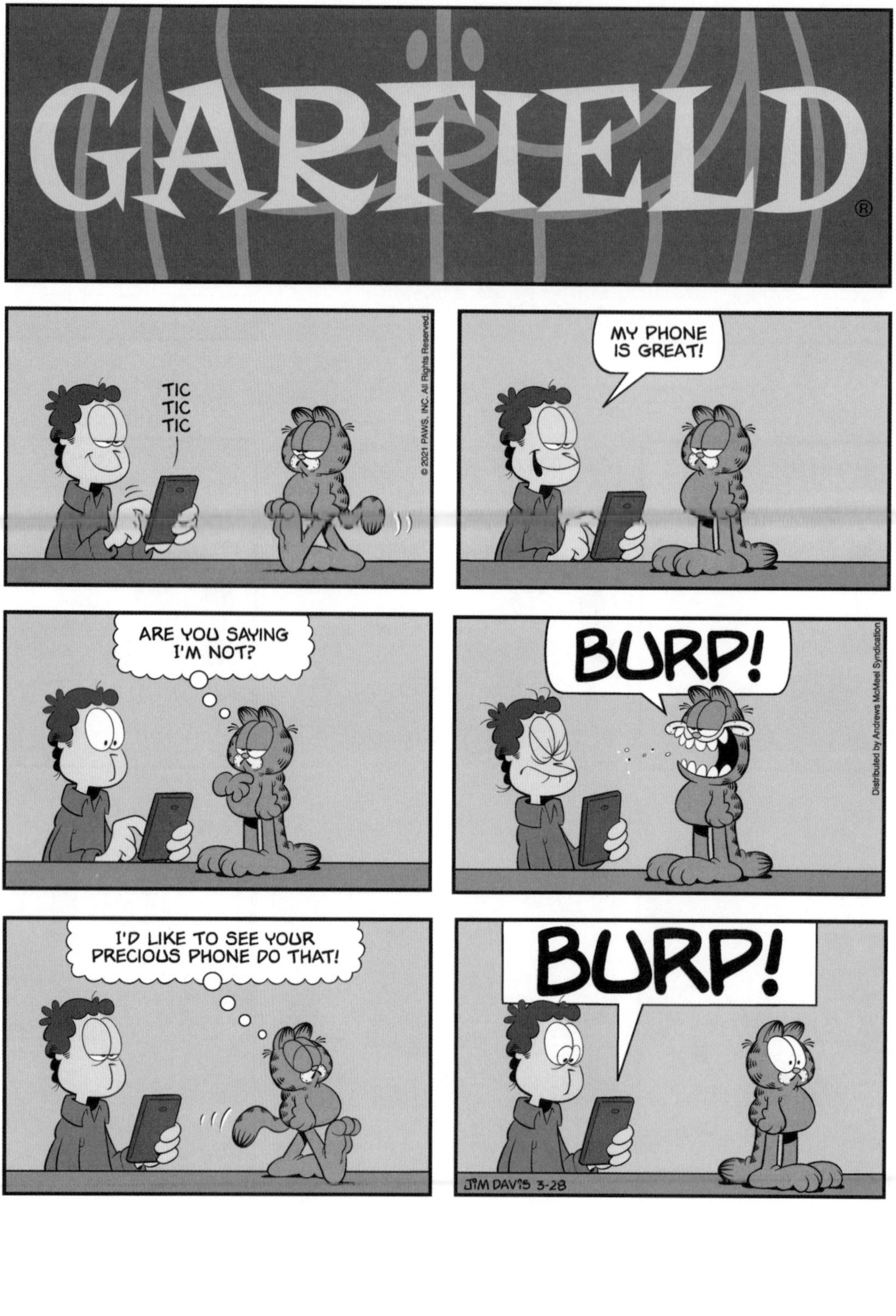
GARFIELD®
TIC
TIC
TIC
© 2021 PAWS, INC. All Rights Reserved.
MY PHONE IS GREAT!
ARE YOU SAYING I'M NOT?
BURP!
Distributed by Andrews McMeel Syndication
I'D LIKE TO SEE YOUR PRECIOUS PHONE DO THAT!
BURP!
JIM DAVIS 3-28

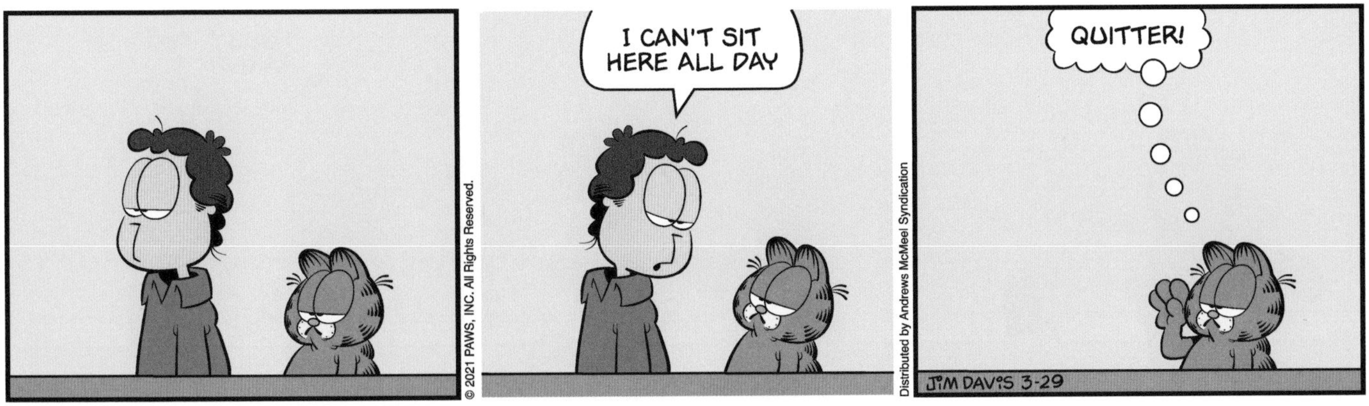

I CAN'T SIT HERE ALL DAY
QUITTER!
© 2021 PAWS, INC. All Rights Reserved.
Distributed by Andrews McMeel Syndication
JIM DAVIS 3-29

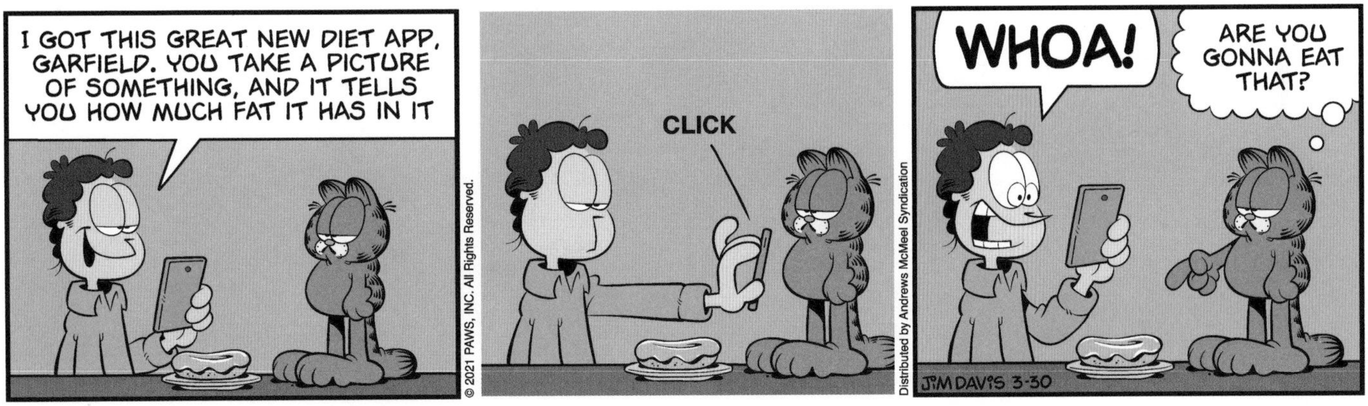

I GOT THIS GREAT NEW DIET APP, GARFIELD. YOU TAKE A PICTURE OF SOMETHING, AND IT TELLS YOU HOW MUCH FAT IT HAS IN IT
CLICK
WHOA!
ARE YOU GONNA EAT THAT?
© 2021 PAWS, INC. All Rights Reserved.
Distributed by Andrews McMeel Syndication
JIM DAVIS 3-30

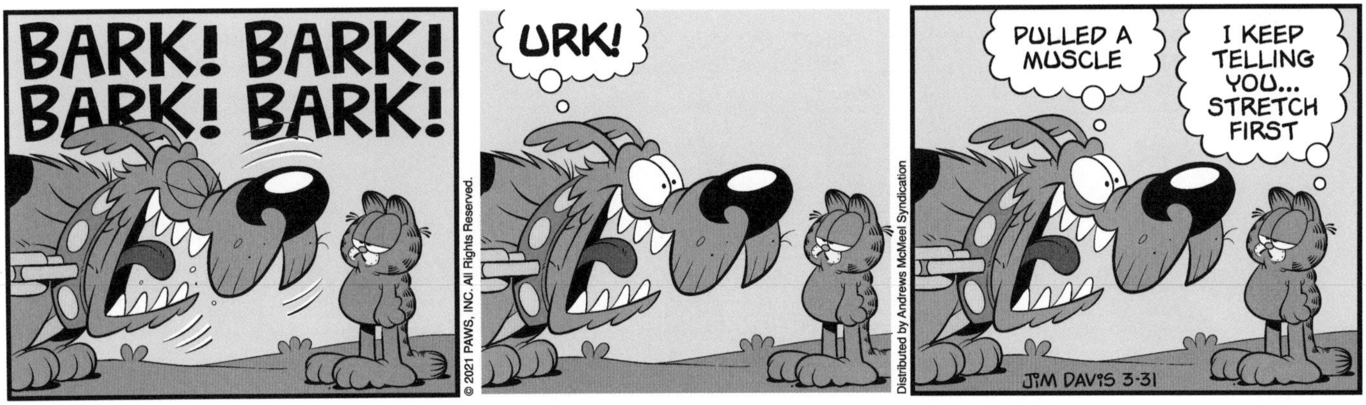

BARK! BARK! BARK! BARK!
URK!
PULLED A MUSCLE
I KEEP TELLING YOU... STRETCH FIRST
© 2021 PAWS, INC. All Rights Reserved.
Distributed by Andrews McMeel Syndication
JIM DAVIS 3-31

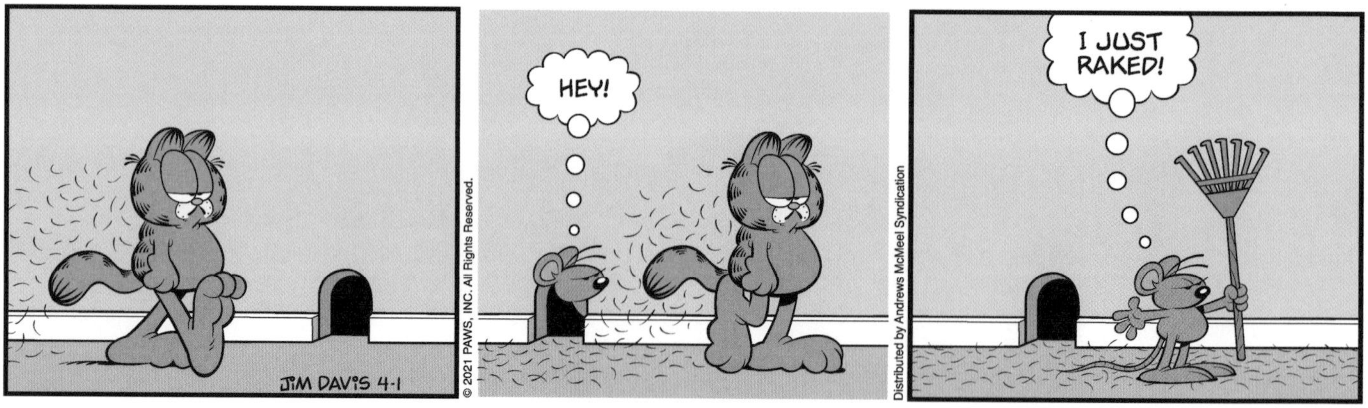
JIM DAVIS 4-1
© 2021 PAWS, INC. All Rights Reserved.
HEY!
Distributed by Andrews McMeel Syndication
I JUST RAKED!

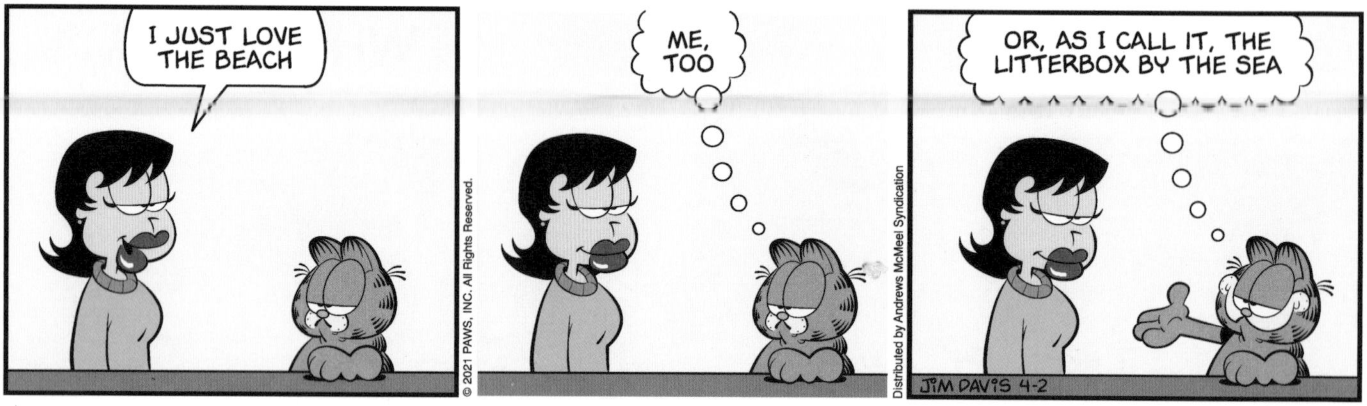
I JUST LOVE THE BEACH
© 2021 PAWS, INC. All Rights Reserved.
ME, TOO
Distributed by Andrews McMeel Syndication
OR, AS I CALL IT, THE LITTERBOX BY THE SEA
JIM DAVIS 4-2

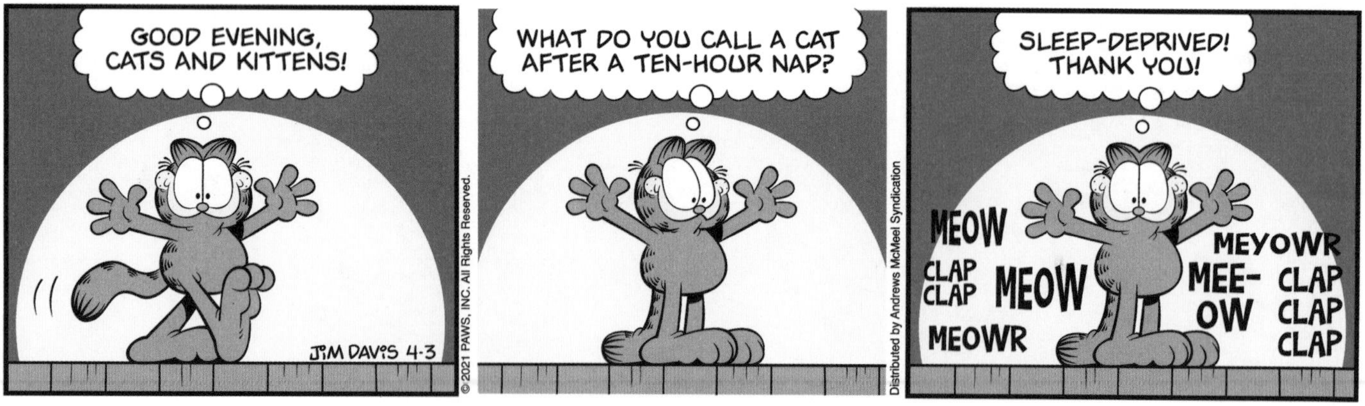
GOOD EVENING, CATS AND KITTENS!
JIM DAVIS 4-3
© 2021 PAWS, INC. All Rights Reserved.
WHAT DO YOU CALL A CAT AFTER A TEN-HOUR NAP?
Distributed by Andrews McMeel Syndication
SLEEP-DEPRIVED! THANK YOU!
MEOW
CLAP CLAP
MEOW
MEOWR
MEYOWR
MEE-OW
CLAP CLAP CLAP

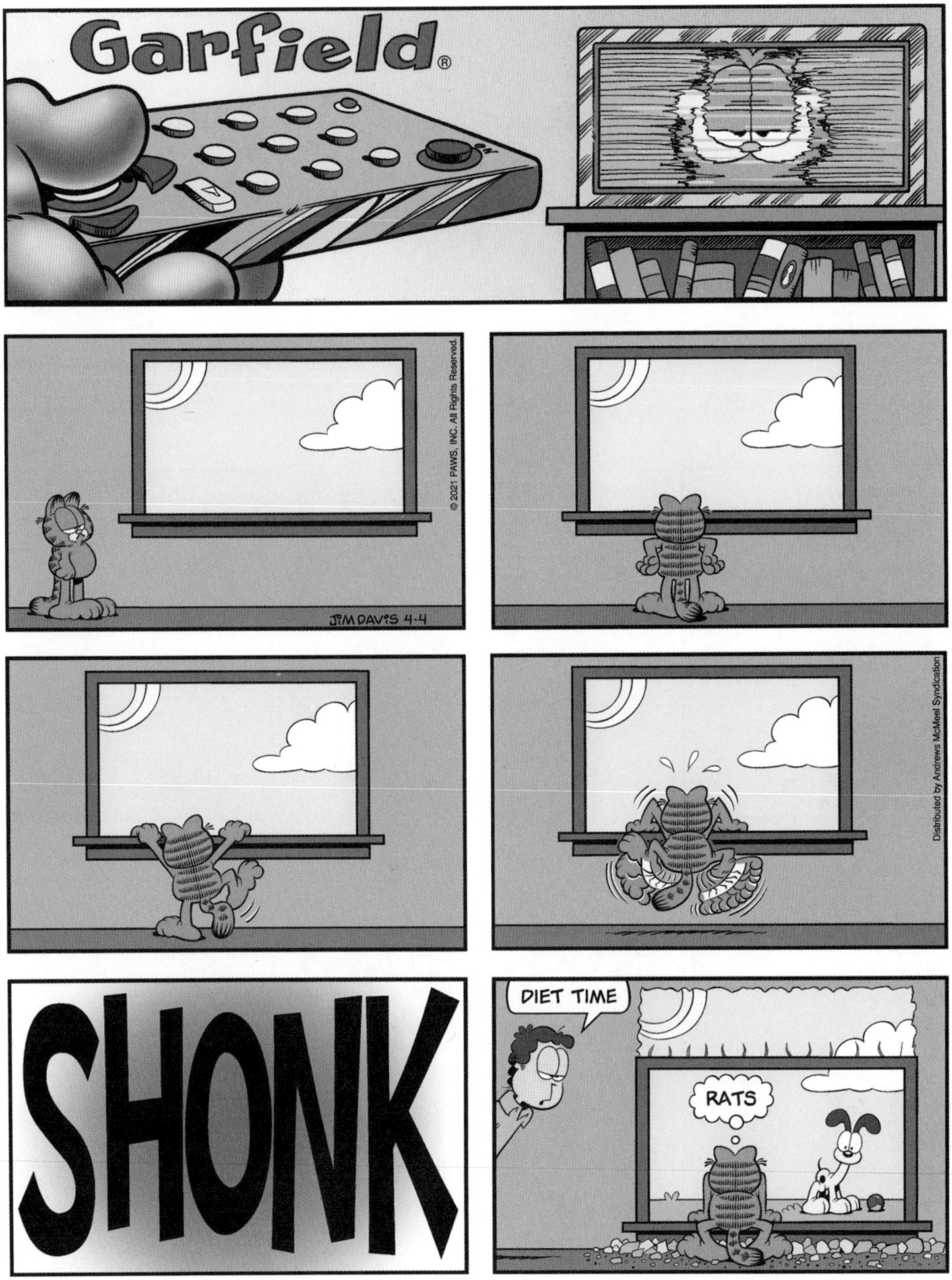
Garfield®
© 2021 PAWS, INC. All Rights Reserved.
JIM DAVIS 4-4
Distributed by Andrews McMeel Syndication
SHONK
DIET TIME
RATS

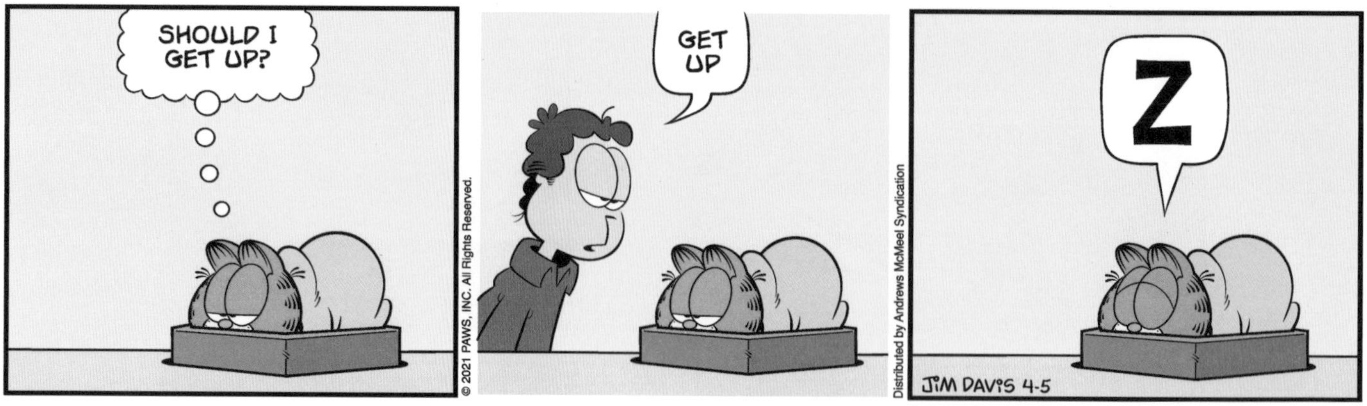
SHOULD I GET UP?
GET UP
Z
© 2021 PAWS, INC. All Rights Reserved.
Distributed by Andrews McMeel Syndication
JIM DAVIS 4-5

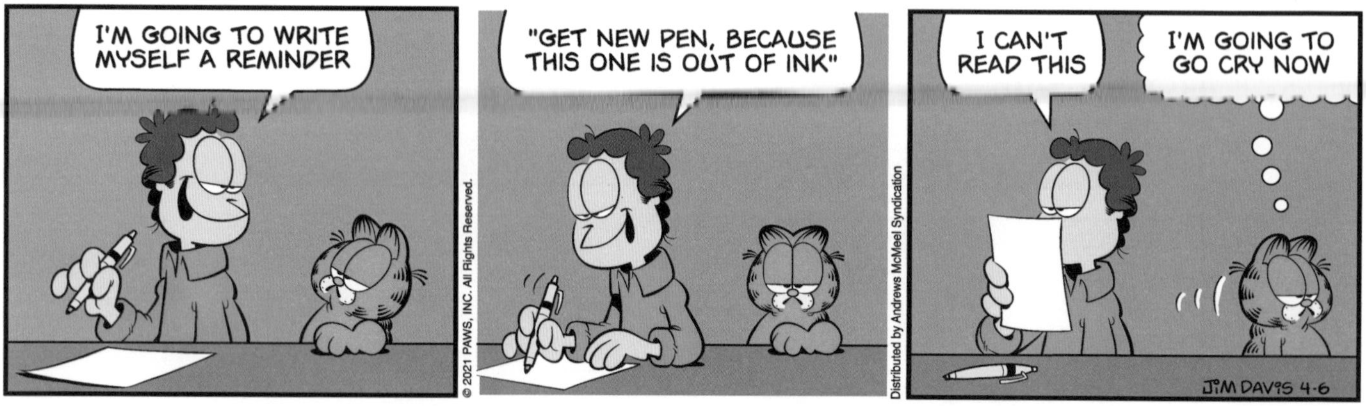
I'M GOING TO WRITE MYSELF A REMINDER
"GET NEW PEN, BECAUSE THIS ONE IS OUT OF INK"
I CAN'T READ THIS
I'M GOING TO GO CRY NOW
© 2021 PAWS, INC. All Rights Reserved.
Distributed by Andrews McMeel Syndication
JIM DAVIS 4-6

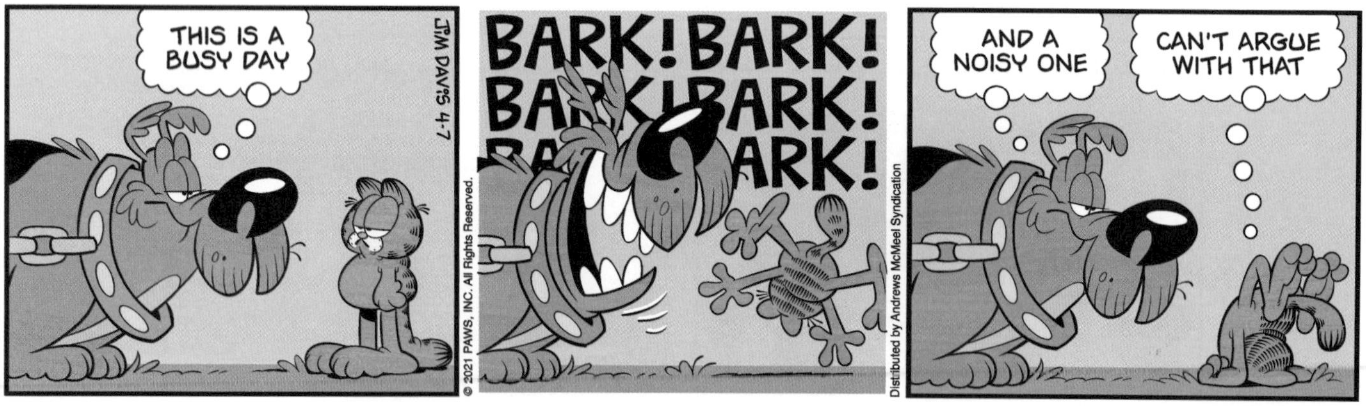
THIS IS A BUSY DAY
JIM DAVIS 4-7
BARK! BARK!
BARK!
AND A NOISY ONE
CAN'T ARGUE WITH THAT
© 2021 PAWS, INC. All Rights Reserved.
Distributed by Andrews McMeel Syndication

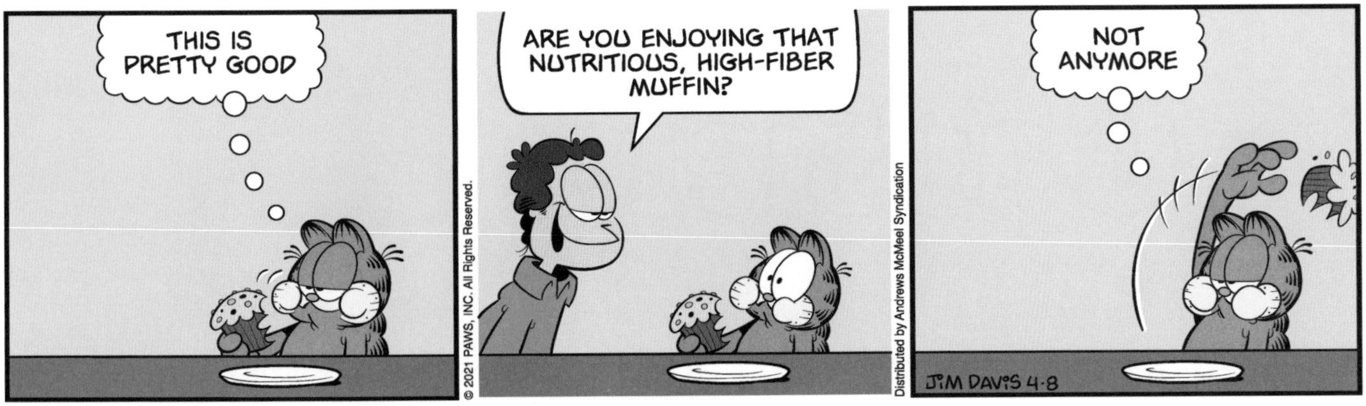
THIS IS PRETTY GOOD
ARE YOU ENJOYING THAT NUTRITIOUS, HIGH-FIBER MUFFIN?
NOT ANYMORE
© 2021 PAWS, INC. All Rights Reserved.
Distributed by Andrews McMeel Syndication
JIM DAVIS 4-8

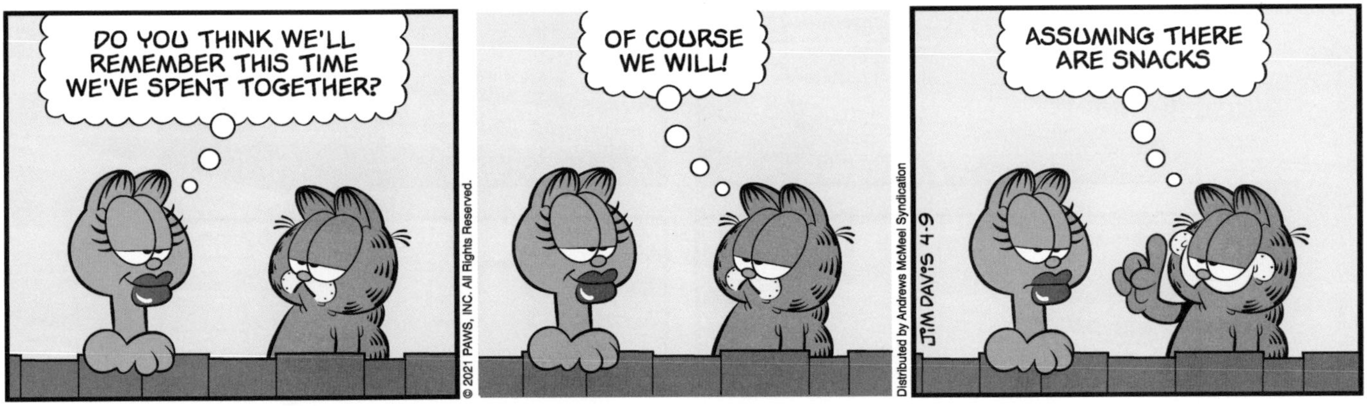
DO YOU THINK WE'LL REMEMBER THIS TIME WE'VE SPENT TOGETHER?
OF COURSE WE WILL!
ASSUMING THERE ARE SNACKS
© 2021 PAWS, INC. All Rights Reserved.
Distributed by Andrews McMeel Syndication
JIM DAVIS 4-9

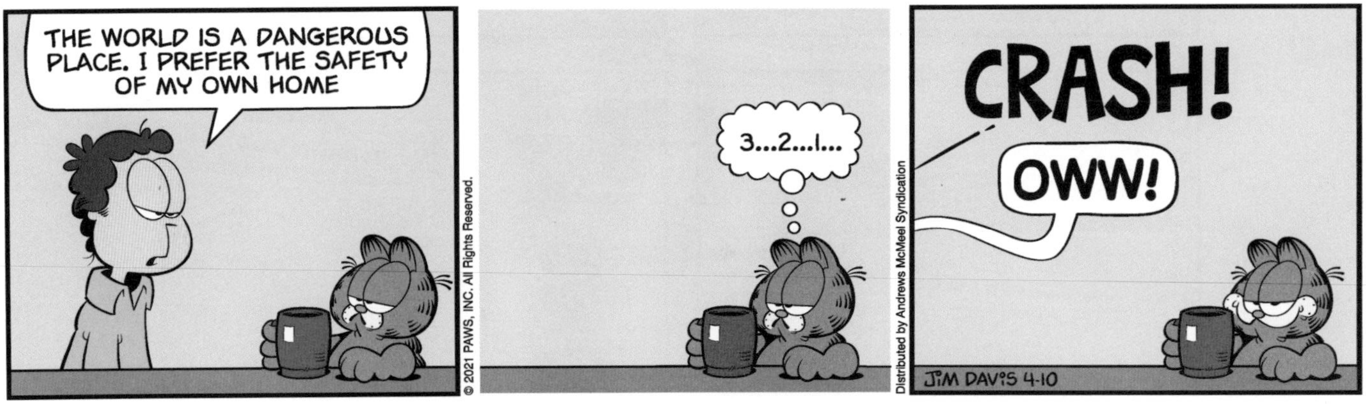
THE WORLD IS A DANGEROUS PLACE. I PREFER THE SAFETY OF MY OWN HOME
3...2...1...
CRASH!
OWW!
© 2021 PAWS, INC. All Rights Reserved.
Distributed by Andrews McMeel Syndication
JIM DAVIS 4-10

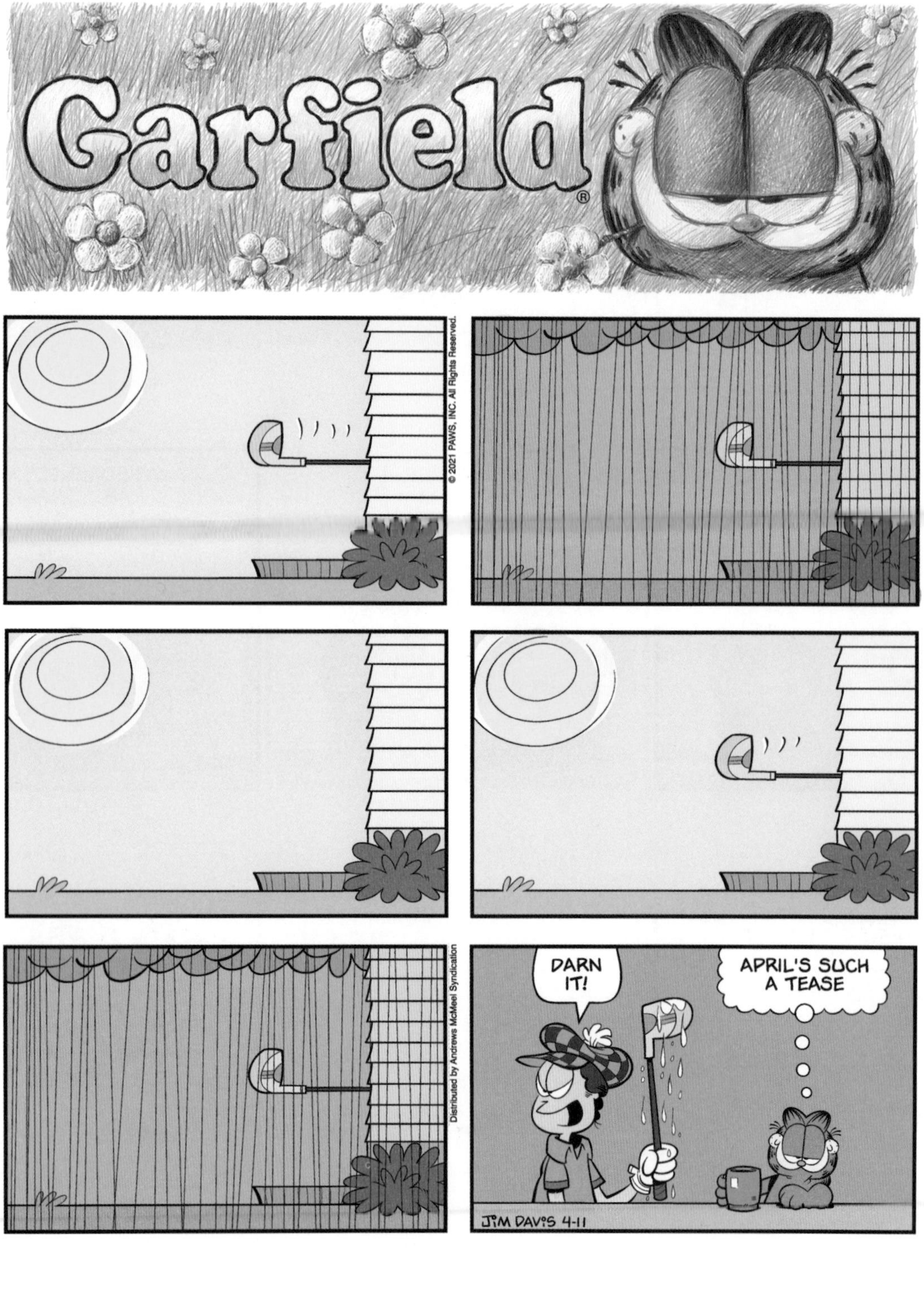
Garfield®
© 2021 PAWS, INC. All Rights Reserved.
Distributed by Andrews McMeel Syndication
DARN IT!
APRIL'S SUCH A TEASE
JIM DAVIS 4-11

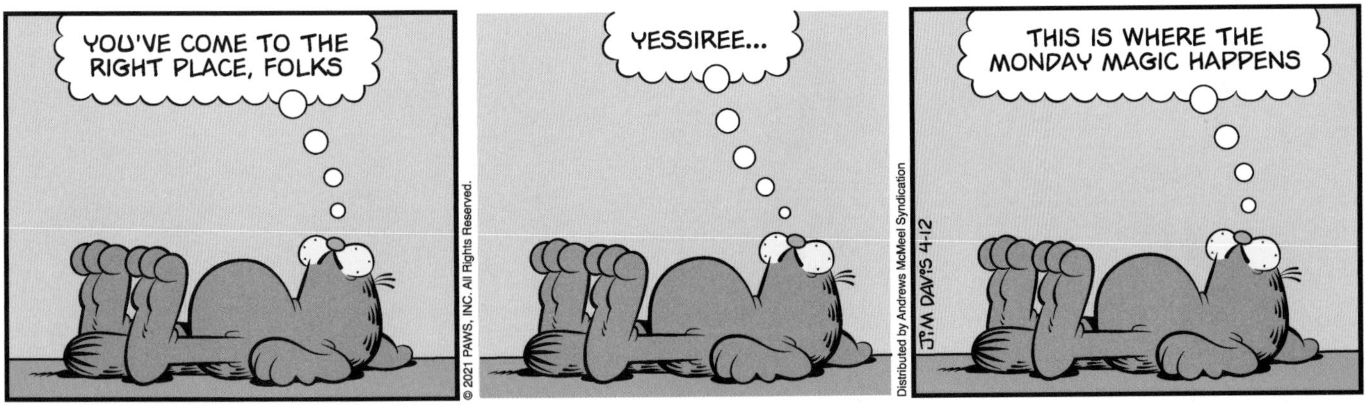
YOU'VE COME TO THE RIGHT PLACE, FOLKS
YESSIREE...
THIS IS WHERE THE MONDAY MAGIC HAPPENS
© 2021 PAWS, INC. All Rights Reserved.
Distributed by Andrews McMeel Syndication
JIM DAVIS 4-12

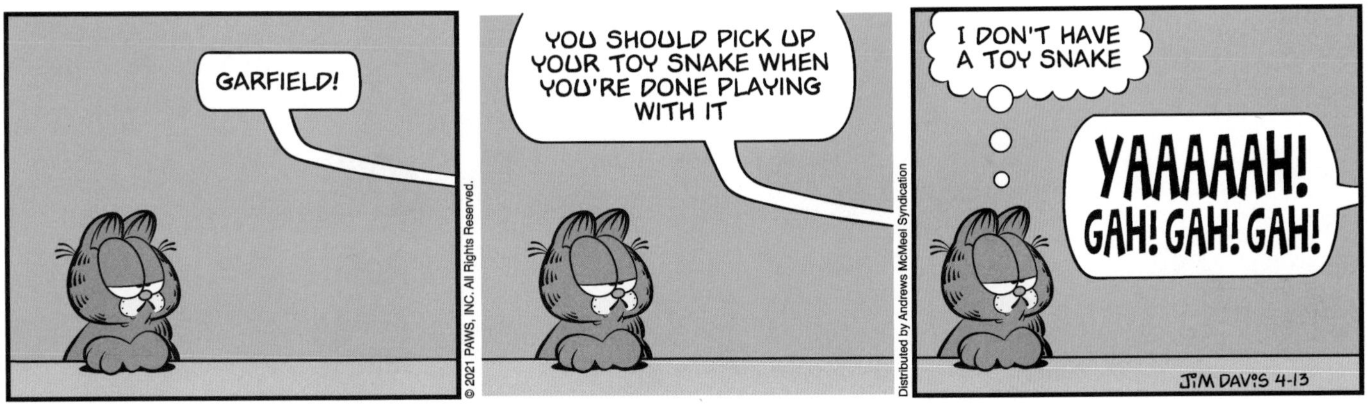
GARFIELD!
YOU SHOULD PICK UP YOUR TOY SNAKE WHEN YOU'RE DONE PLAYING WITH IT
I DON'T HAVE A TOY SNAKE
YAAAAAH! GAH! GAH! GAH!
© 2021 PAWS, INC. All Rights Reserved.
Distributed by Andrews McMeel Syndication
JIM DAVIS 4-13

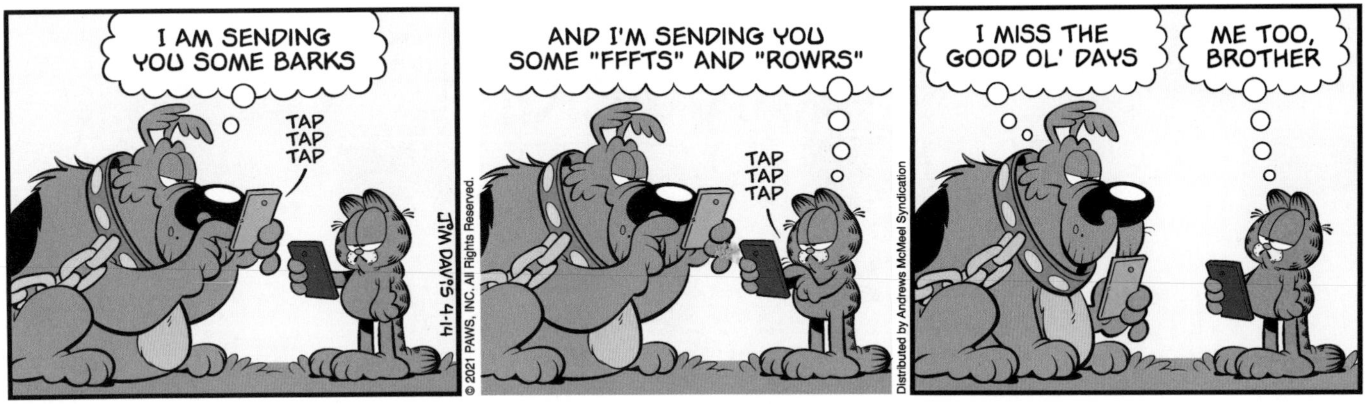
I AM SENDING YOU SOME BARKS
TAP TAP TAP
JIM DAVIS 4-14
AND I'M SENDING YOU SOME "FFFTS" AND "ROWRS"
TAP TAP TAP
I MISS THE GOOD OL' DAYS
ME TOO, BROTHER
© 2021 PAWS, INC. All Rights Reserved.
Distributed by Andrews McMeel Syndication

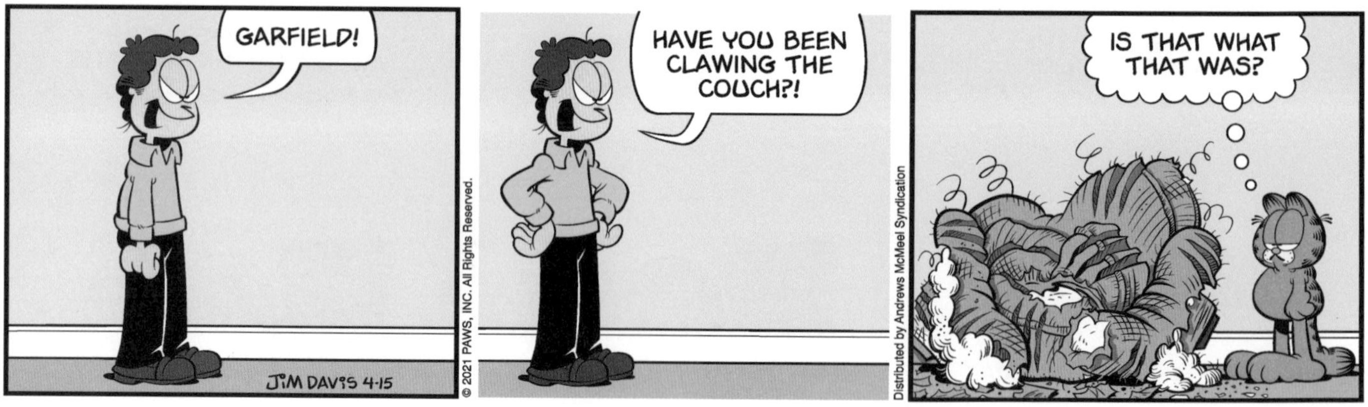
GARFIELD!
JIM DAVIS 4-15
© 2021 PAWS, INC. All Rights Reserved.
HAVE YOU BEEN CLAWING THE COUCH?!
Distributed by Andrews McMeel Syndication
IS THAT WHAT THAT WAS?

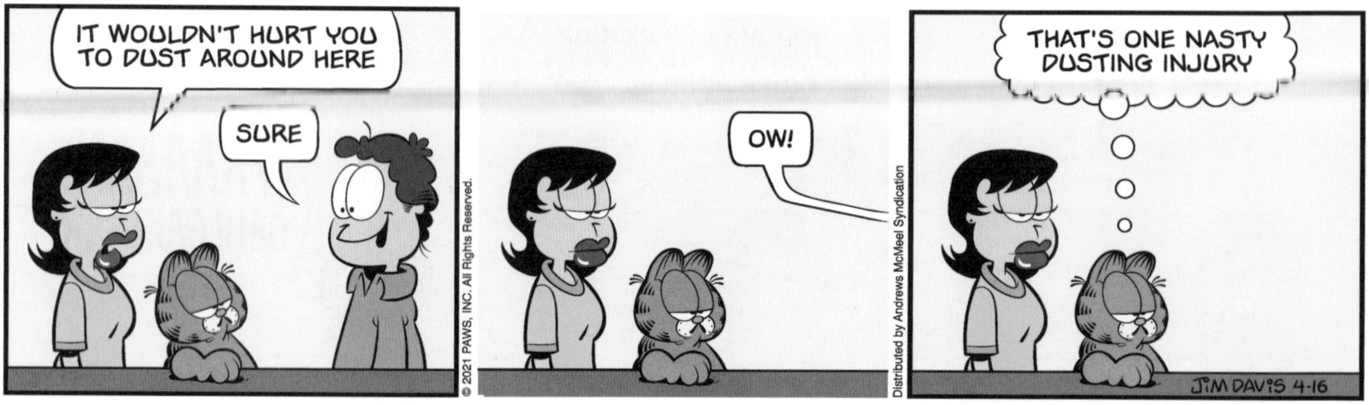
IT WOULDN'T HURT YOU TO DUST AROUND HERE
SURE
© 2021 PAWS, INC. All Rights Reserved.
OW!
Distributed by Andrews McMeel Syndication
THAT'S ONE NASTY DUSTING INJURY
JIM DAVIS 4-16

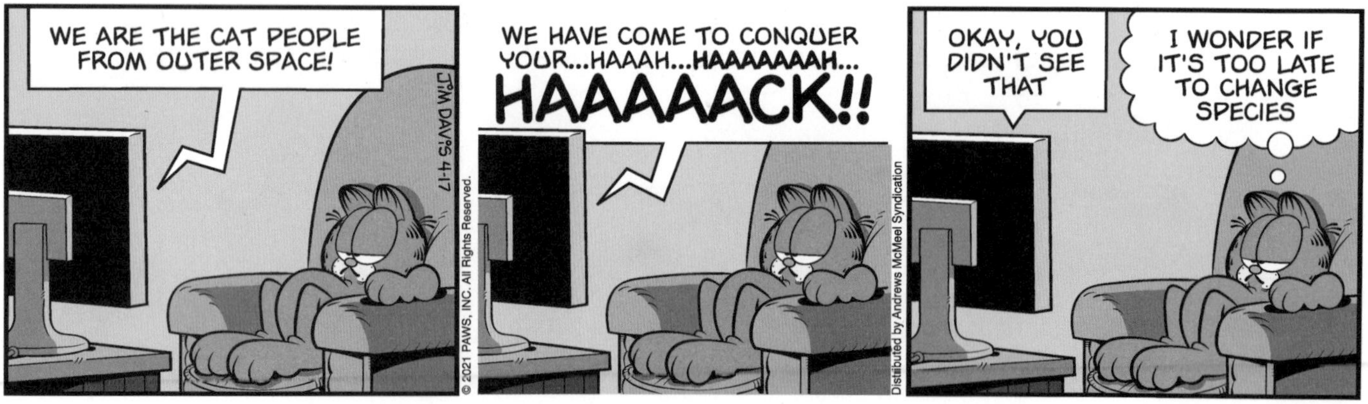
WE ARE THE CAT PEOPLE FROM OUTER SPACE!
JIM DAVIS 4-17
© 2021 PAWS, INC. All Rights Reserved.
WE HAVE COME TO CONQUER YOUR...HAAAH...HAAAAAAAH...
HAAAAACK!!
Distributed by Andrews McMeel Syndication
OKAY, YOU DIDN'T SEE THAT
I WONDER IF IT'S TOO LATE TO CHANGE SPECIES

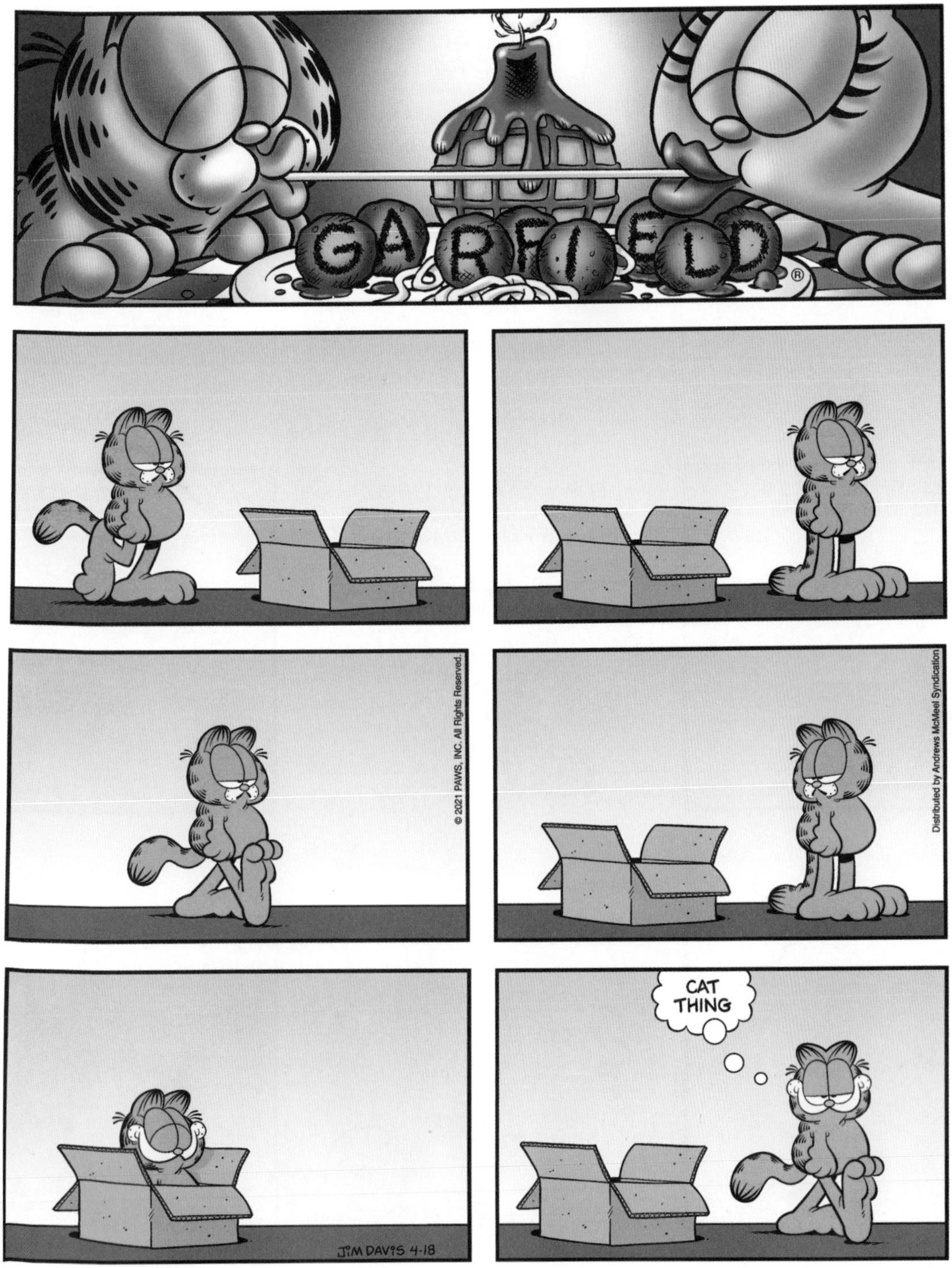
GARFIELD®
© 2021 PAWS, INC. All Rights Reserved.
Distributed by Andrews McMeel Syndication
CAT
THING
JIM DAVIS 4-18

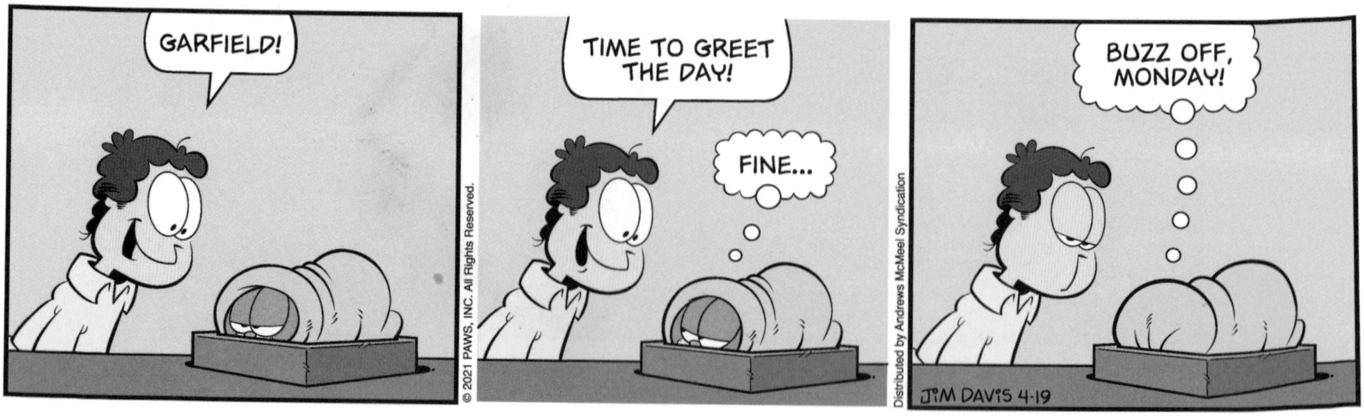
GARFIELD!
TIME TO GREET THE DAY!
FINE...
BUZZ OFF, MONDAY!
© 2021 PAWS, INC. All Rights Reserved.
Distributed by Andrews McMeel Syndication
JIM DAVIS 4-19

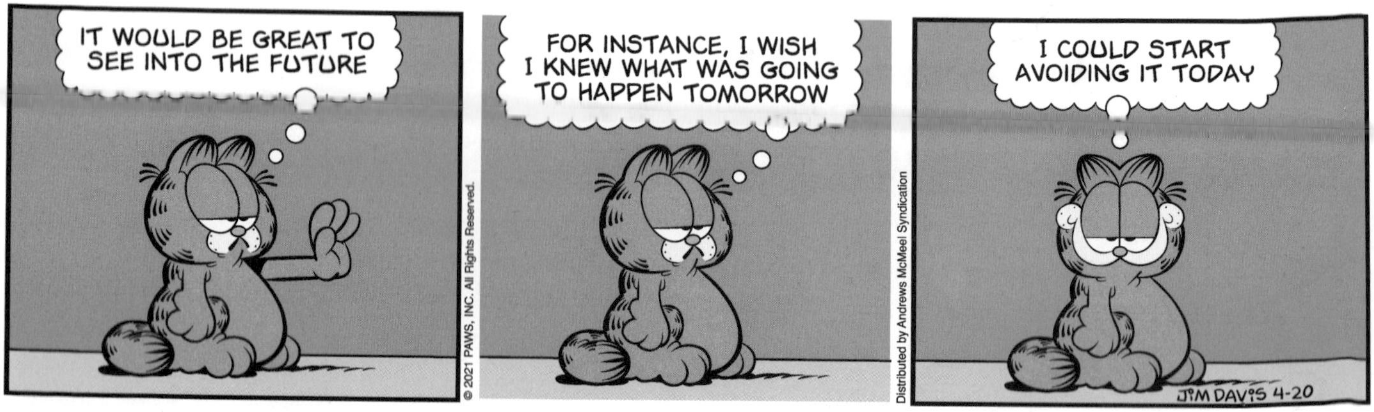
IT WOULD BE GREAT TO SEE INTO THE FUTURE
FOR INSTANCE, I WISH I KNEW WHAT WAS GOING TO HAPPEN TOMORROW
I COULD START AVOIDING IT TODAY
© 2021 PAWS, INC. All Rights Reserved.
Distributed by Andrews McMeel Syndication
JIM DAVIS 4-20

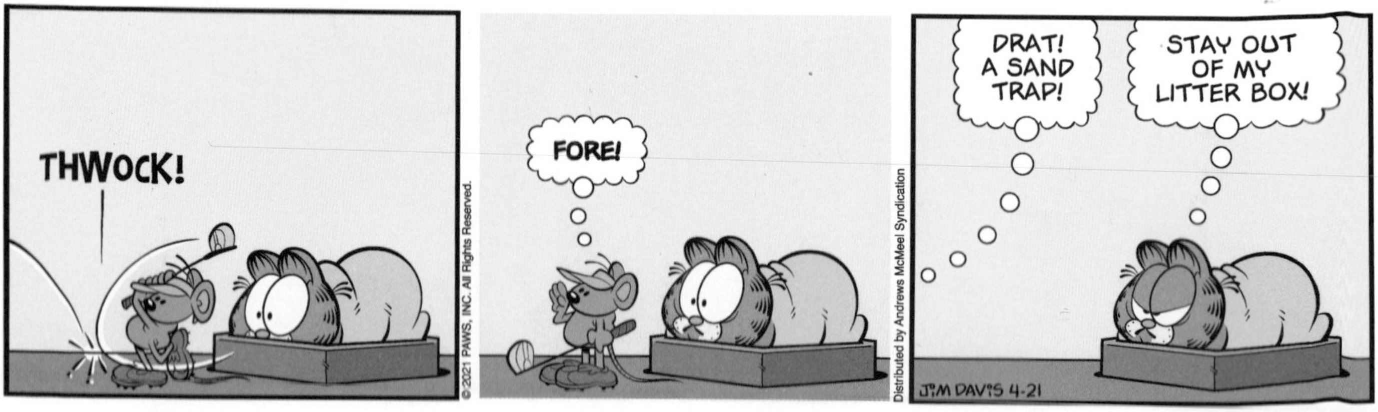
THWOCK!
FORE!
DRAT! A SAND TRAP!
STAY OUT OF MY LITTER BOX!
© 2021 PAWS, INC. All Rights Reserved.
Distributed by Andrews McMeel Syndication
JIM DAVIS 4-21

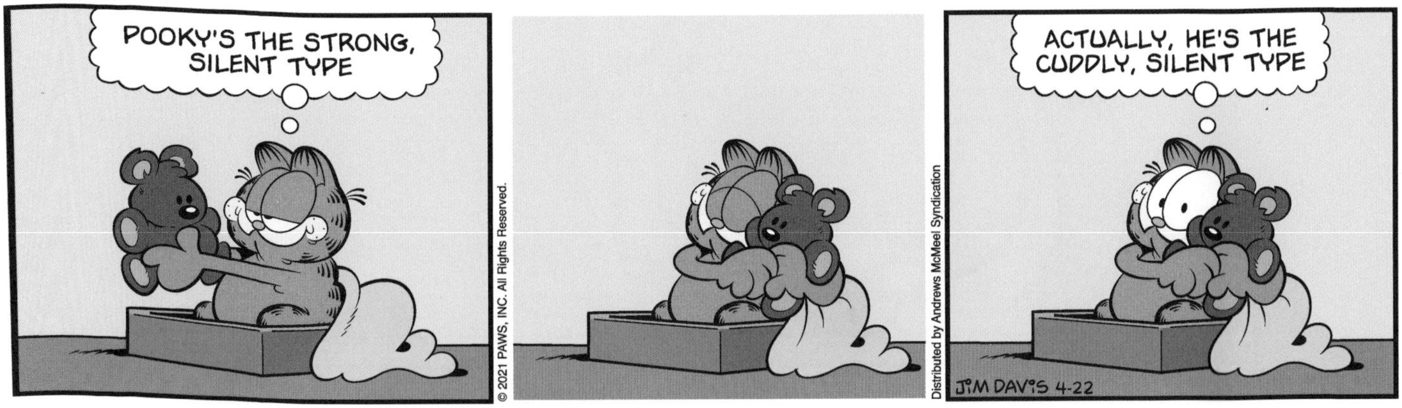
POOKY'S THE STRONG, SILENT TYPE
© 2021 PAWS, INC. All Rights Reserved.
Distributed by Andrews McMeel Syndication
ACTUALLY, HE'S THE CUDDLY, SILENT TYPE
JIM DAVIS 4-22

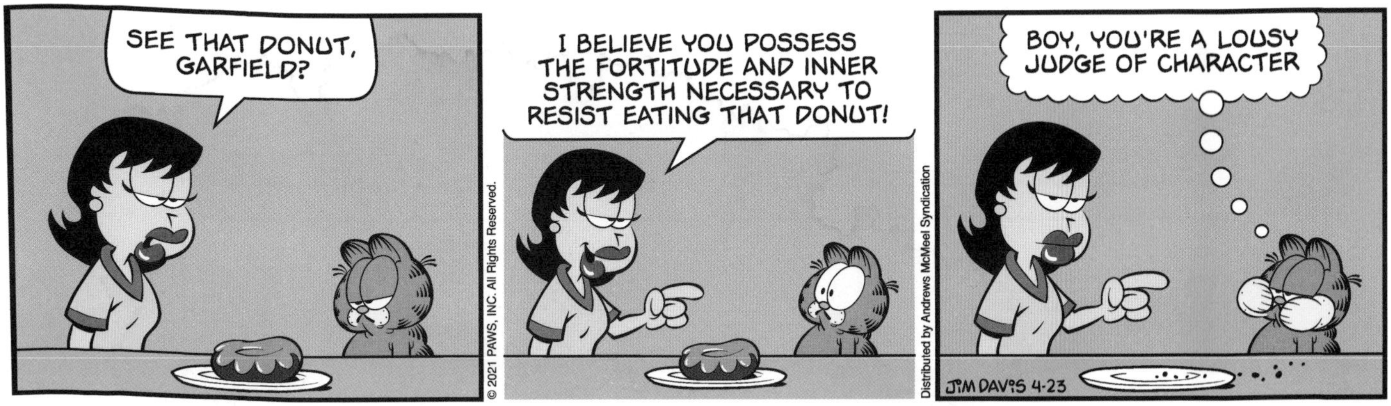
SEE THAT DONUT, GARFIELD?
© 2021 PAWS, INC. All Rights Reserved.
I BELIEVE YOU POSSESS THE FORTITUDE AND INNER STRENGTH NECESSARY TO RESIST EATING THAT DONUT!
Distributed by Andrews McMeel Syndication
BOY, YOU'RE A LOUSY JUDGE OF CHARACTER
JIM DAVIS 4-23

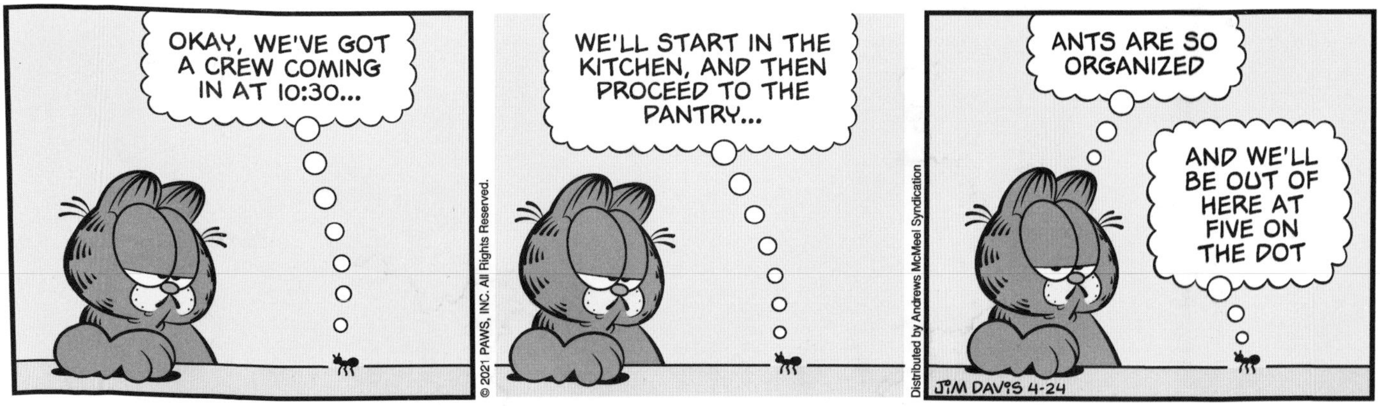
OKAY, WE'VE GOT A CREW COMING IN AT 10:30...
© 2021 PAWS, INC. All Rights Reserved.
WE'LL START IN THE KITCHEN, AND THEN PROCEED TO THE PANTRY...
Distributed by Andrews McMeel Syndication
ANTS ARE SO ORGANIZED
AND WE'LL BE OUT OF HERE AT FIVE ON THE DOT
JIM DAVIS 4-24

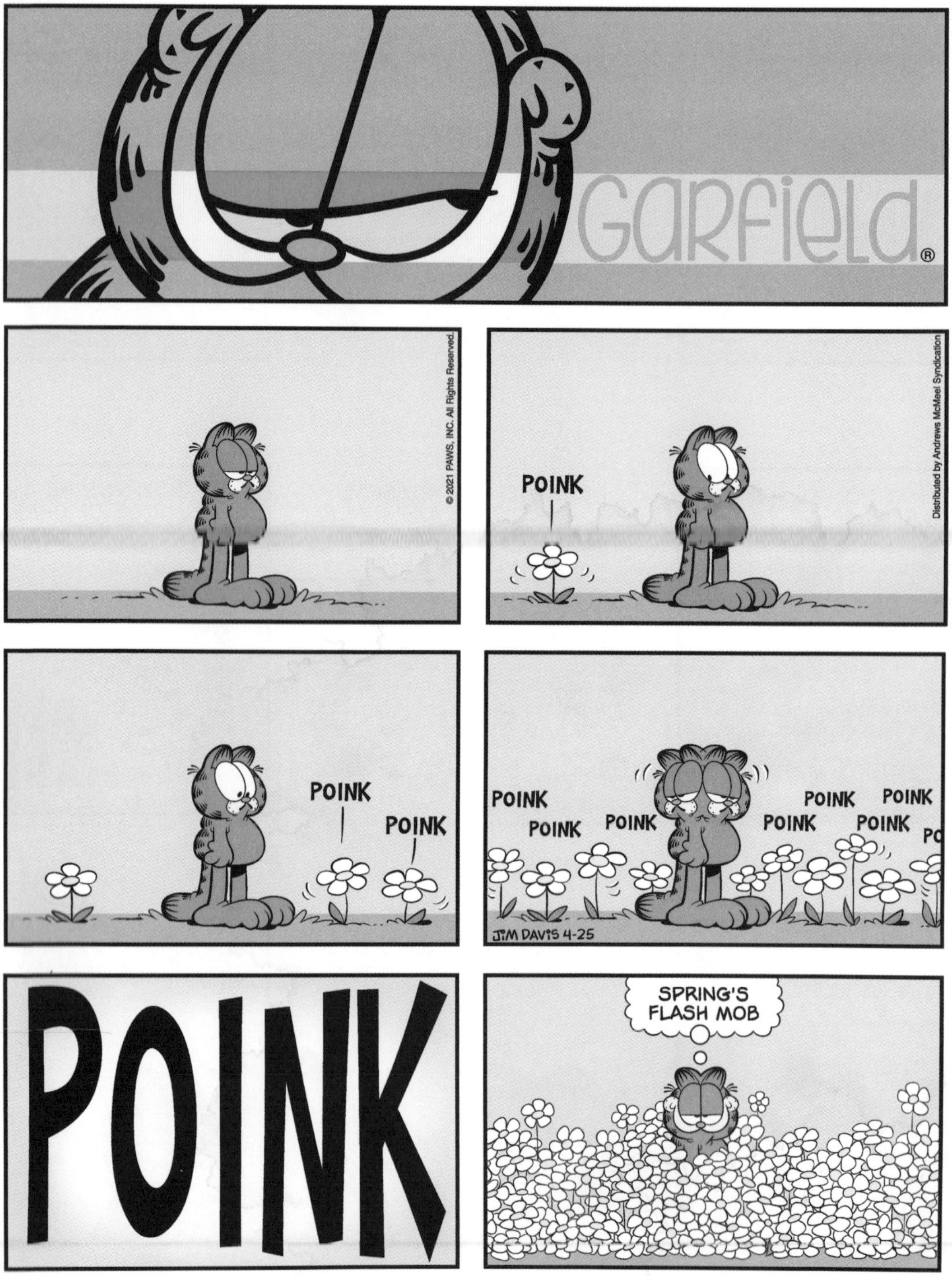
GARFIELD®
© 2021 PAWS, INC. All Rights Reserved.
Distributed by Andrews McMeel Syndication
POINK
POINK
POINK
POINK
POINK
POINK
POINK
POINK
POINK
POINK
JIM DAVIS 4-25
POINK
SPRING'S FLASH MOB

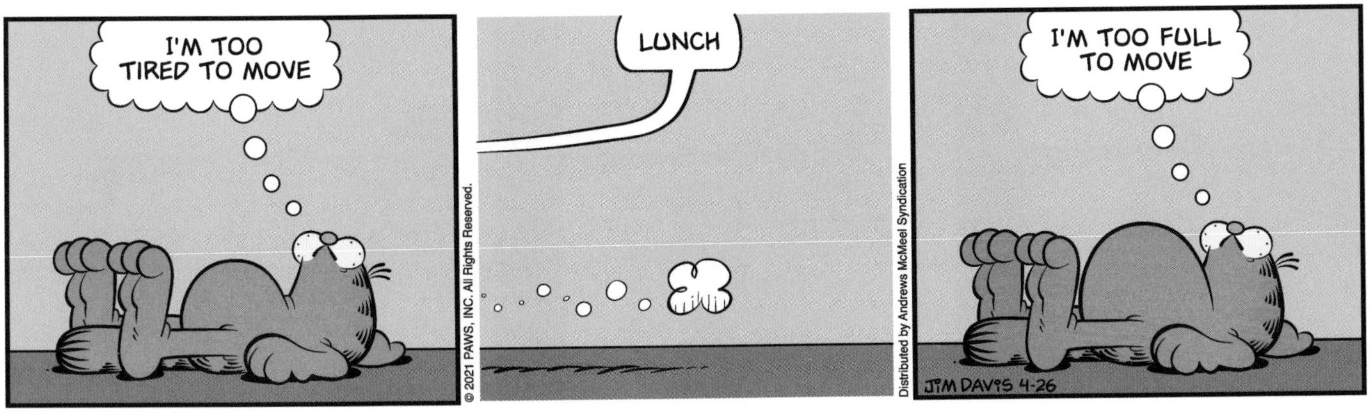
I'M TOO TIRED TO MOVE
LUNCH
I'M TOO FULL TO MOVE
JIM DAVIS 4-26
© 2021 PAWS, INC. All Rights Reserved.
Distributed by Andrews McMeel Syndication

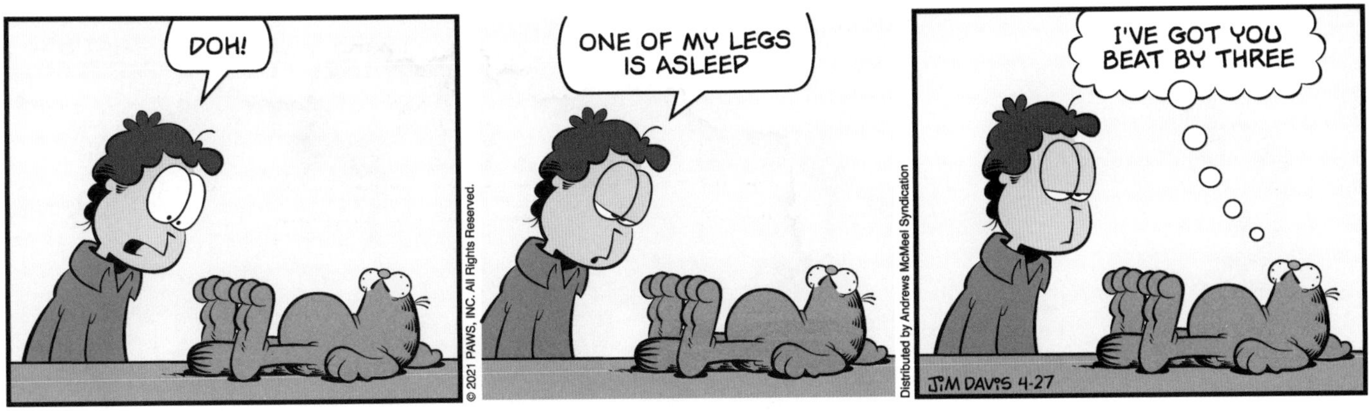
DOH!
ONE OF MY LEGS IS ASLEEP
I'VE GOT YOU BEAT BY THREE
JIM DAVIS 4-27
© 2021 PAWS, INC. All Rights Reserved.
Distributed by Andrews McMeel Syndication

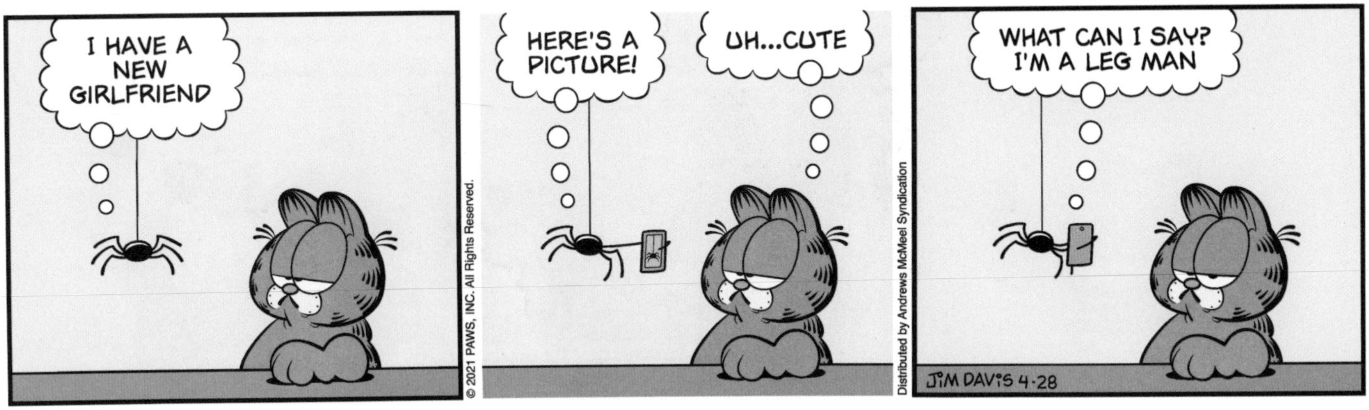
I HAVE A NEW GIRLFRIEND
HERE'S A PICTURE!
UH...CUTE
WHAT CAN I SAY? I'M A LEG MAN
JIM DAVIS 4-28
© 2021 PAWS, INC. All Rights Reserved.
Distributed by Andrews McMeel Syndication

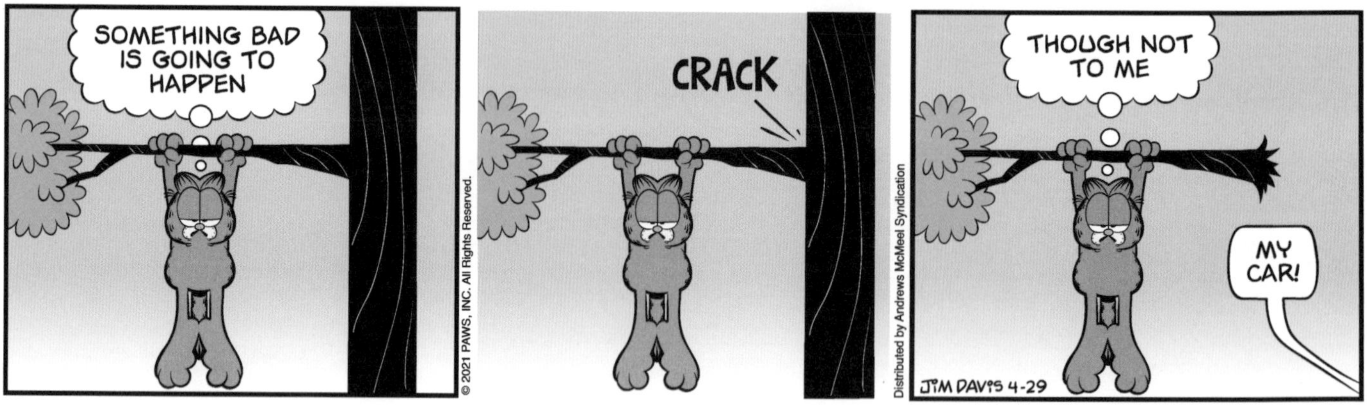
SOMETHING BAD IS GOING TO HAPPEN
CRACK
THOUGH NOT TO ME
MY CAR!
© 2021 PAWS, INC. All Rights Reserved.
Distributed by Andrews McMeel Syndication
JIM DAVIS 4-29

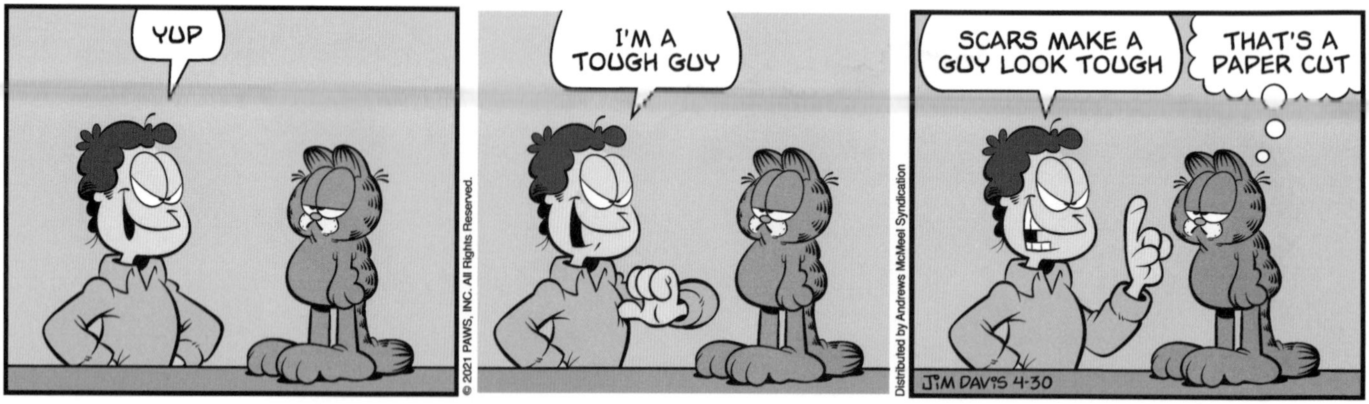
YUP
I'M A TOUGH GUY
SCARS MAKE A GUY LOOK TOUGH
THAT'S A PAPER CUT
© 2021 PAWS, INC. All Rights Reserved.
Distributed by Andrews McMeel Syndication
JIM DAVIS 4-30

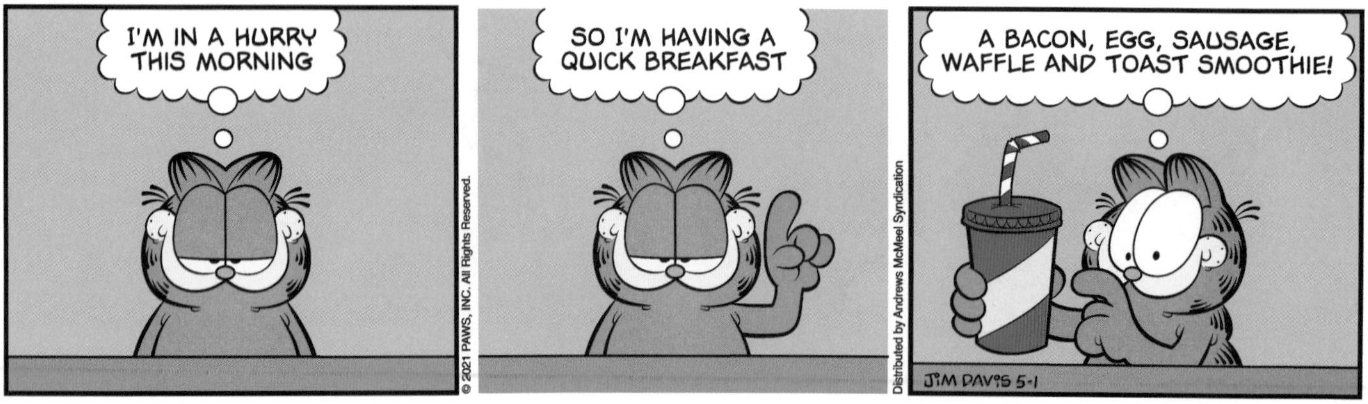
I'M IN A HURRY THIS MORNING
SO I'M HAVING A QUICK BREAKFAST
A BACON, EGG, SAUSAGE, WAFFLE AND TOAST SMOOTHIE!
© 2021 PAWS, INC. All Rights Reserved.
Distributed by Andrews McMeel Syndication
JIM DAVIS 5-1

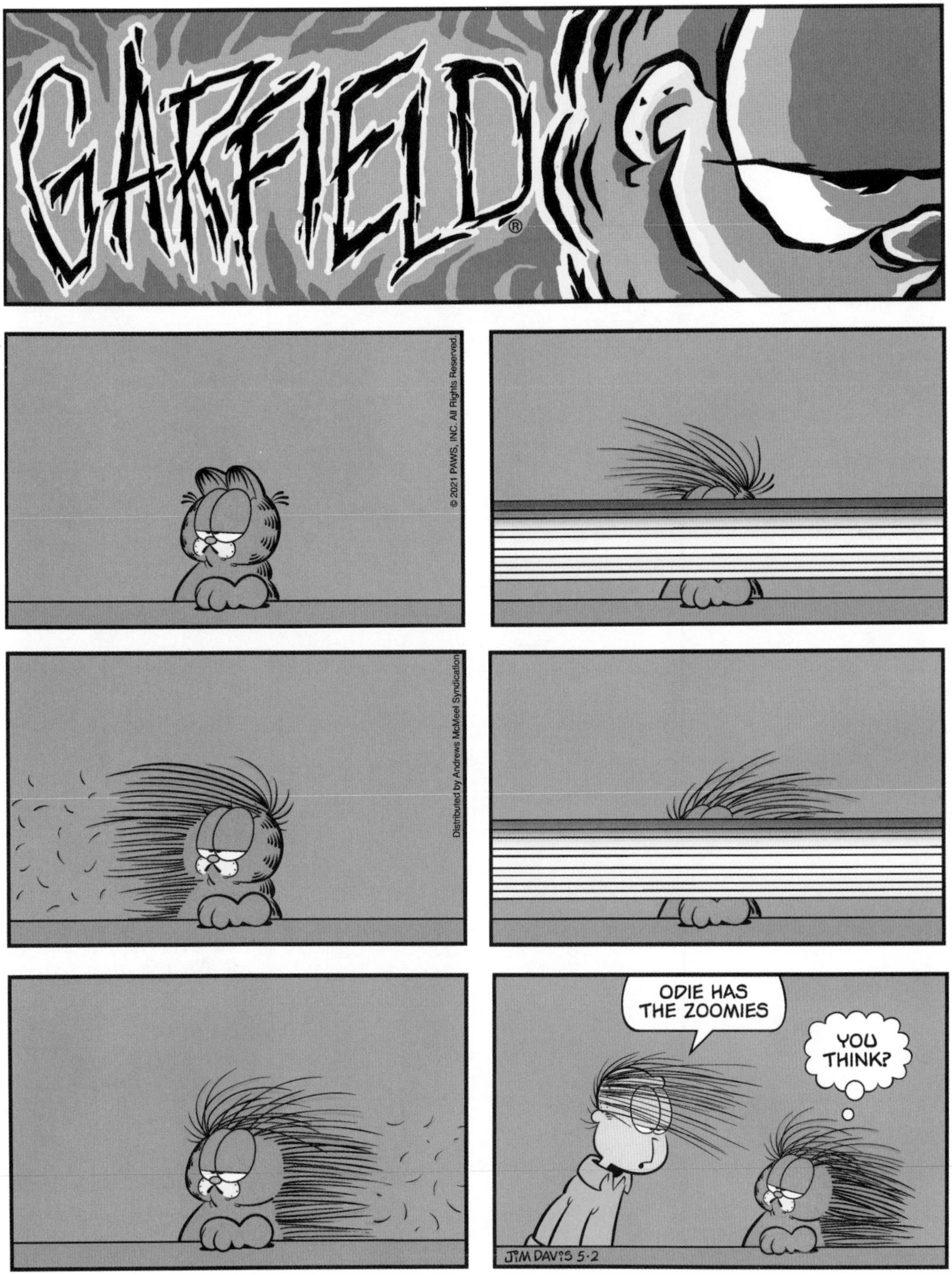
GARFIELD®
© 2021 PAWS, INC. All Rights Reserved.
Distributed by Andrews McMeel Syndication
ODIE HAS THE ZOOMIES
YOU THINK?
JIM DAVIS 5-2

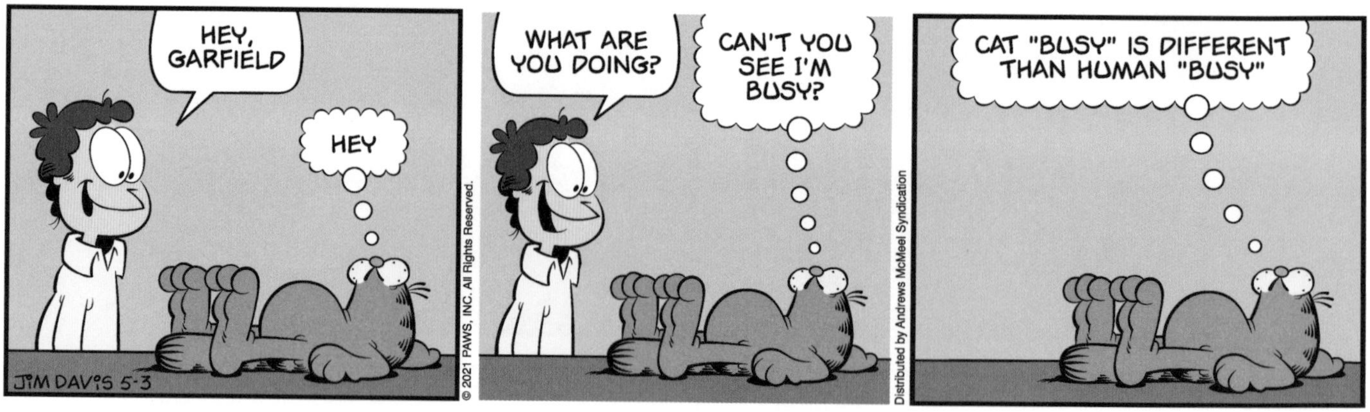
HEY, GARFIELD
HEY
WHAT ARE YOU DOING?
CAN'T YOU SEE I'M BUSY?
CAT "BUSY" IS DIFFERENT THAN HUMAN "BUSY"
JIM DAVIS 5-3
© 2021 PAWS, INC. All Rights Reserved.
Distributed by Andrews McMeel Syndication

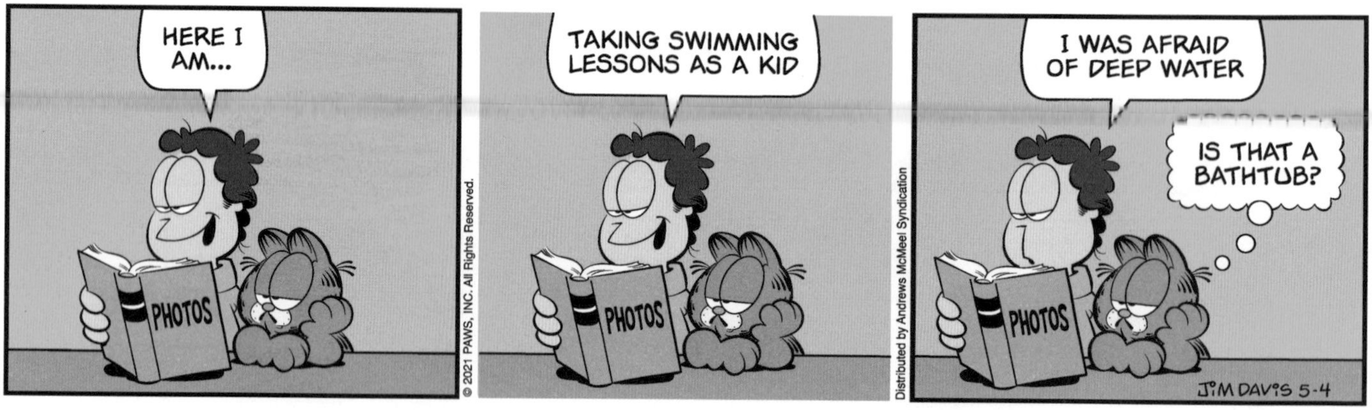
HERE I AM...
PHOTOS
TAKING SWIMMING LESSONS AS A KID
I WAS AFRAID OF DEEP WATER
IS THAT A BATHTUB?
JIM DAVIS 5-4
© 2021 PAWS, INC. All Rights Reserved.
Distributed by Andrews McMeel Syndication

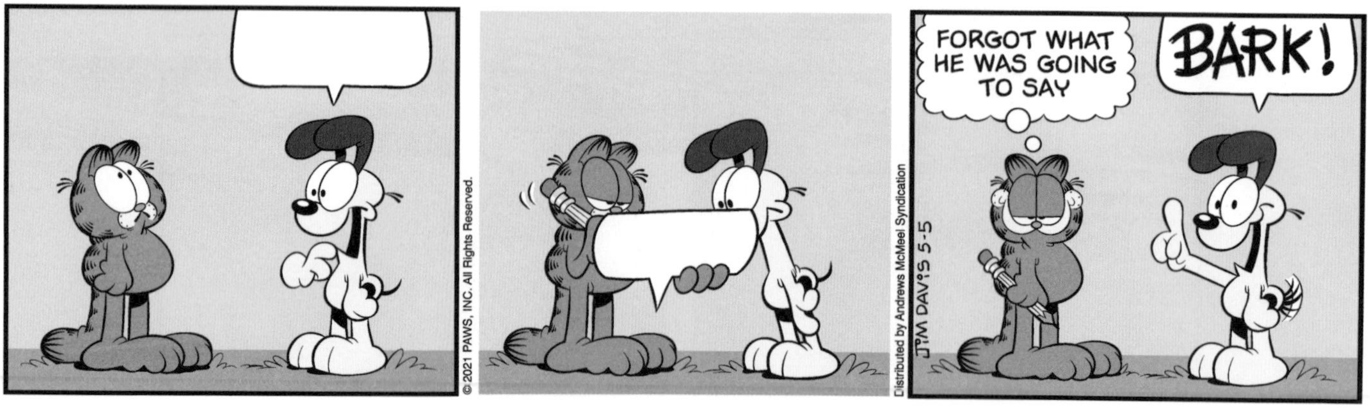
FORGOT WHAT HE WAS GOING TO SAY
BARK!
JIM DAVIS 5-5
© 2021 PAWS, INC. All Rights Reserved.
Distributed by Andrews McMeel Syndication

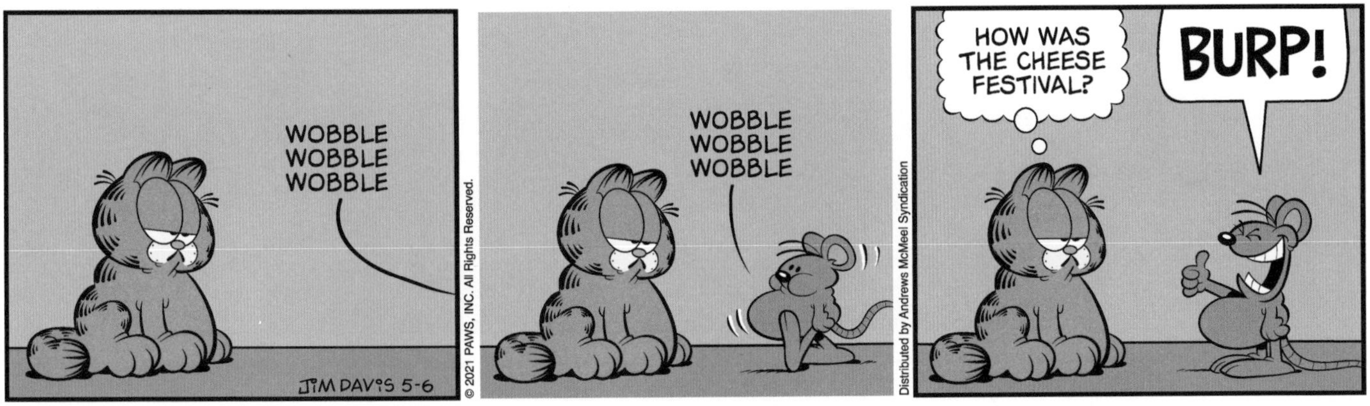
WOBBLE
WOBBLE
WOBBLE
JIM DAVIS 5-6
WOBBLE
WOBBLE
WOBBLE
© 2021 PAWS, INC. All Rights Reserved.
HOW WAS THE CHEESE FESTIVAL?
BURP!
Distributed by Andrews McMeel Syndication

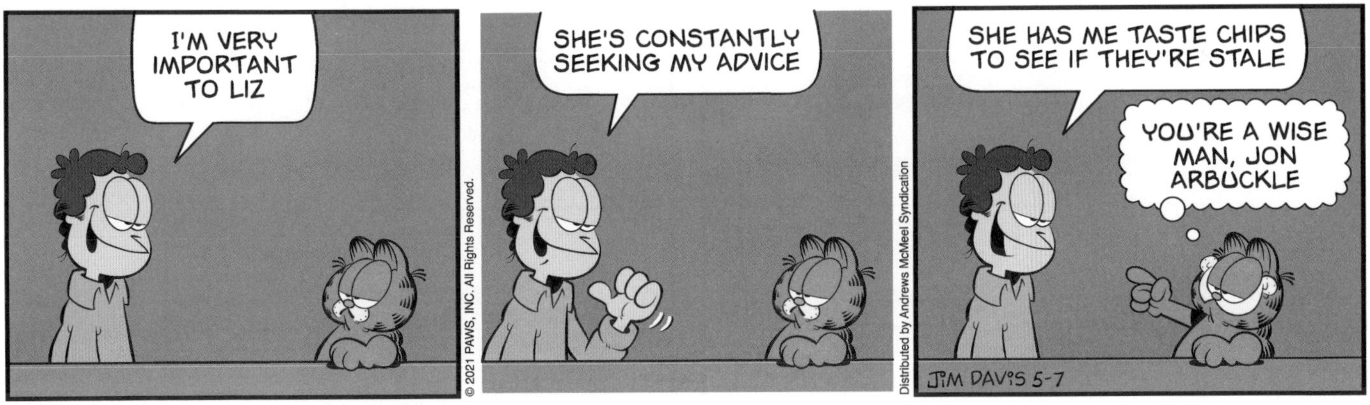
I'M VERY IMPORTANT TO LIZ
SHE'S CONSTANTLY SEEKING MY ADVICE
© 2021 PAWS, INC. All Rights Reserved.
SHE HAS ME TASTE CHIPS TO SEE IF THEY'RE STALE
YOU'RE A WISE MAN, JON ARBUCKLE
Distributed by Andrews McMeel Syndication
JIM DAVIS 5-7

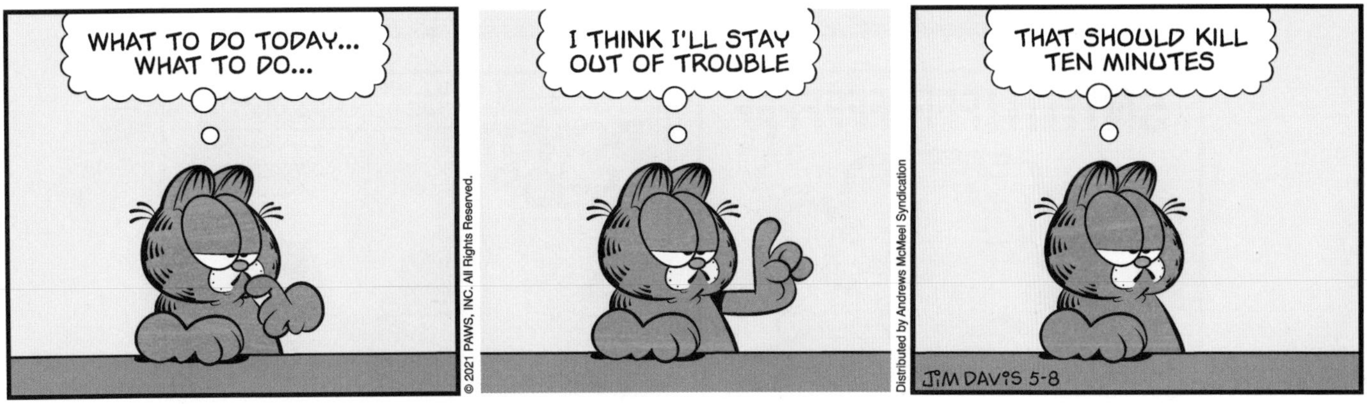
WHAT TO DO TODAY... WHAT TO DO...
I THINK I'LL STAY OUT OF TROUBLE
© 2021 PAWS, INC. All Rights Reserved.
THAT SHOULD KILL TEN MINUTES
Distributed by Andrews McMeel Syndication
JIM DAVIS 5-8

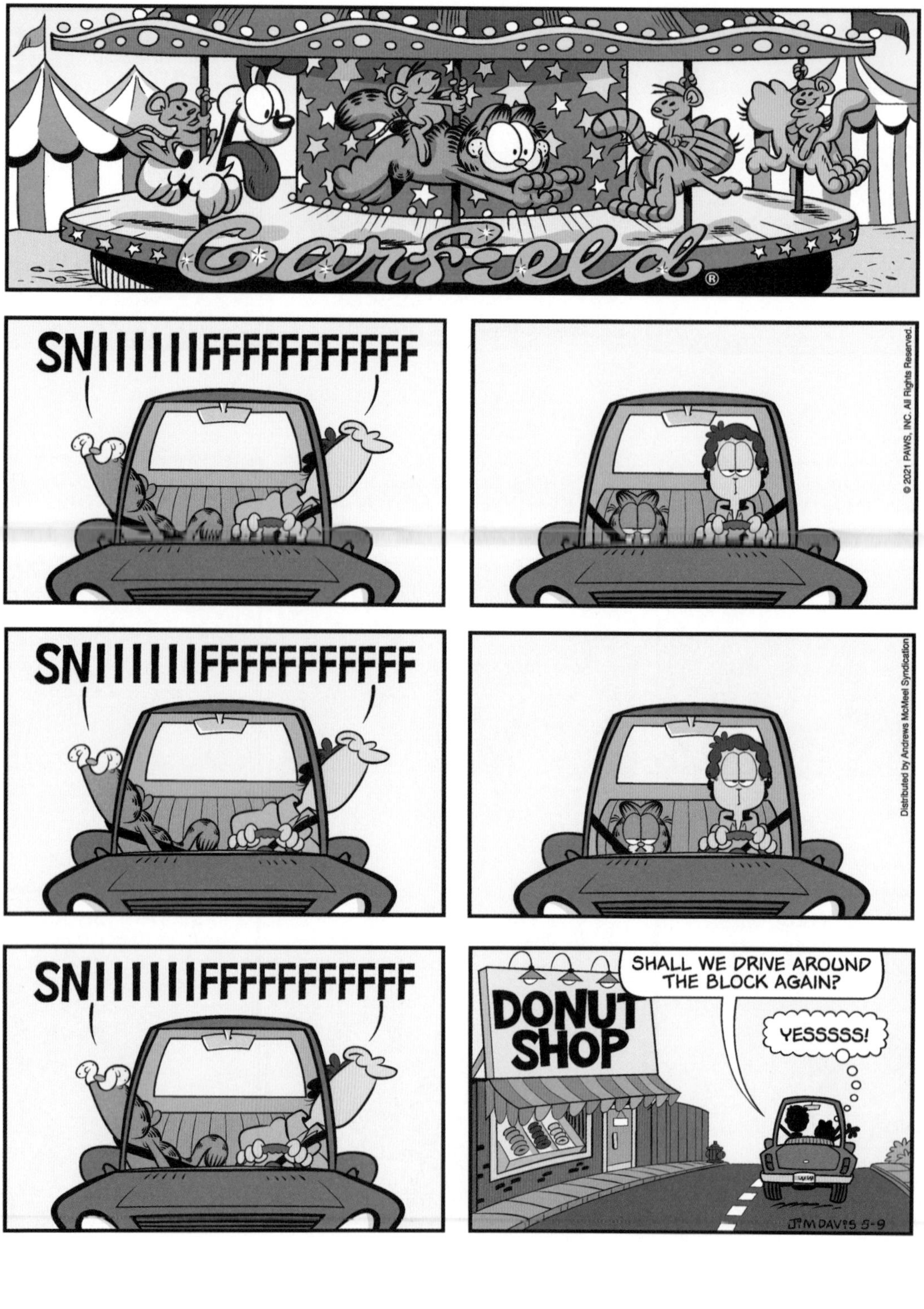
Garfield®
SNIIIIIIFFFFFFFFFFF
© 2021 PAWS, INC. All Rights Reserved.
SNIIIIIIFFFFFFFFFFF
Distributed by Andrews McMeel Syndication
SNIIIIIIFFFFFFFFFFF
DONUT SHOP
SHALL WE DRIVE AROUND THE BLOCK AGAIN?
YESSSSS!
JIM DAVIS 5-9

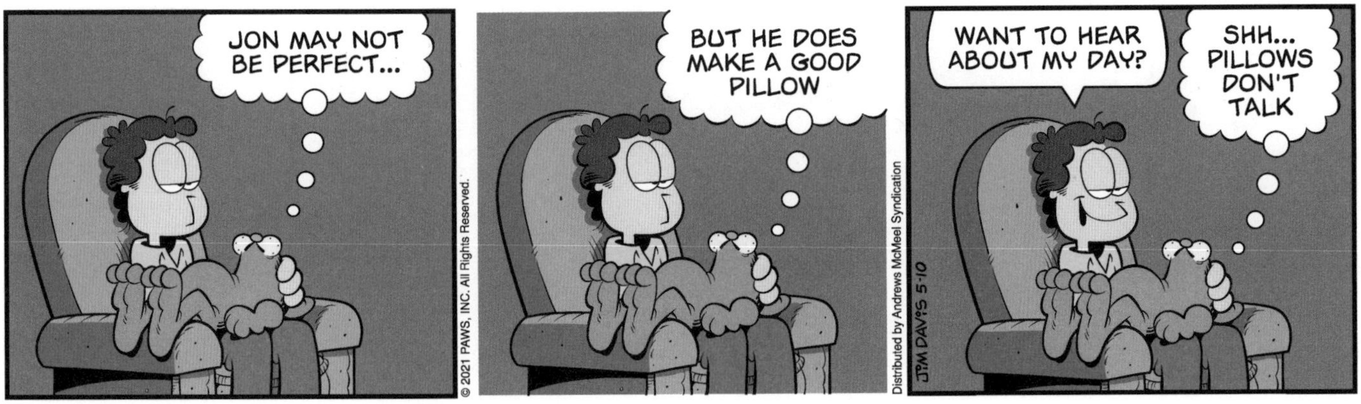
JON MAY NOT BE PERFECT...
BUT HE DOES MAKE A GOOD PILLOW
WANT TO HEAR ABOUT MY DAY?
SHH... PILLOWS DON'T TALK
JIM DAVIS 5-10
© 2021 PAWS, INC. All Rights Reserved.
Distributed by Andrews McMeel Syndication

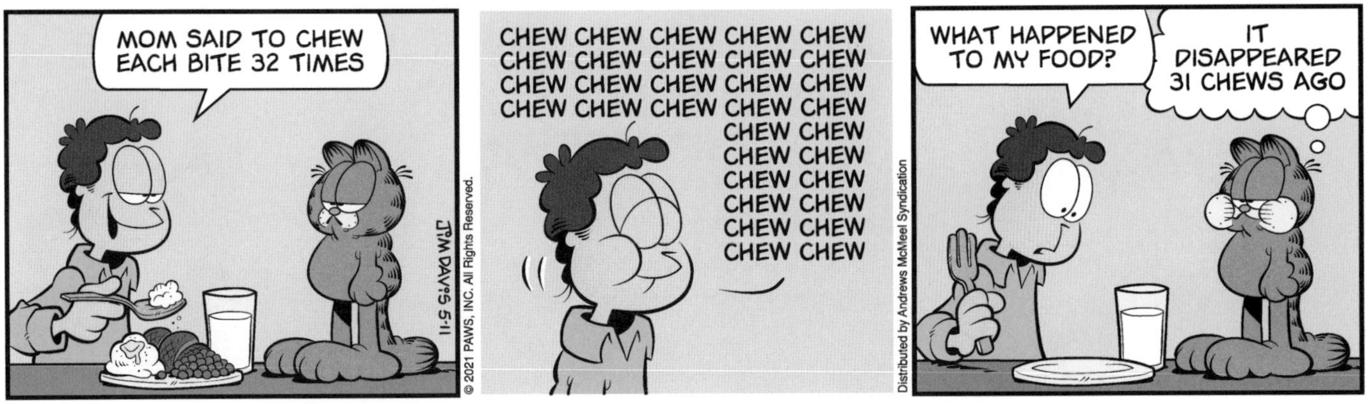
MOM SAID TO CHEW EACH BITE 32 TIMES
JIM DAVIS 5-11
CHEW CHEW CHEW CHEW CHEW
CHEW CHEW CHEW CHEW CHEW
CHEW CHEW CHEW CHEW CHEW
CHEW CHEW CHEW CHEW CHEW
CHEW CHEW
CHEW CHEW
CHEW CHEW
CHEW CHEW
CHEW CHEW
CHEW CHEW
WHAT HAPPENED TO MY FOOD?
IT DISAPPEARED 31 CHEWS AGO
© 2021 PAWS, INC. All Rights Reserved.
Distributed by Andrews McMeel Syndication

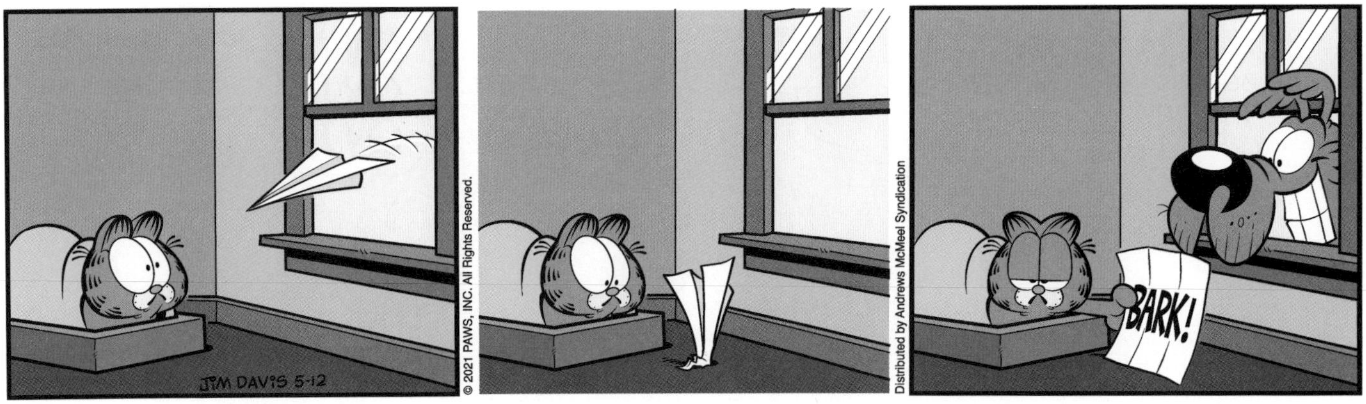
JIM DAVIS 5-12
BARK!
© 2021 PAWS, INC. All Rights Reserved.
Distributed by Andrews McMeel Syndication

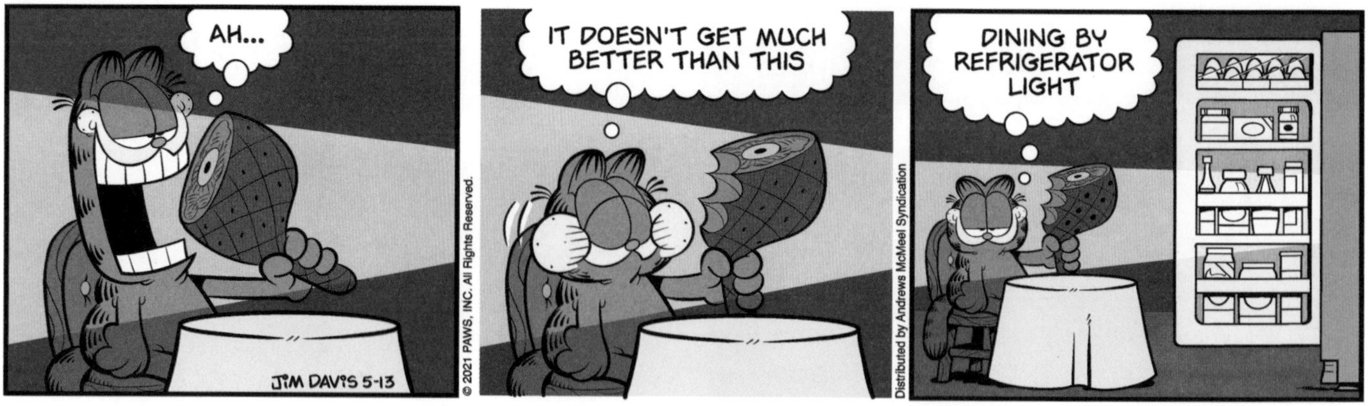
AH...
IT DOESN'T GET MUCH BETTER THAN THIS
DINING BY REFRIGERATOR LIGHT
JIM DAVIS 5-13
© 2021 PAWS, INC. All Rights Reserved.
Distributed by Andrews McMeel Syndication

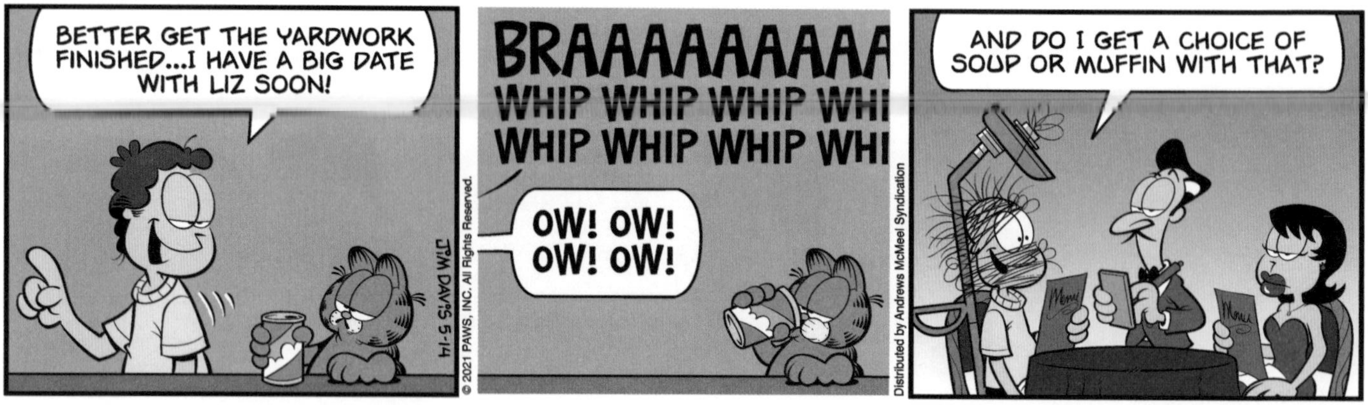
BETTER GET THE YARDWORK FINISHED...I HAVE A BIG DATE WITH LIZ SOON!
JIM DAVIS 5-14
BRAAAAAAAAA
WHIP WHIP WHIP WHI
WHIP WHIP WHIP WHI
OW! OW! OW! OW!
AND DO I GET A CHOICE OF SOUP OR MUFFIN WITH THAT?
Menu
Menu
© 2021 PAWS, INC. All Rights Reserved.
Distributed by Andrews McMeel Syndication

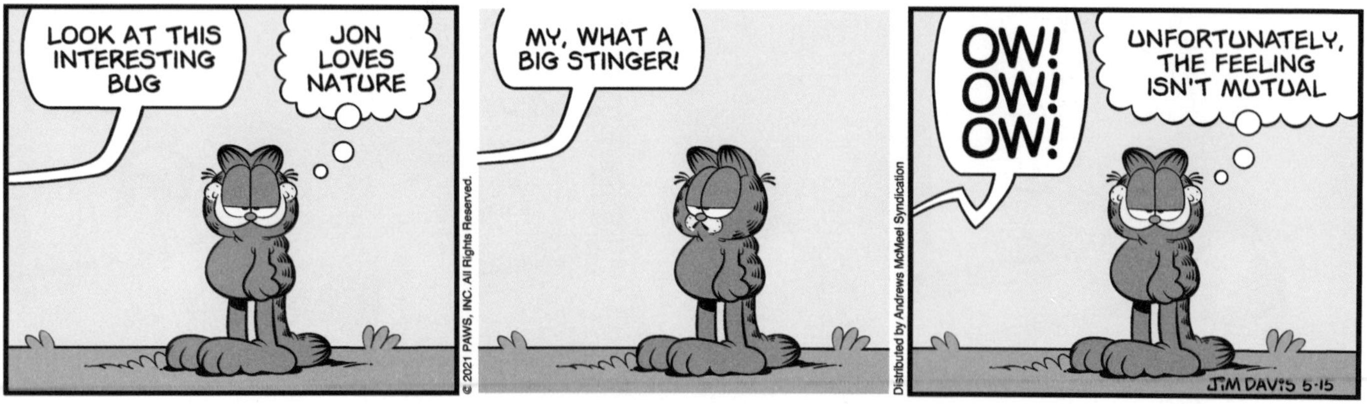
LOOK AT THIS INTERESTING BUG
JON LOVES NATURE
MY, WHAT A BIG STINGER!
OW! OW! OW!
UNFORTUNATELY, THE FEELING ISN'T MUTUAL
JIM DAVIS 5-15
© 2021 PAWS, INC. All Rights Reserved.
Distributed by Andrews McMeel Syndication

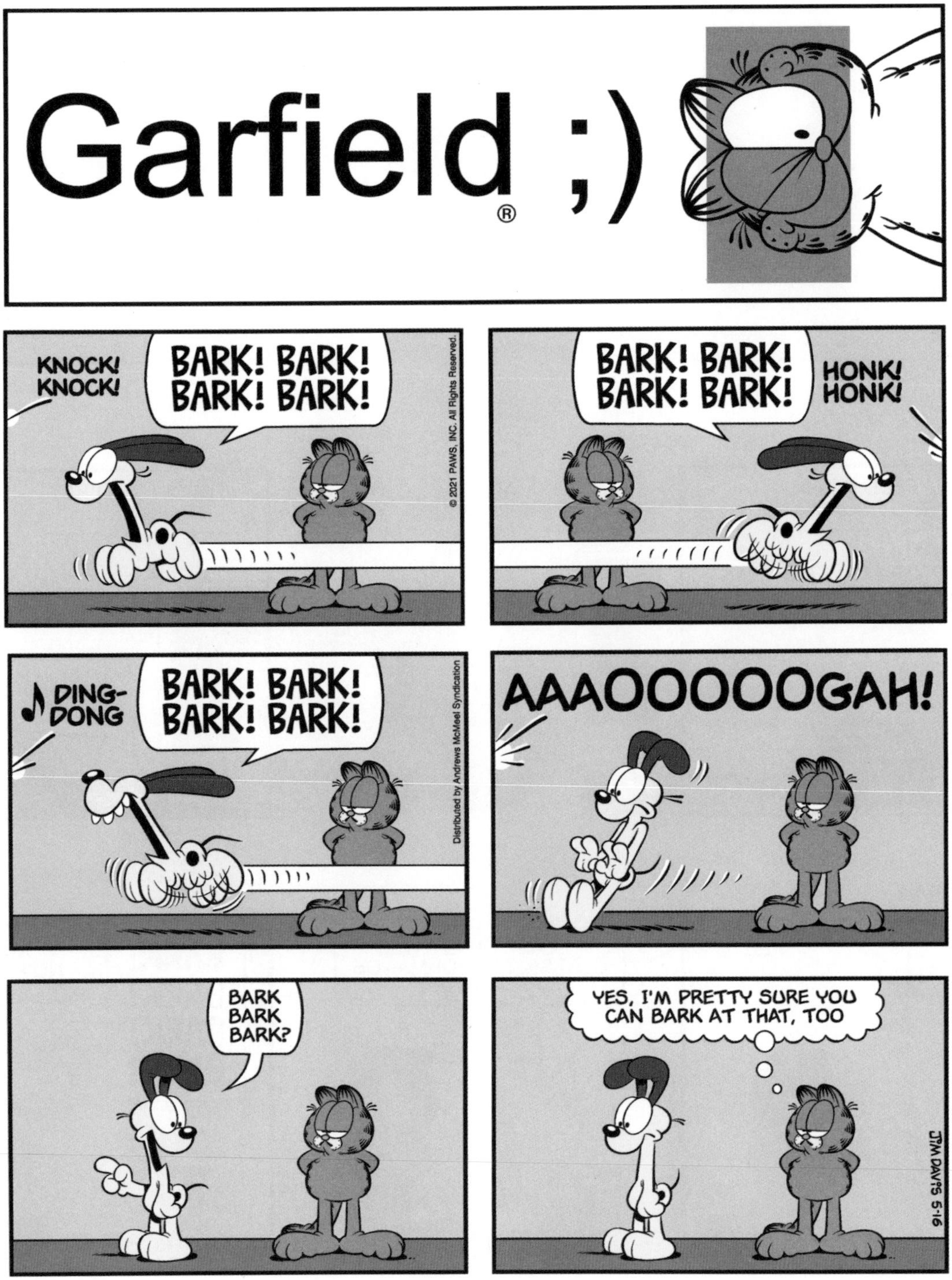
Garfield ;)
KNOCK! KNOCK!
BARK! BARK! BARK! BARK!
© 2021 PAWS, INC. All Rights Reserved.
BARK! BARK! BARK! BARK!
HONK! HONK!
DING-DONG
BARK! BARK! BARK! BARK!
Distributed by Andrews McMeel Syndication
AAAOOOOOGAH!
BARK BARK BARK?
YES, I'M PRETTY SURE YOU CAN BARK AT THAT, TOO
JIM DAVIS 5-16

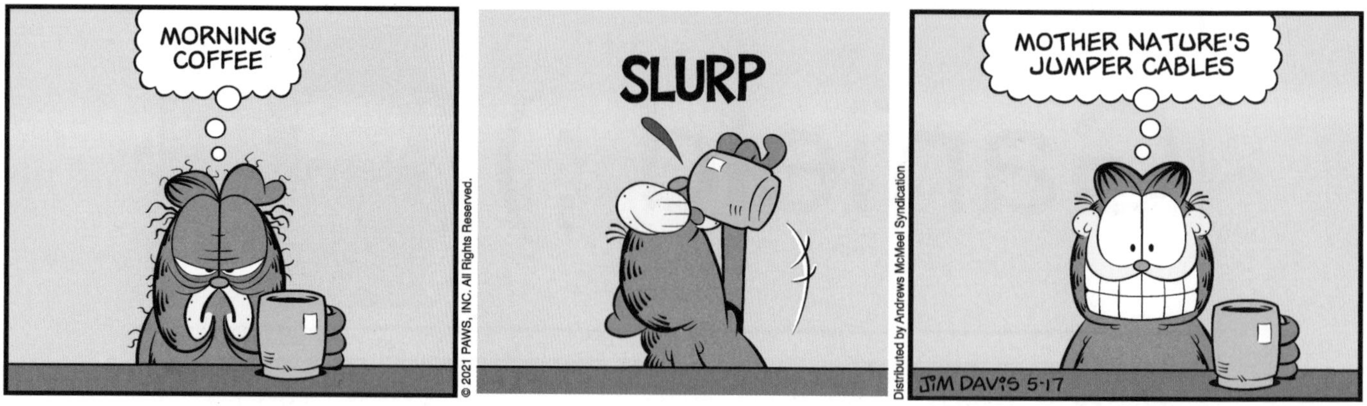
MORNING COFFEE
SLURP
MOTHER NATURE'S JUMPER CABLES
© 2021 PAWS, INC. All Rights Reserved.
Distributed by Andrews McMeel Syndication
JIM DAVIS 5-17

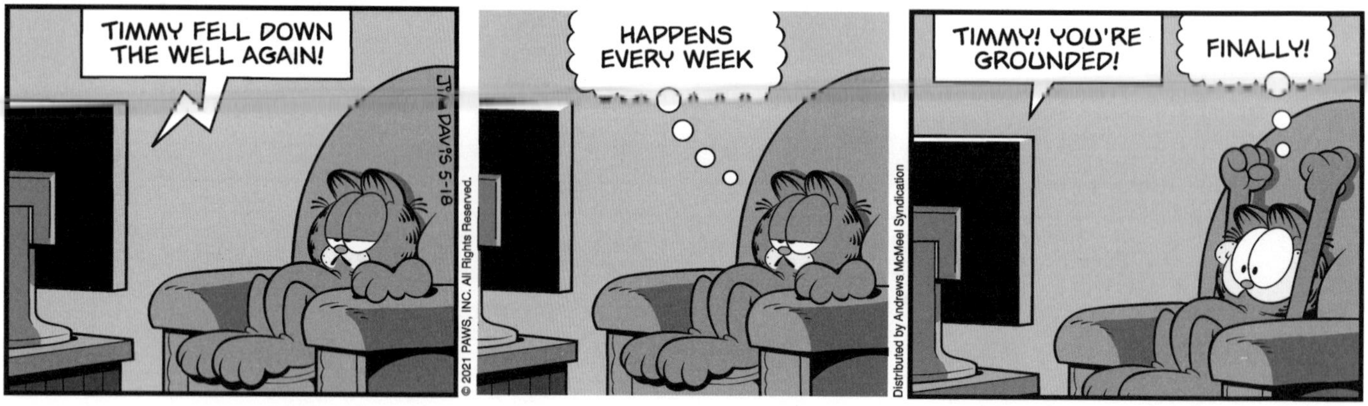
TIMMY FELL DOWN THE WELL AGAIN!
JIM DAVIS 5-18
HAPPENS EVERY WEEK
TIMMY! YOU'RE GROUNDED!
FINALLY!
© 2021 PAWS, INC. All Rights Reserved.
Distributed by Andrews McMeel Syndication

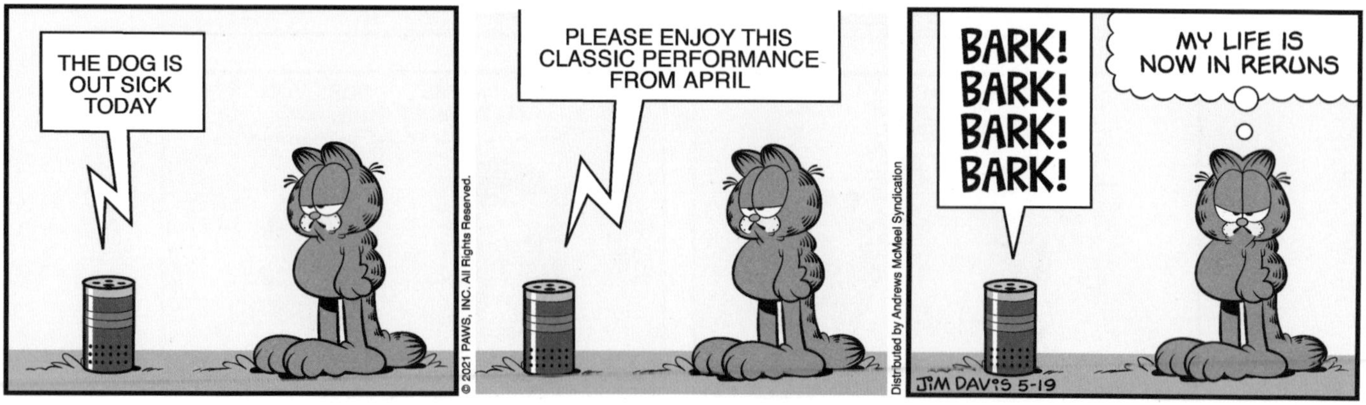
THE DOG IS OUT SICK TODAY
PLEASE ENJOY THIS CLASSIC PERFORMANCE FROM APRIL
BARK! BARK! BARK! BARK!
MY LIFE IS NOW IN RERUNS
© 2021 PAWS, INC. All Rights Reserved.
Distributed by Andrews McMeel Syndication
JIM DAVIS 5-19

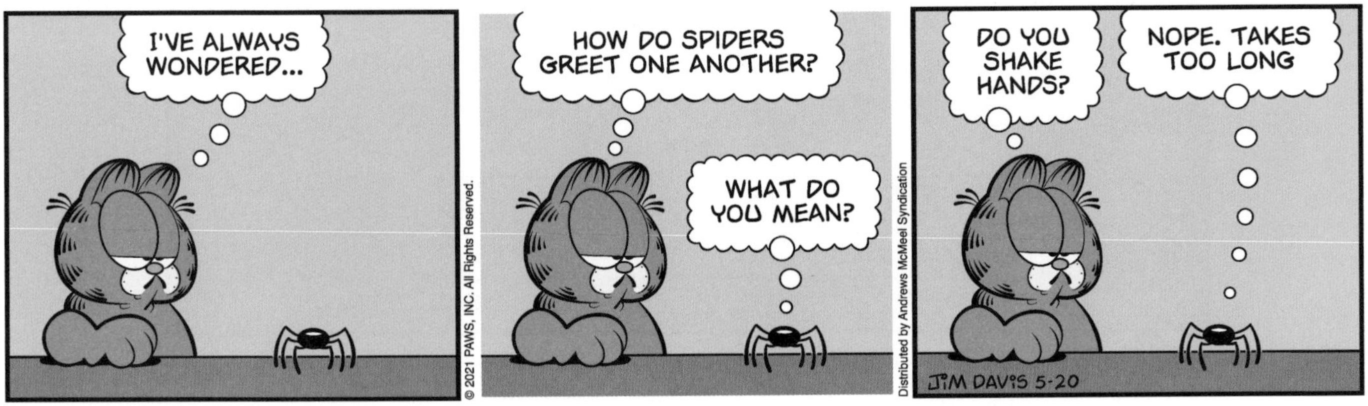
I'VE ALWAYS WONDERED...
HOW DO SPIDERS GREET ONE ANOTHER?
WHAT DO YOU MEAN?
DO YOU SHAKE HANDS?
NOPE. TAKES TOO LONG
JIM DAVIS 5-20
© 2021 PAWS, INC. All Rights Reserved.
Distributed by Andrews McMeel Syndication

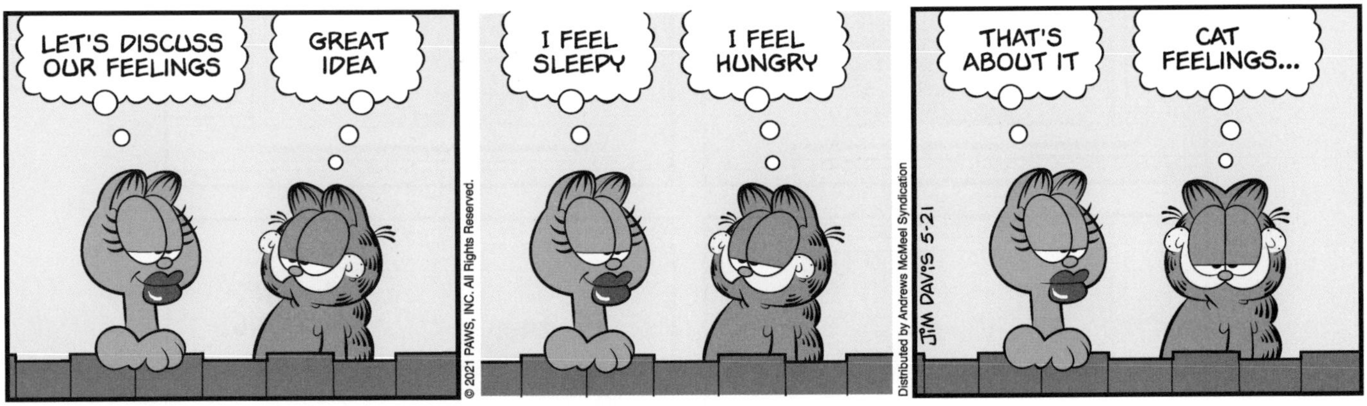
LET'S DISCUSS OUR FEELINGS
GREAT IDEA
I FEEL SLEEPY
I FEEL HUNGRY
THAT'S ABOUT IT
CAT FEELINGS...
JIM DAVIS 5-21
© 2021 PAWS, INC. All Rights Reserved.
Distributed by Andrews McMeel Syndication

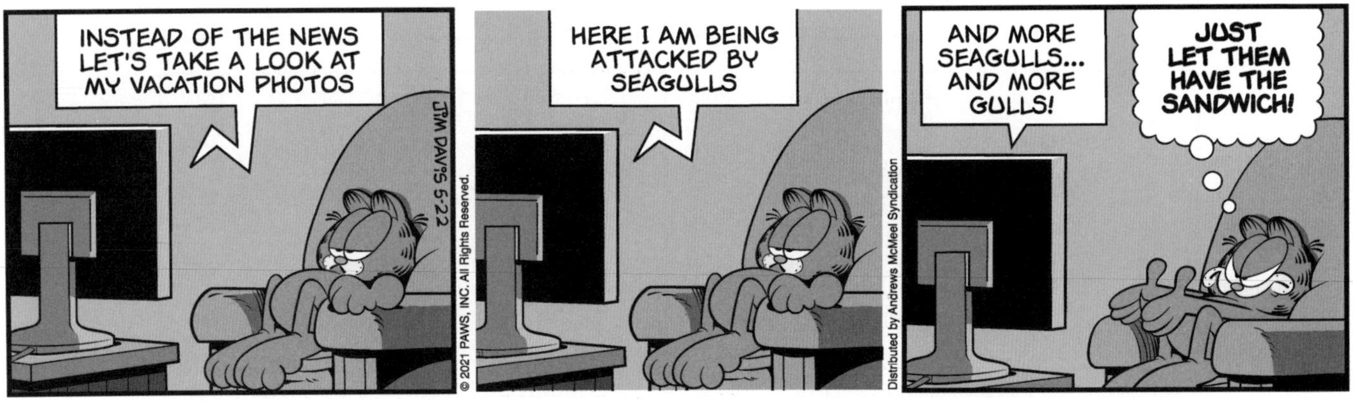
INSTEAD OF THE NEWS LET'S TAKE A LOOK AT MY VACATION PHOTOS
HERE I AM BEING ATTACKED BY SEAGULLS
AND MORE SEAGULLS... AND MORE GULLS!
JUST LET THEM HAVE THE SANDWICH!
JIM DAVIS 5-22
© 2021 PAWS, INC. All Rights Reserved.
Distributed by Andrews McMeel Syndication

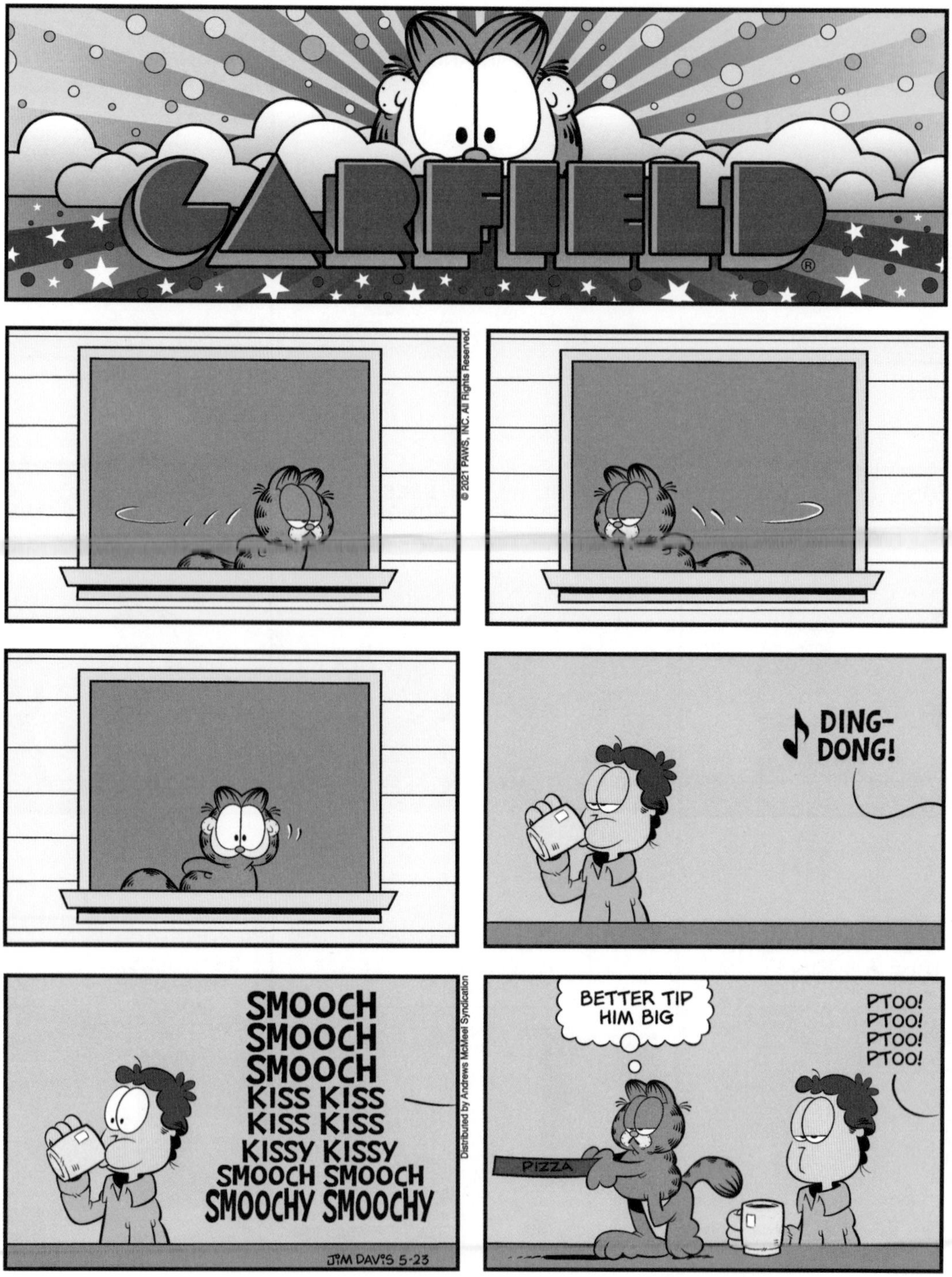
GARFIELD®
© 2021 PAWS, INC. All Rights Reserved.
DING-DONG!
SMOOCH SMOOCH SMOOCH KISS KISS KISS KISS KISSY KISSY SMOOCH SMOOCH SMOOCHY SMOOCHY
Distributed by Andrews McMeel Syndication
JIM DAVIS 5-23
BETTER TIP HIM BIG
PIZZA
PTOO! PTOO! PTOO! PTOO!

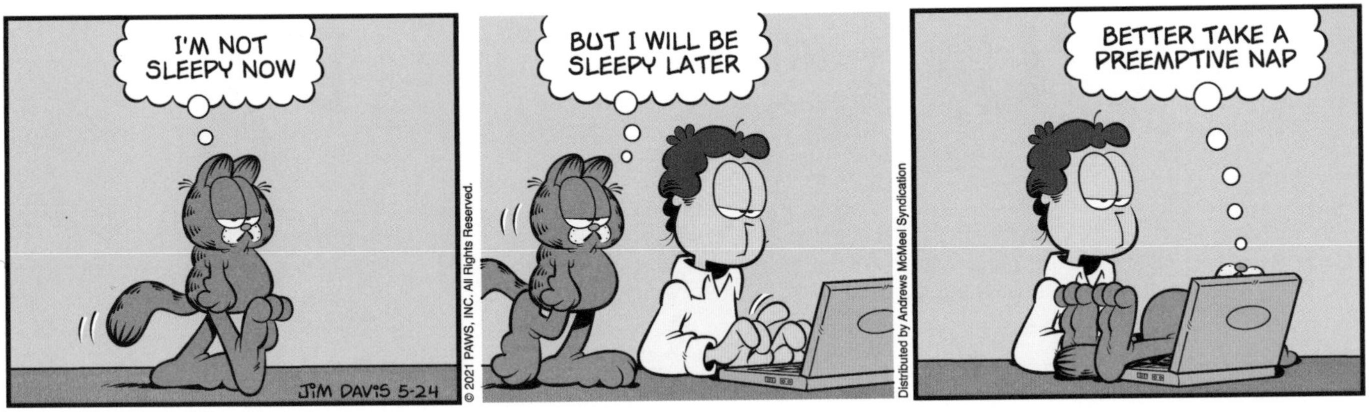
I'M NOT SLEEPY NOW
JIM DAVIS 5-24
BUT I WILL BE SLEEPY LATER
BETTER TAKE A PREEMPTIVE NAP
© 2021 PAWS, INC. All Rights Reserved.
Distributed by Andrews McMeel Syndication

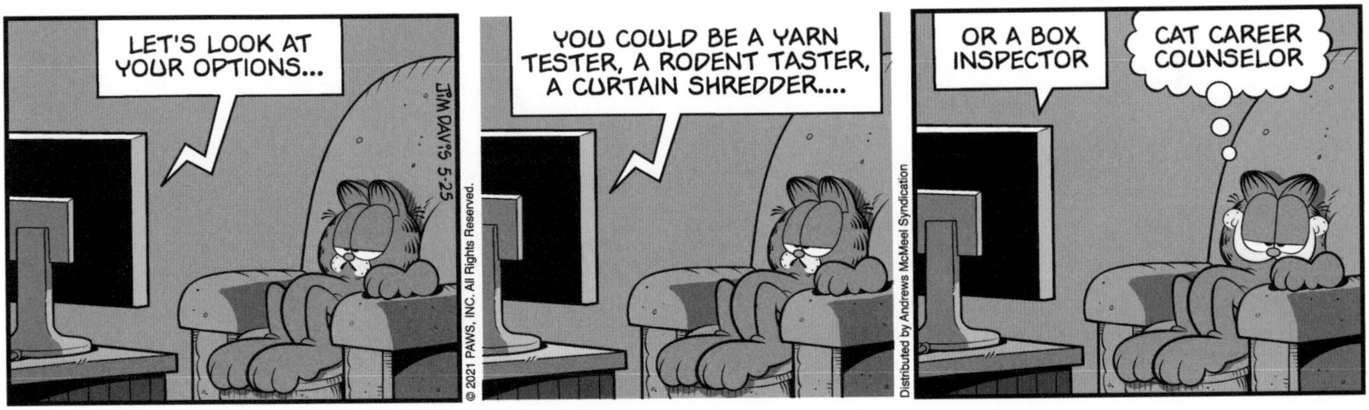
LET'S LOOK AT YOUR OPTIONS...
JIM DAVIS 5-25
YOU COULD BE A YARN TESTER, A RODENT TASTER, A CURTAIN SHREDDER....
OR A BOX INSPECTOR
CAT CAREER COUNSELOR
© 2021 PAWS, INC. All Rights Reserved.
Distributed by Andrews McMeel Syndication

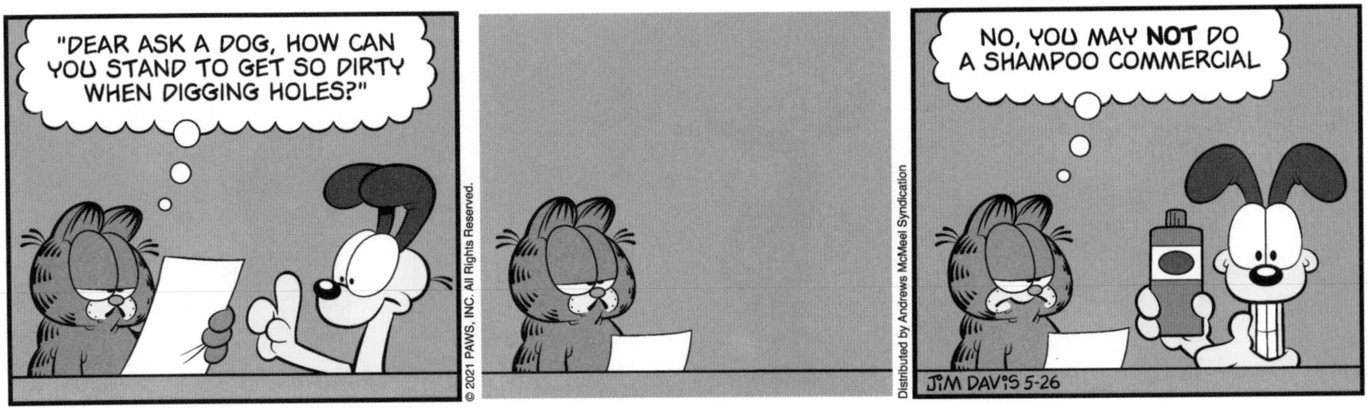
"DEAR ASK A DOG, HOW CAN YOU STAND TO GET SO DIRTY WHEN DIGGING HOLES?"
NO, YOU MAY **NOT** DO A SHAMPOO COMMERCIAL
JIM DAVIS 5-26
© 2021 PAWS, INC. All Rights Reserved.
Distributed by Andrews McMeel Syndication

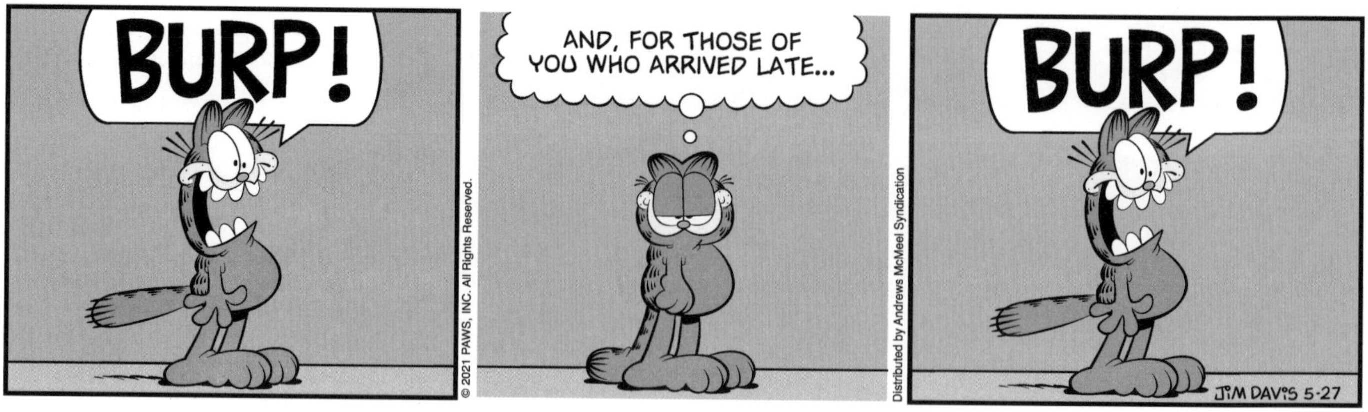
BURP!
AND, FOR THOSE OF YOU WHO ARRIVED LATE...
BURP!
JIM DAVIS 5-27
© 2021 PAWS, INC. All Rights Reserved.
Distributed by Andrews McMeel Syndication

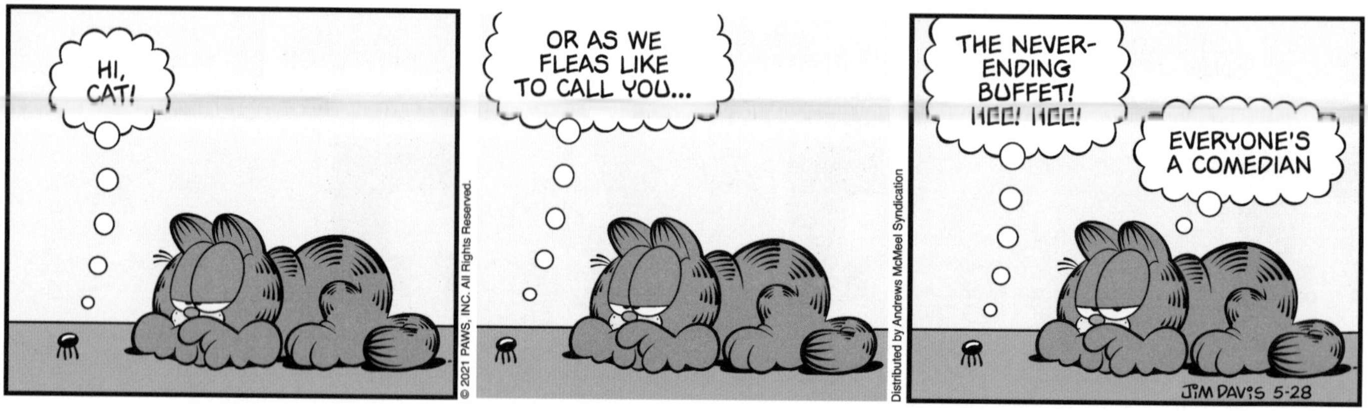
HI, CAT!
OR AS WE FLEAS LIKE TO CALL YOU...
THE NEVER-ENDING BUFFET! HEE! HEE!
EVERYONE'S A COMEDIAN
JIM DAVIS 5-28
© 2021 PAWS, INC. All Rights Reserved.
Distributed by Andrews McMeel Syndication

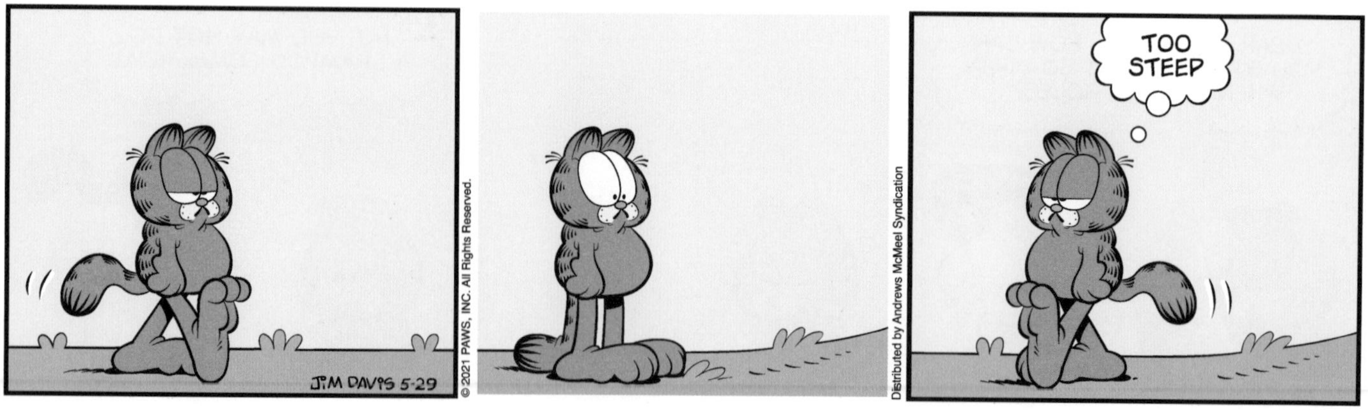
TOO STEEP
JIM DAVIS 5-29
© 2021 PAWS, INC. All Rights Reserved.
Distributed by Andrews McMeel Syndication

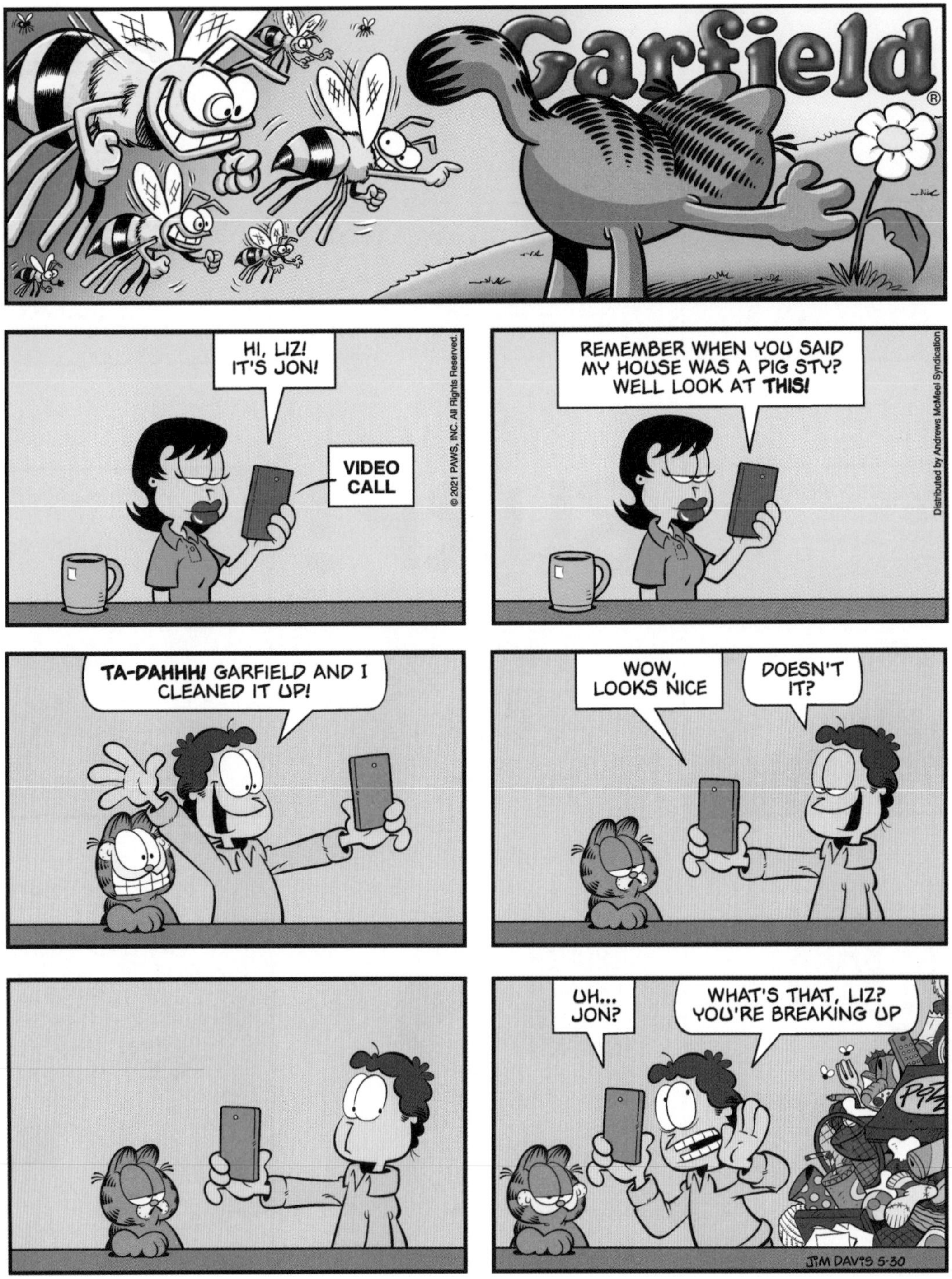
Garfield®
HI, LIZ! IT'S JON!
VIDEO CALL
© 2021 PAWS, INC. All Rights Reserved.
REMEMBER WHEN YOU SAID MY HOUSE WAS A PIG STY? WELL LOOK AT THIS!
Distributed by Andrews McMeel Syndication
TA-DAHHH! GARFIELD AND I CLEANED IT UP!
WOW, LOOKS NICE
DOESN'T IT?
UH... JON?
WHAT'S THAT, LIZ? YOU'RE BREAKING UP
JIM DAVIS 5-30

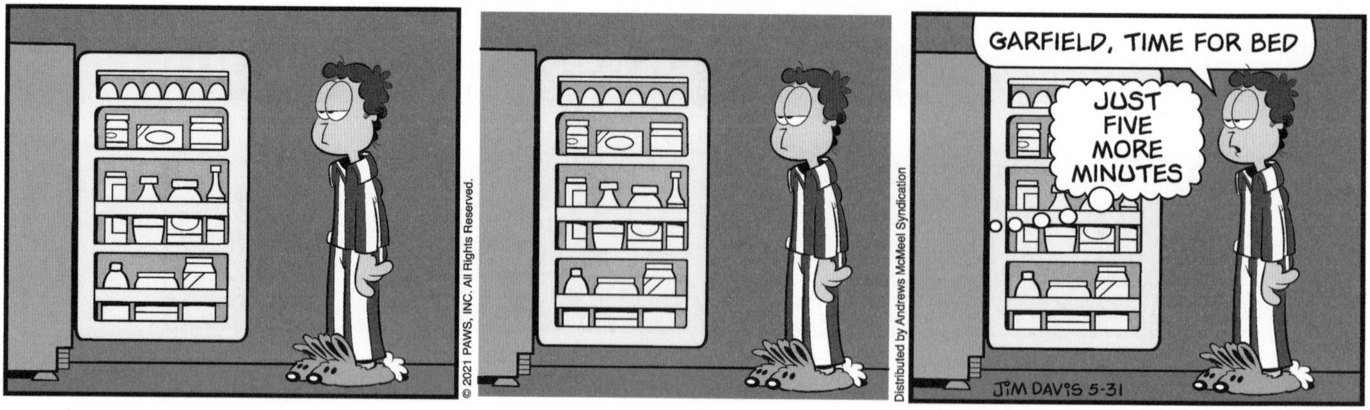
GARFIELD, TIME FOR BED
JUST FIVE MORE MINUTES
© 2021 PAWS, INC. All Rights Reserved.
Distributed by Andrews McMeel Syndication
JIM DAVIS 5-31

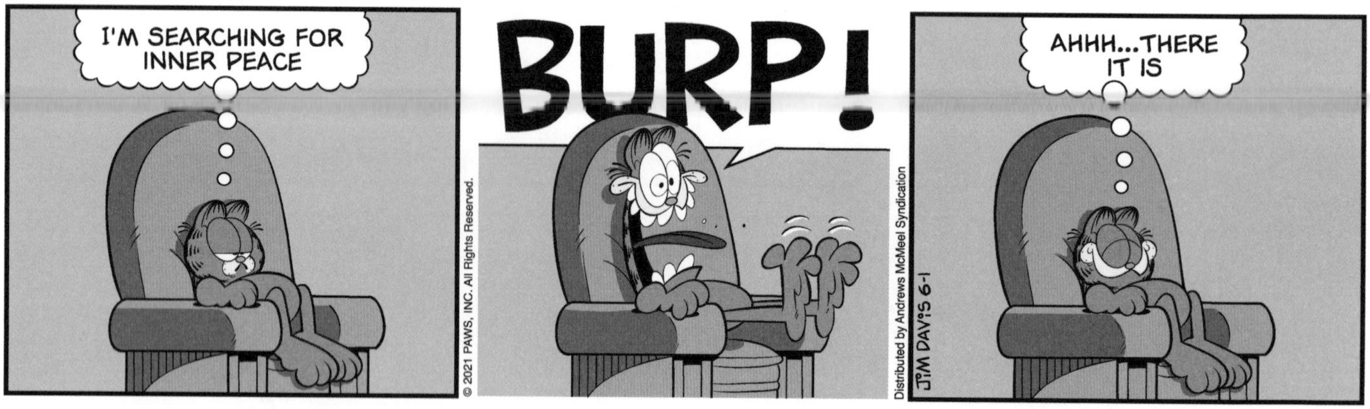
I'M SEARCHING FOR INNER PEACE
BURP!
AHHH...THERE IT IS
© 2021 PAWS, INC. All Rights Reserved.
Distributed by Andrews McMeel Syndication
JIM DAVIS 6-1

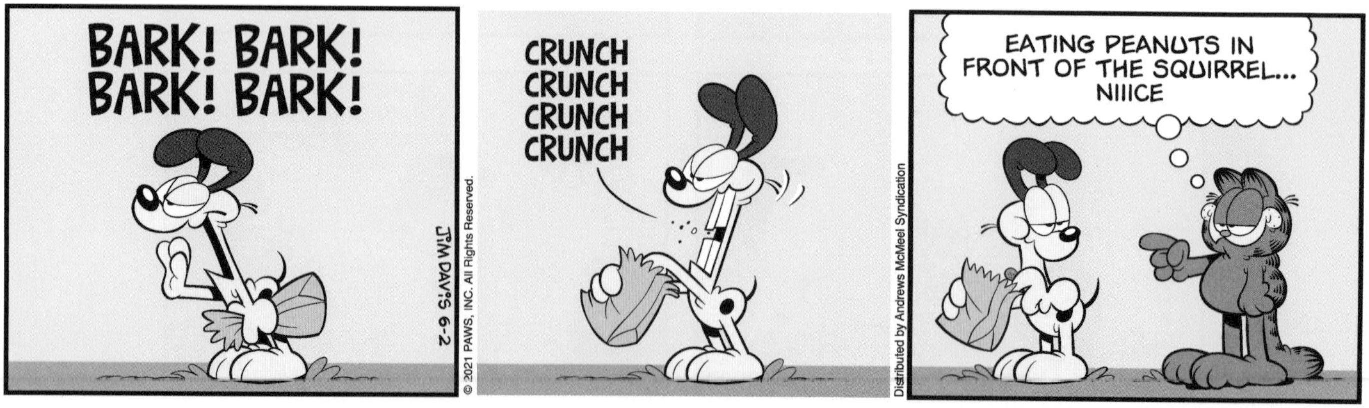
BARK! BARK! BARK! BARK!
CRUNCH CRUNCH CRUNCH CRUNCH
EATING PEANUTS IN FRONT OF THE SQUIRREL... NIIICE
© 2021 PAWS, INC. All Rights Reserved.
Distributed by Andrews McMeel Syndication
JIM DAVIS 6-2

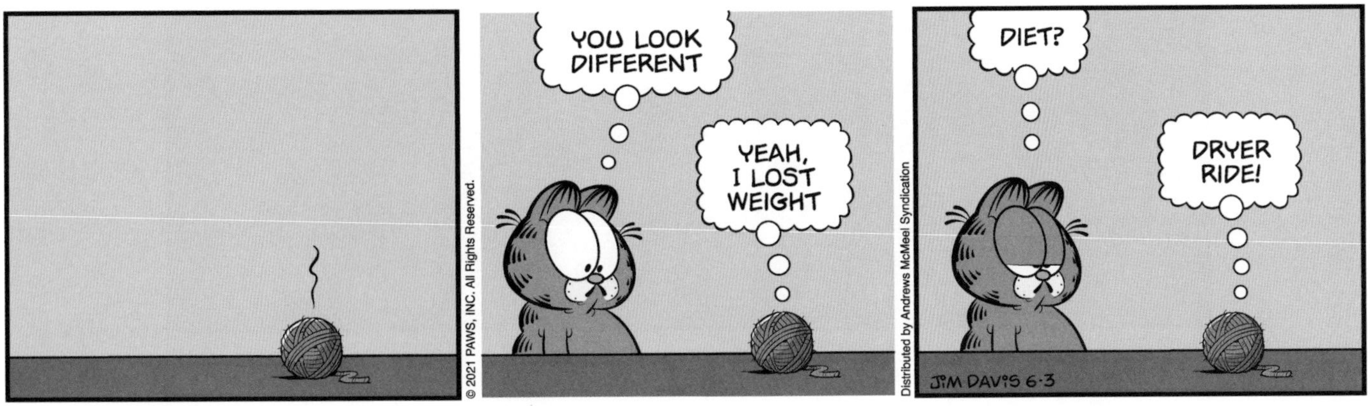
YOU LOOK DIFFERENT
YEAH, I LOST WEIGHT
DIET?
DRYER RIDE!
JIM DAVIS 6-3

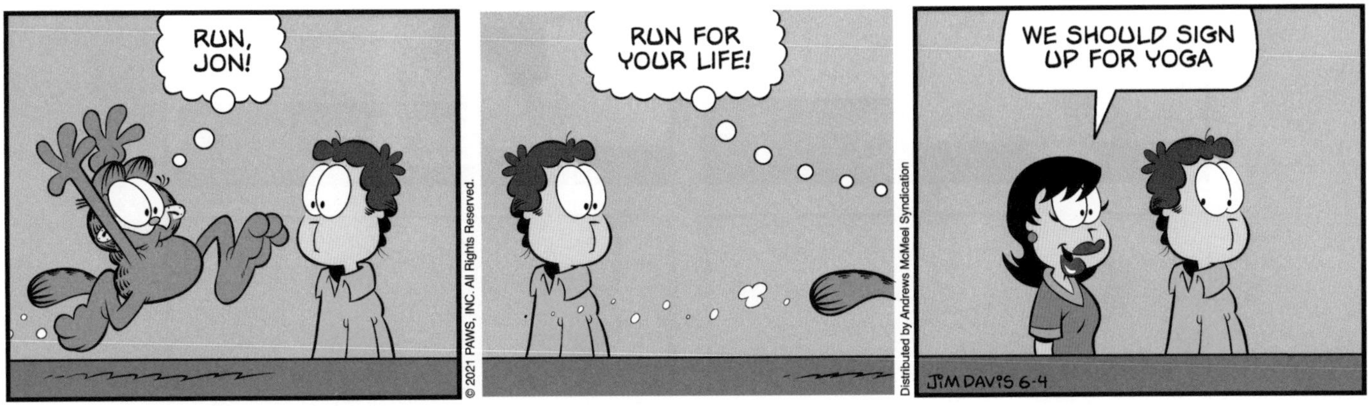
RUN, JON!
RUN FOR YOUR LIFE!
WE SHOULD SIGN UP FOR YOGA
JIM DAVIS 6-4

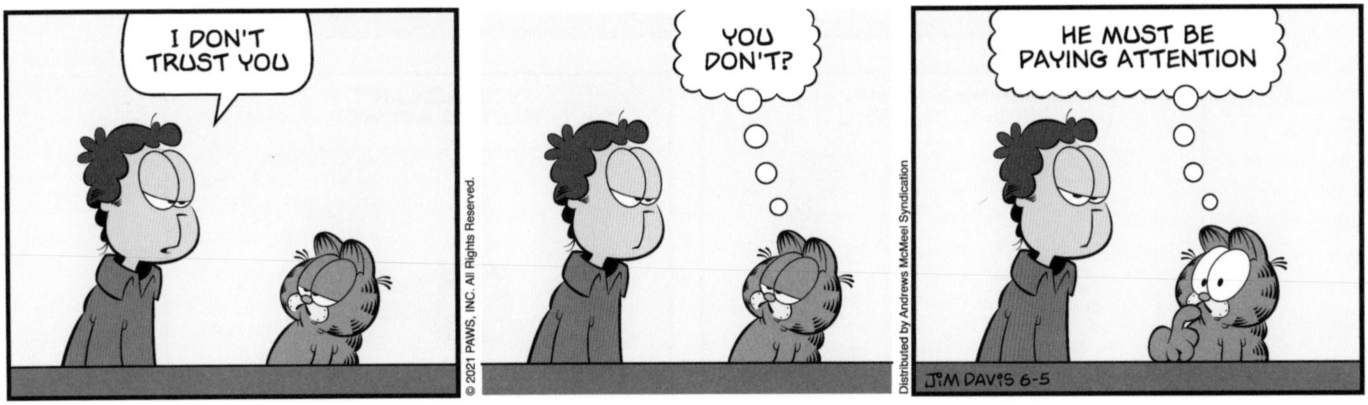
I DON'T TRUST YOU
YOU DON'T?
HE MUST BE PAYING ATTENTION
JIM DAVIS 6-5

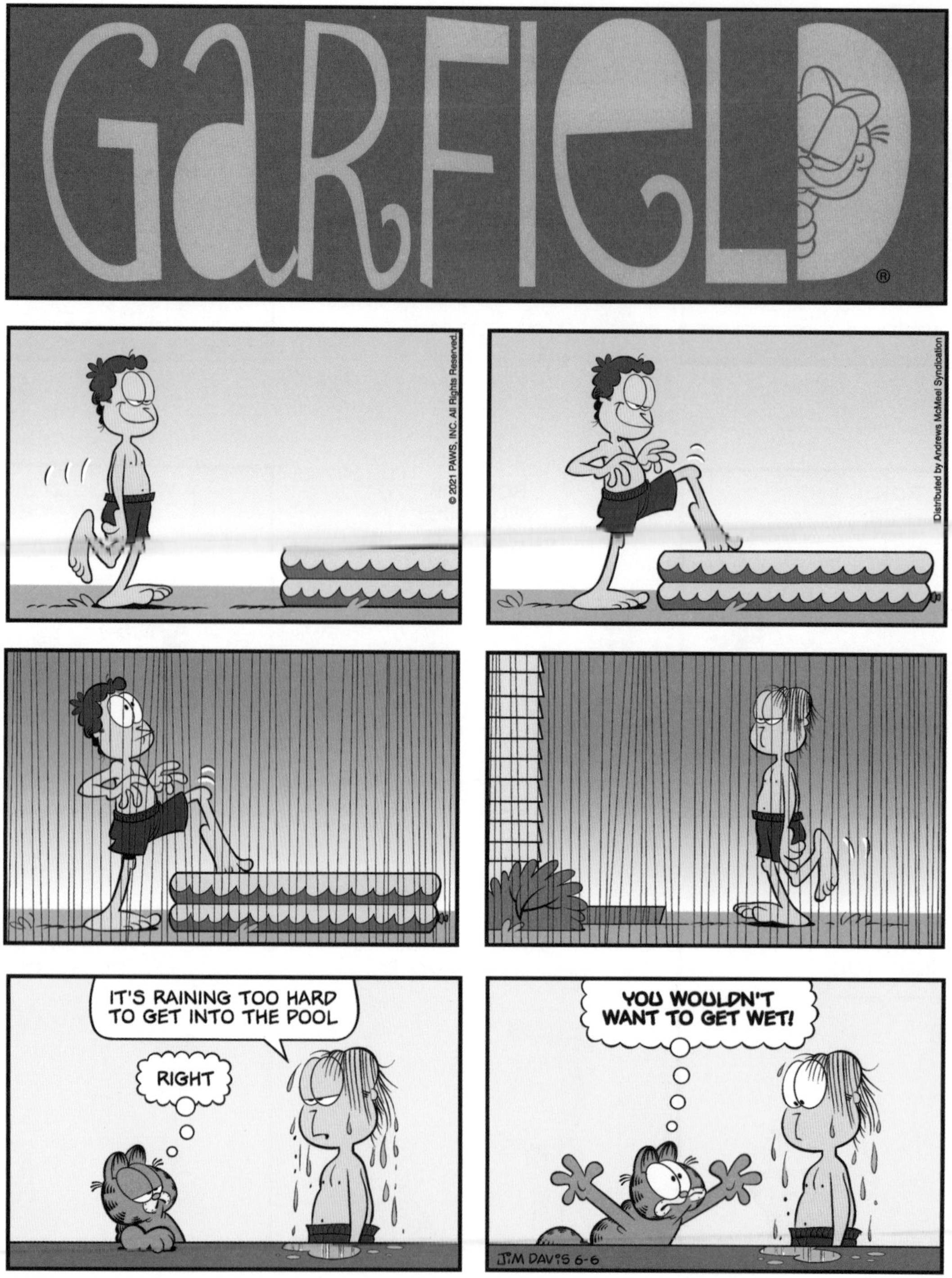
GARFIELD
© 2021 PAWS, INC. All Rights Reserved.
Distributed by Andrews McMeel Syndication
IT'S RAINING TOO HARD TO GET INTO THE POOL
RIGHT
YOU WOULDN'T WANT TO GET WET!
JIM DAVIS 6-6

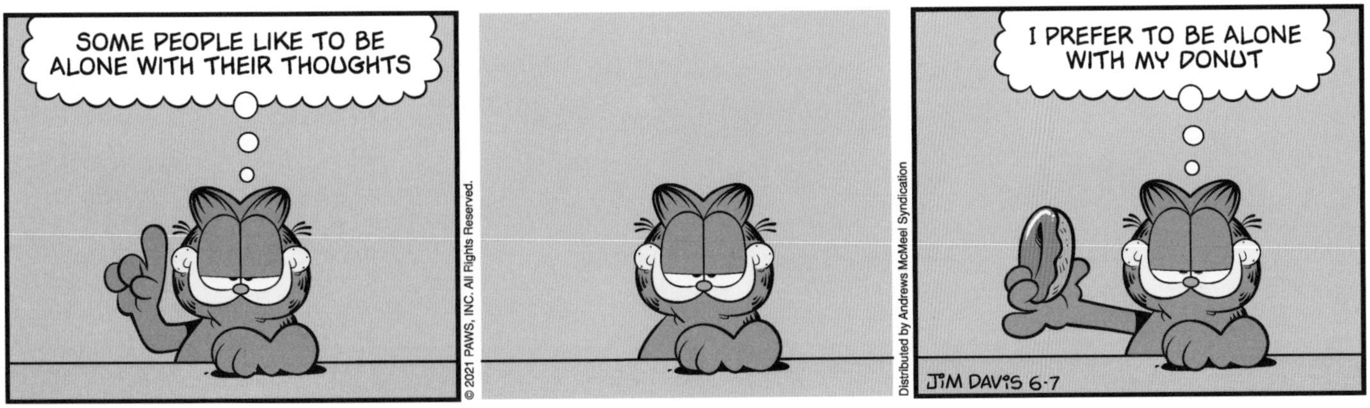
SOME PEOPLE LIKE TO BE ALONE WITH THEIR THOUGHTS
© 2021 PAWS, INC. All Rights Reserved.
Distributed by Andrews McMeel Syndication
I PREFER TO BE ALONE WITH MY DONUT
JIM DAVIS 6-7

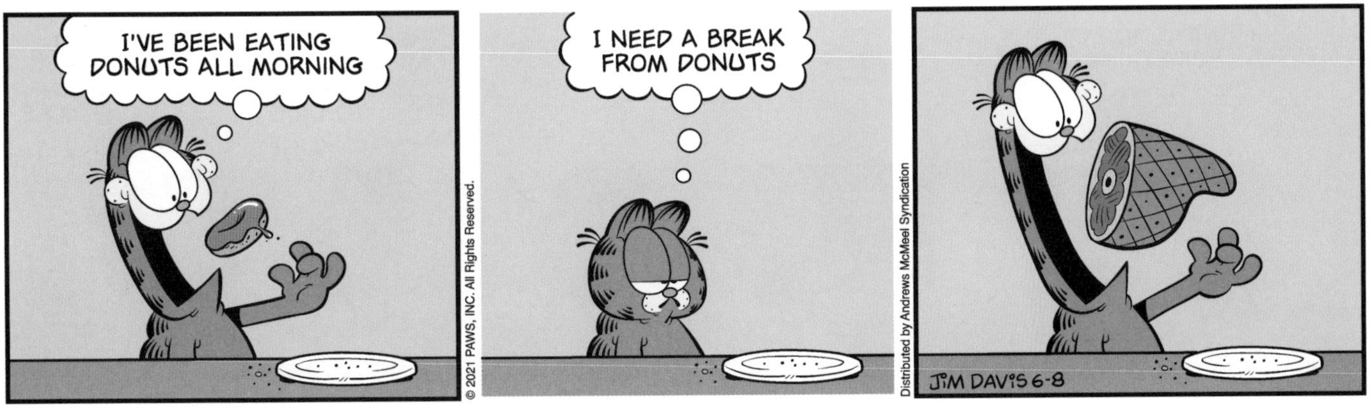
I'VE BEEN EATING DONUTS ALL MORNING
© 2021 PAWS, INC. All Rights Reserved.
I NEED A BREAK FROM DONUTS
Distributed by Andrews McMeel Syndication
JIM DAVIS 6-8

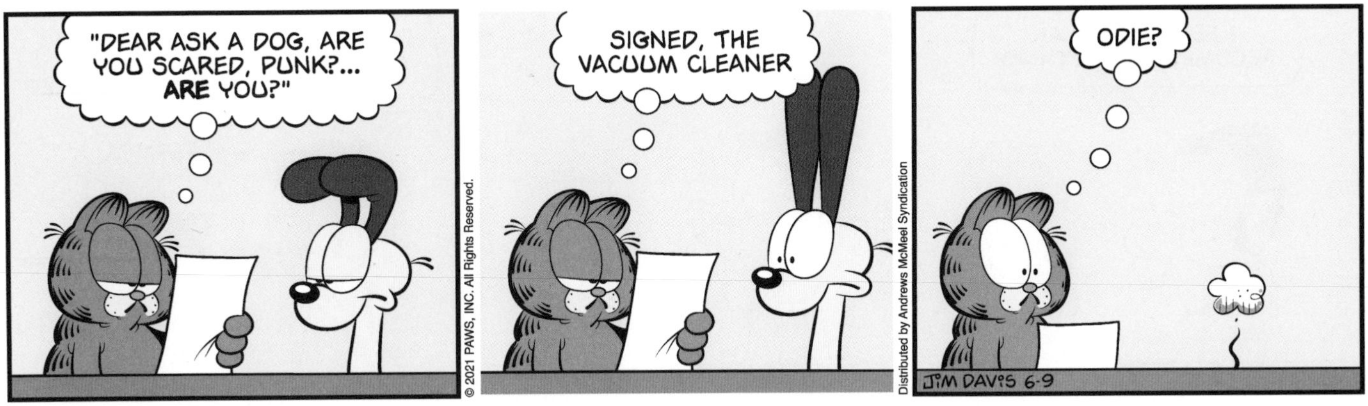
"DEAR ASK A DOG, ARE YOU SCARED, PUNK?... **ARE** YOU?"
© 2021 PAWS, INC. All Rights Reserved.
SIGNED, THE VACUUM CLEANER
Distributed by Andrews McMeel Syndication
ODIE?
JIM DAVIS 6-9

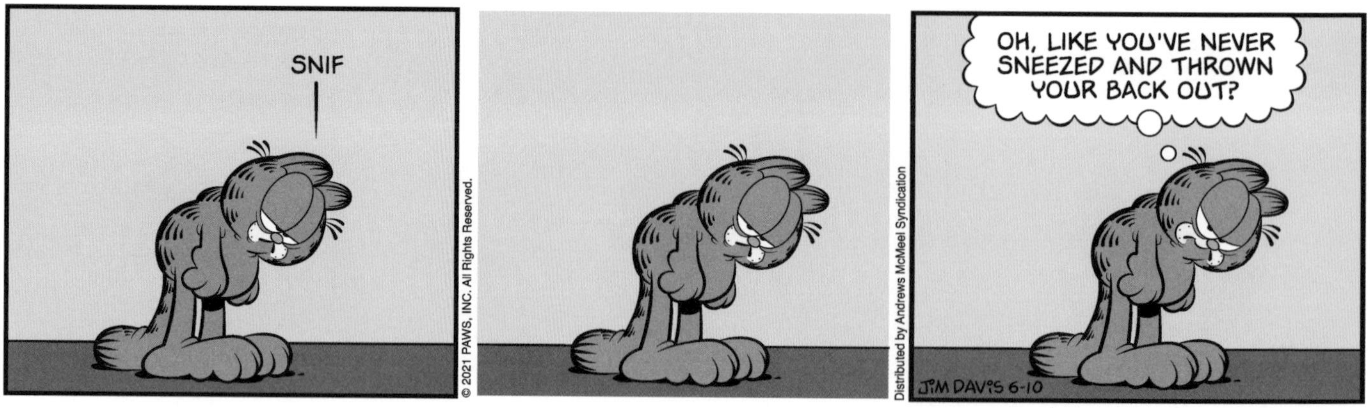
SNIF
OH, LIKE YOU'VE NEVER SNEEZED AND THROWN YOUR BACK OUT?
© 2021 PAWS, INC. All Rights Reserved.
Distributed by Andrews McMeel Syndication
JIM DAVIS 6-10

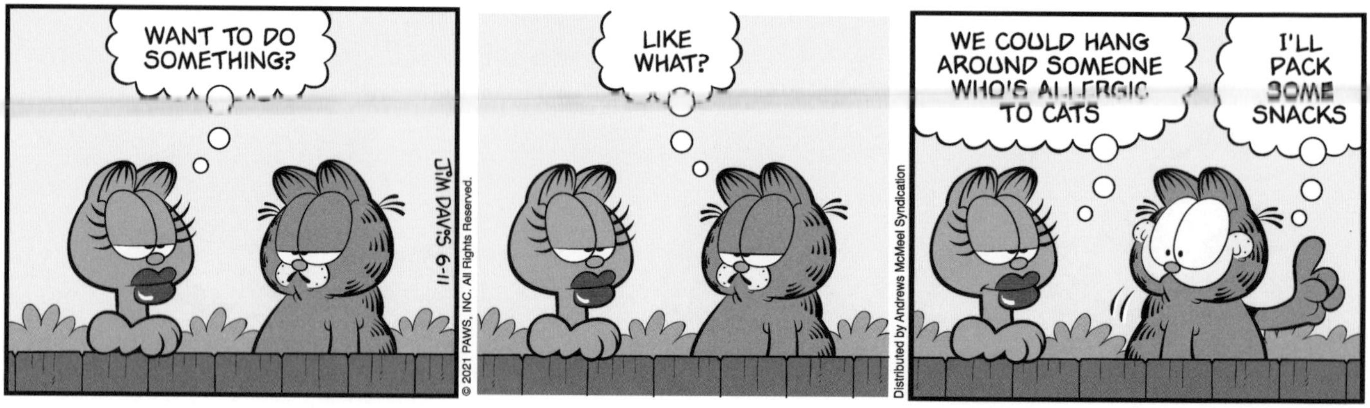
WANT TO DO SOMETHING?
LIKE WHAT?
WE COULD HANG AROUND SOMEONE WHO'S ALLERGIC TO CATS
I'LL PACK SOME SNACKS
JIM DAVIS 6-11
© 2021 PAWS, INC. All Rights Reserved.
Distributed by Andrews McMeel Syndication

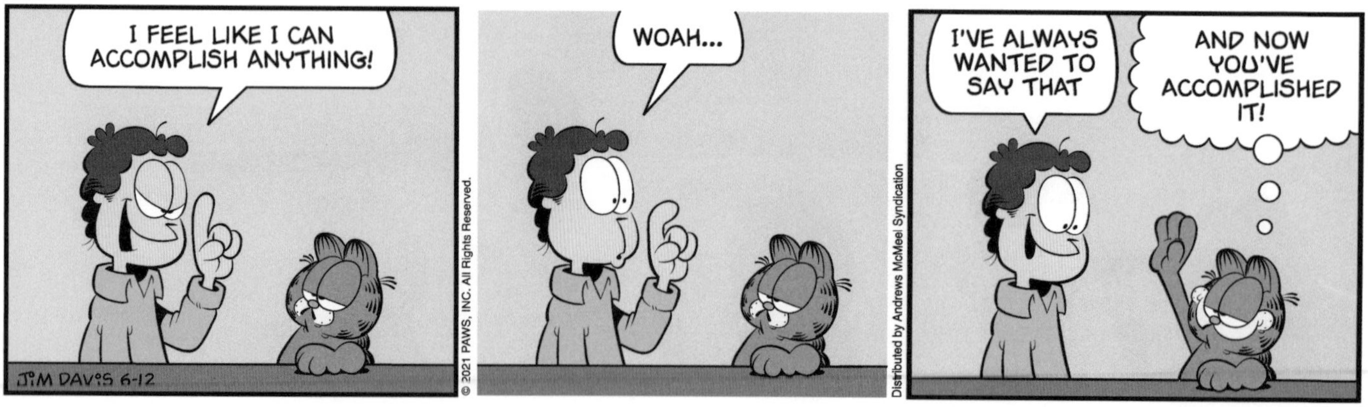
I FEEL LIKE I CAN ACCOMPLISH ANYTHING!
WOAH...
I'VE ALWAYS WANTED TO SAY THAT
AND NOW YOU'VE ACCOMPLISHED IT!
JIM DAVIS 6-12
© 2021 PAWS, INC. All Rights Reserved.
Distributed by Andrews McMeel Syndication

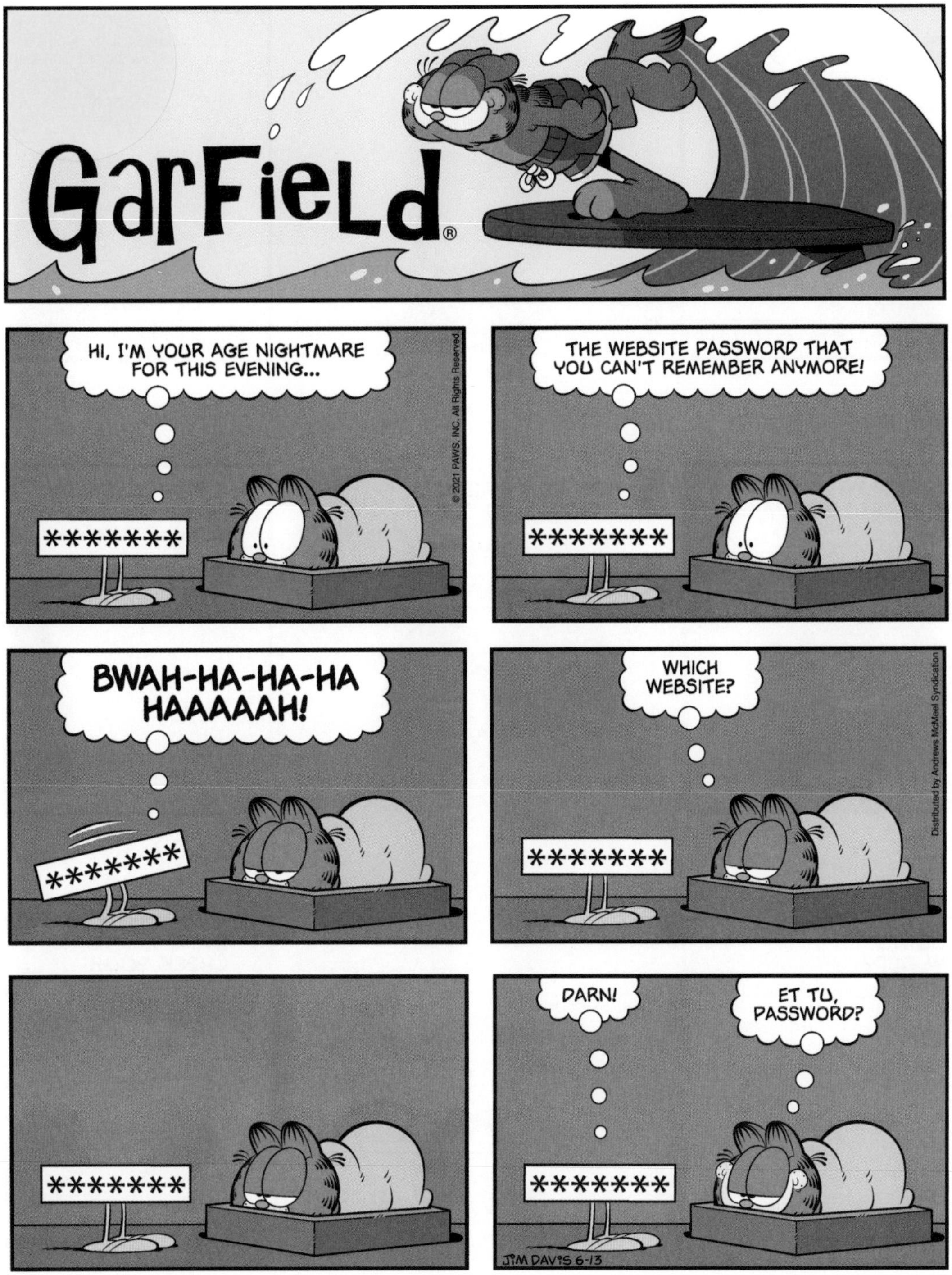
GarField®
HI, I'M YOUR AGE NIGHTMARE FOR THIS EVENING...
****
© 2021 PAWS, INC. All Rights Reserved.
THE WEBSITE PASSWORD THAT YOU CAN'T REMEMBER ANYMORE!
****
BWAH-HA-HA-HA HAAAAAH!
****
WHICH WEBSITE?
****
Distributed by Andrews McMeel Syndication
****
DARN!
ET TU, PASSWORD?
****
JIM DAVIS 6-13

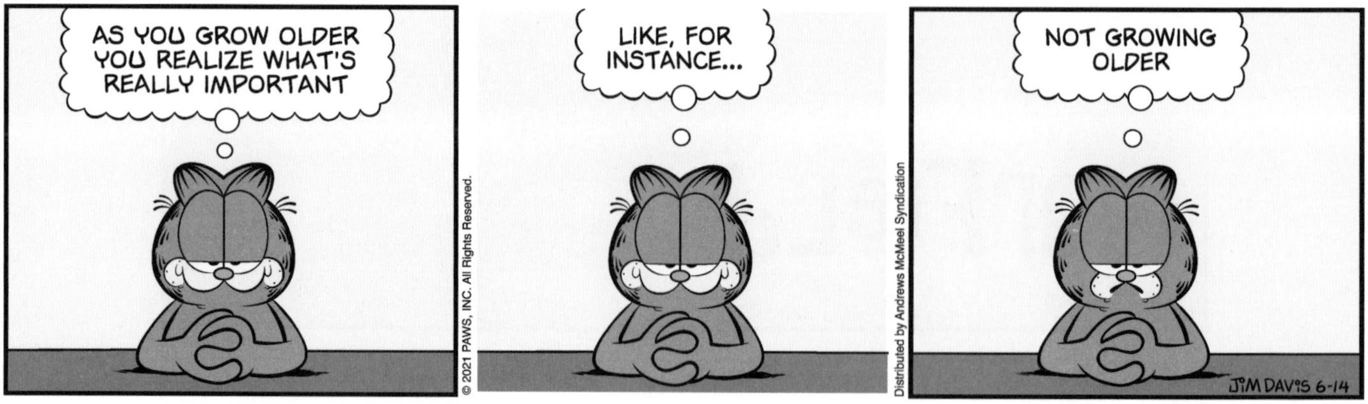
AS YOU GROW OLDER YOU REALIZE WHAT'S REALLY IMPORTANT
LIKE, FOR INSTANCE...
NOT GROWING OLDER
JIM DAVIS 6-14

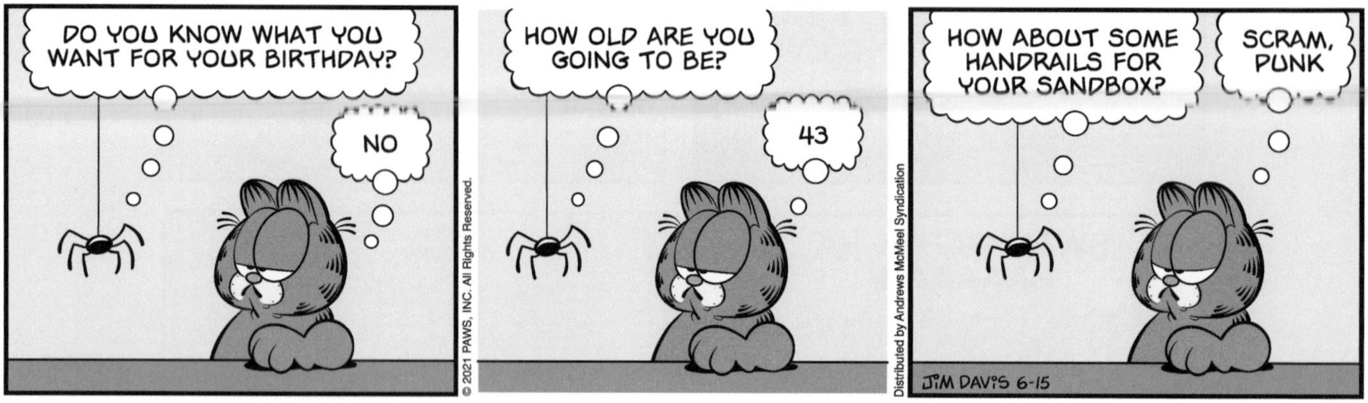
DO YOU KNOW WHAT YOU WANT FOR YOUR BIRTHDAY?
NO
HOW OLD ARE YOU GOING TO BE?
43
HOW ABOUT SOME HANDRAILS FOR YOUR SANDBOX?
SCRAM, PUNK
JIM DAVIS 6-15

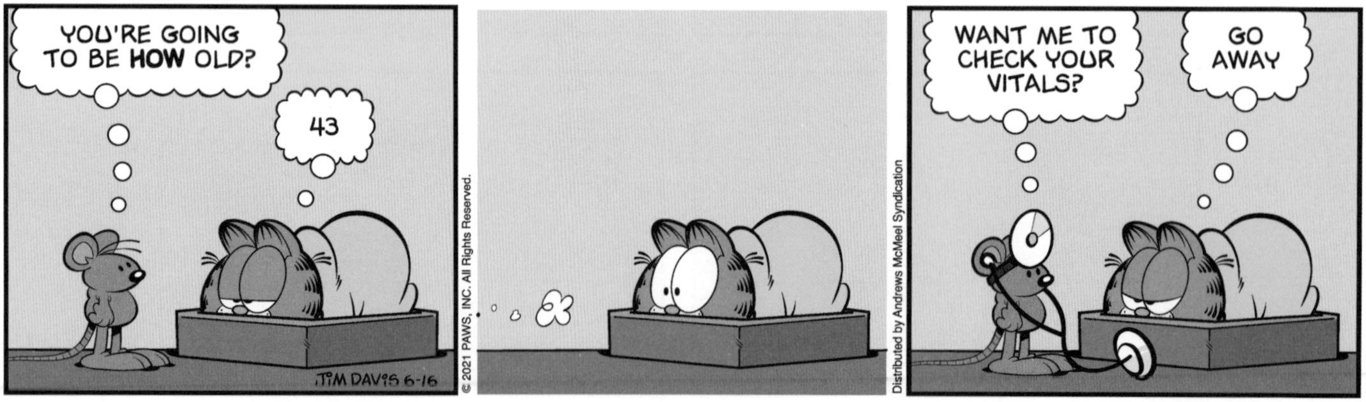
YOU'RE GOING TO BE **HOW** OLD?
43
JIM DAVIS 6-16
WANT ME TO CHECK YOUR VITALS?
GO AWAY

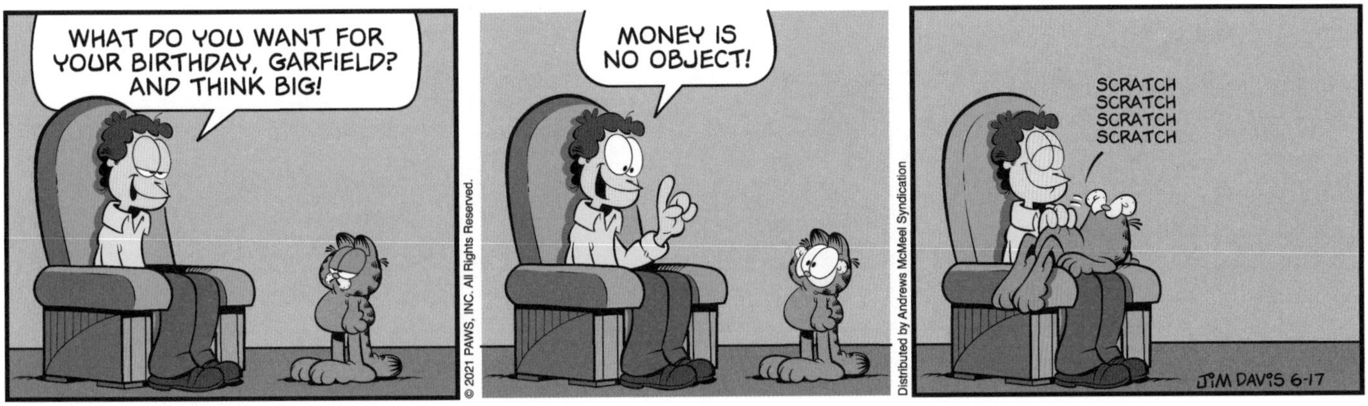
WHAT DO YOU WANT FOR YOUR BIRTHDAY, GARFIELD? AND THINK BIG!
MONEY IS NO OBJECT!
SCRATCH SCRATCH SCRATCH SCRATCH
JIM DAVIS 6-17

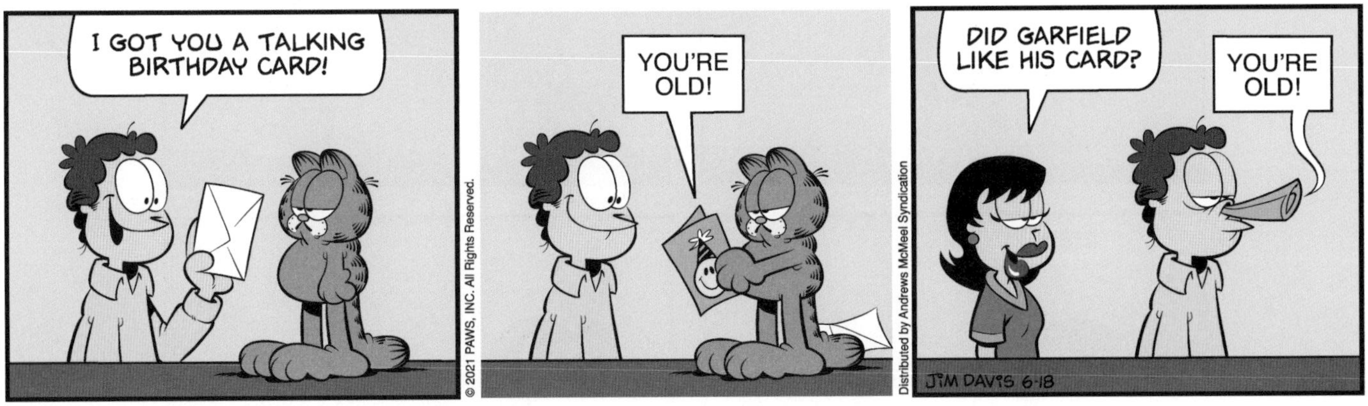
I GOT YOU A TALKING BIRTHDAY CARD!
YOU'RE OLD!
DID GARFIELD LIKE HIS CARD?
YOU'RE OLD!
JIM DAVIS 6-18

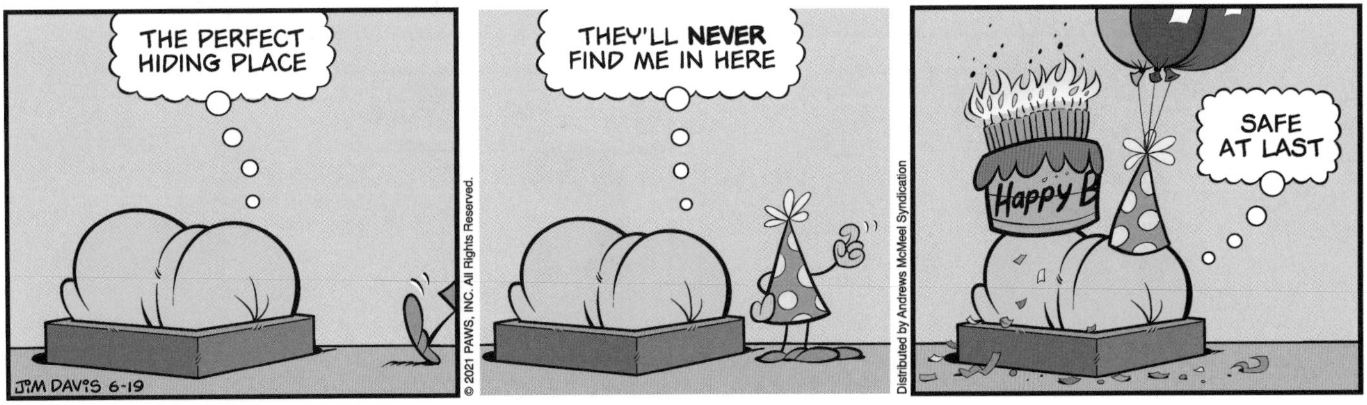
THE PERFECT HIDING PLACE
JIM DAVIS 6-19
THEY'LL NEVER FIND ME IN HERE
Happy B
SAFE AT LAST

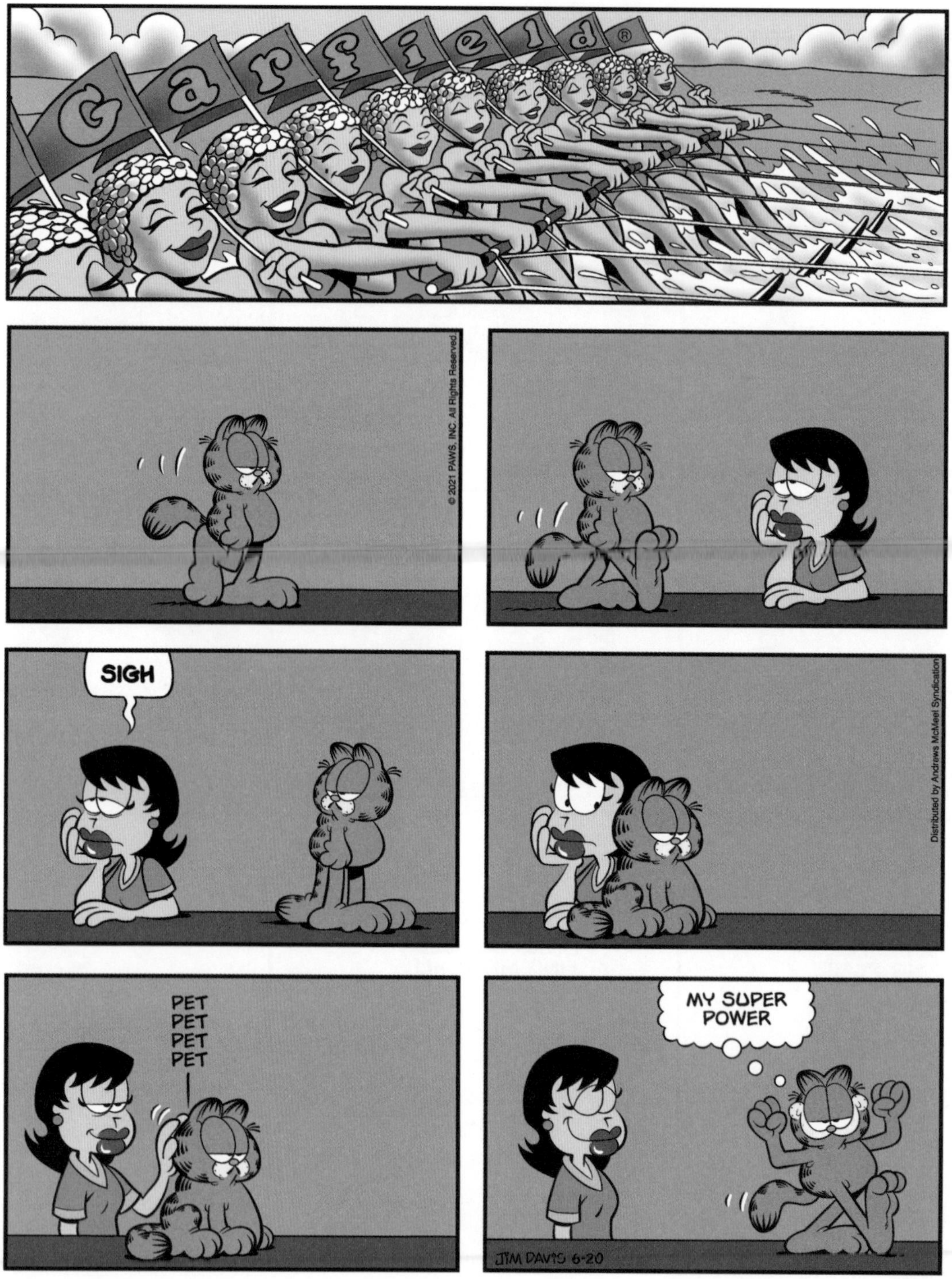
Garfield®
© 2021 PAWS, INC. All Rights Reserved.
Distributed by Andrews McMeel Syndication
SIGH
PET
PET
PET
PET
MY SUPER POWER
JIM DAVIS 6-20

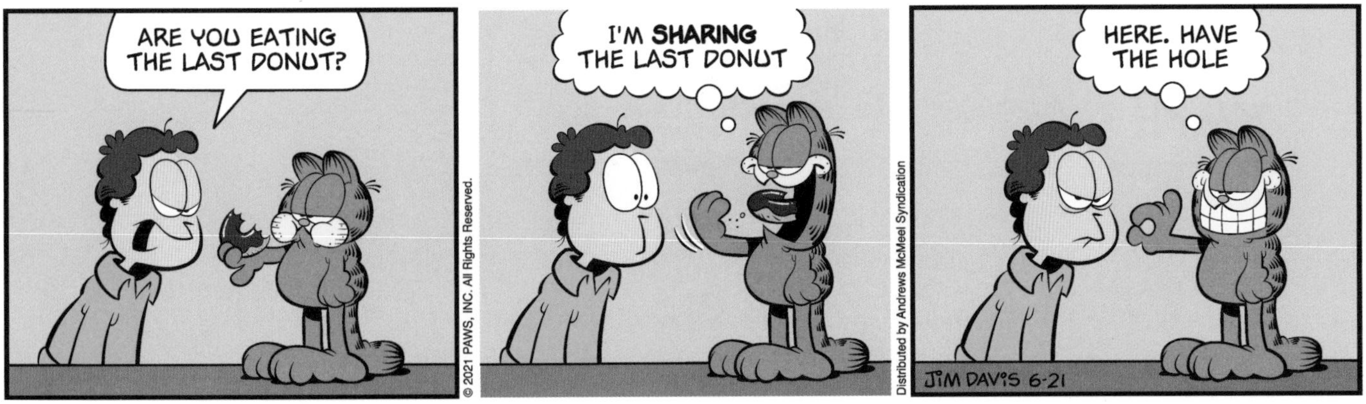
ARE YOU EATING THE LAST DONUT?
I'M **SHARING** THE LAST DONUT
HERE. HAVE THE HOLE
JIM DAVIS 6-21

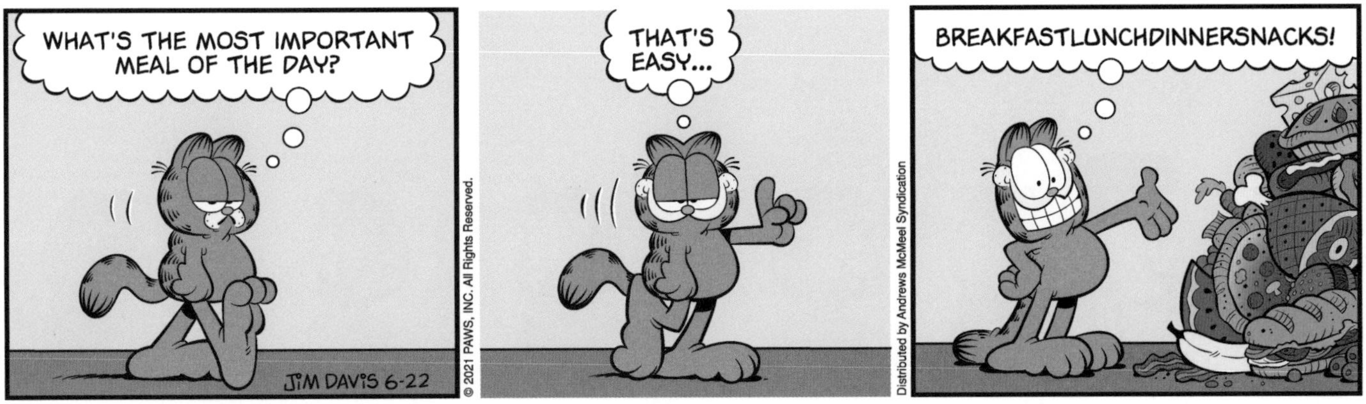
WHAT'S THE MOST IMPORTANT MEAL OF THE DAY?
JIM DAVIS 6-22
THAT'S EASY...
BREAKFASTLUNCHDINNERSNACKS!

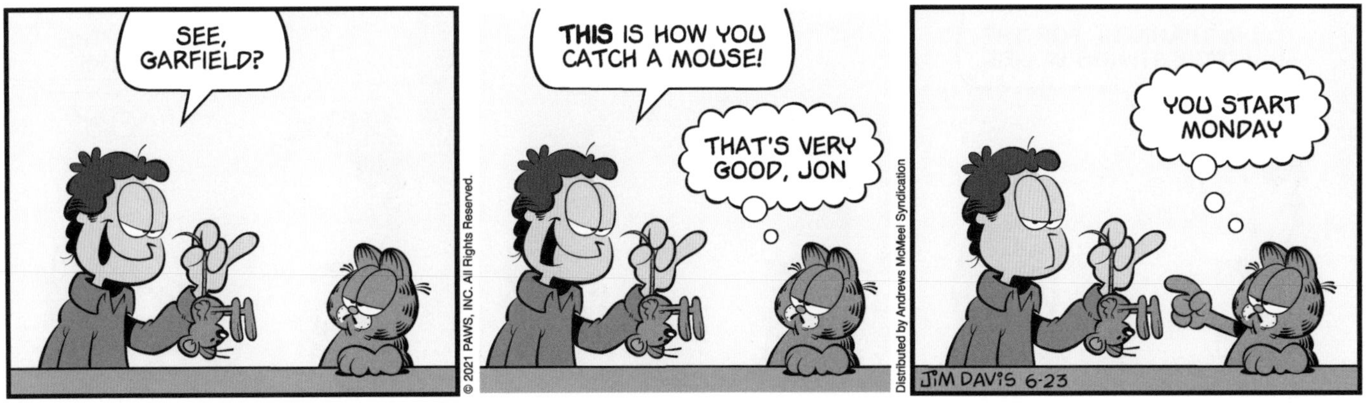
SEE, GARFIELD?
THIS IS HOW YOU CATCH A MOUSE!
THAT'S VERY GOOD, JON
YOU START MONDAY
JIM DAVIS 6-23

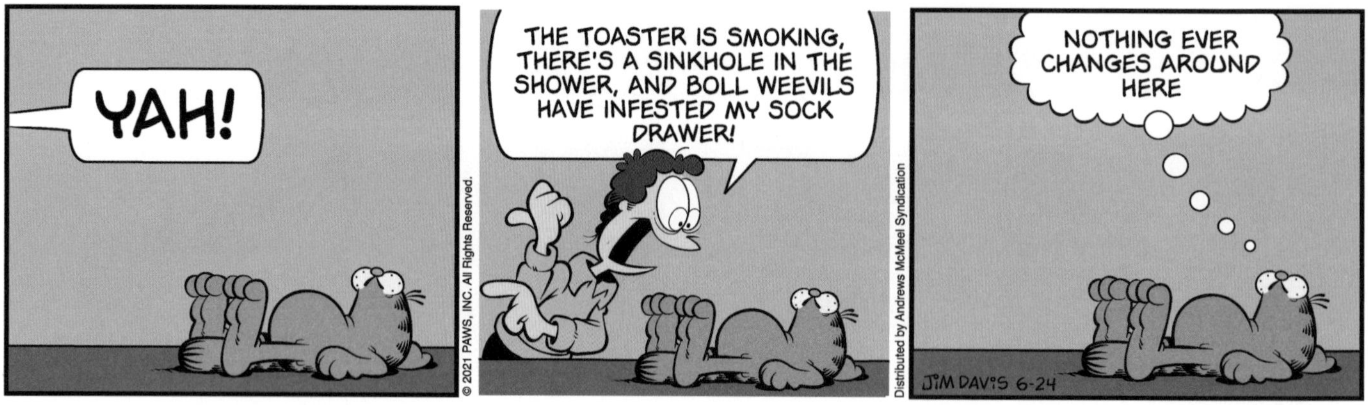
YAH!
THE TOASTER IS SMOKING, THERE'S A SINKHOLE IN THE SHOWER, AND BOLL WEEVILS HAVE INFESTED MY SOCK DRAWER!
NOTHING EVER CHANGES AROUND HERE
© 2021 PAWS, INC. All Rights Reserved.
Distributed by Andrews McMeel Syndication
JIM DAVIS 6-24

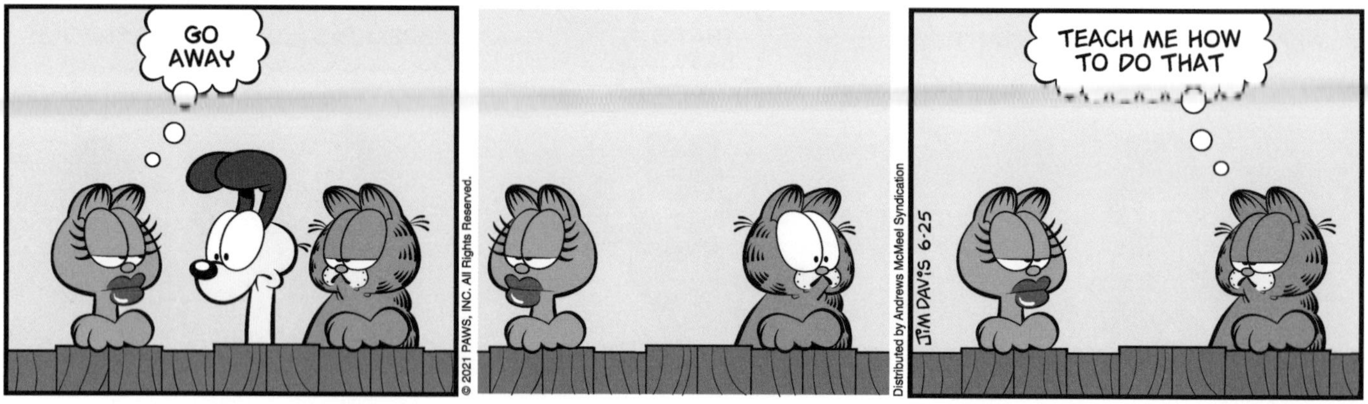
GO AWAY
TEACH ME HOW TO DO THAT
© 2021 PAWS, INC. All Rights Reserved.
Distributed by Andrews McMeel Syndication
JIM DAVIS 6-25

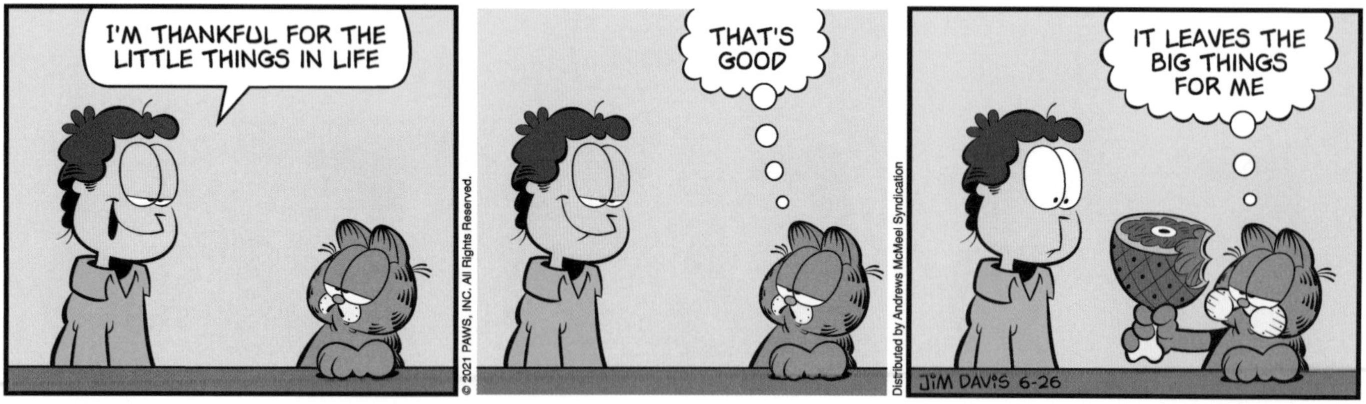
I'M THANKFUL FOR THE LITTLE THINGS IN LIFE
THAT'S GOOD
IT LEAVES THE BIG THINGS FOR ME
© 2021 PAWS, INC. All Rights Reserved.
Distributed by Andrews McMeel Syndication
JIM DAVIS 6-26

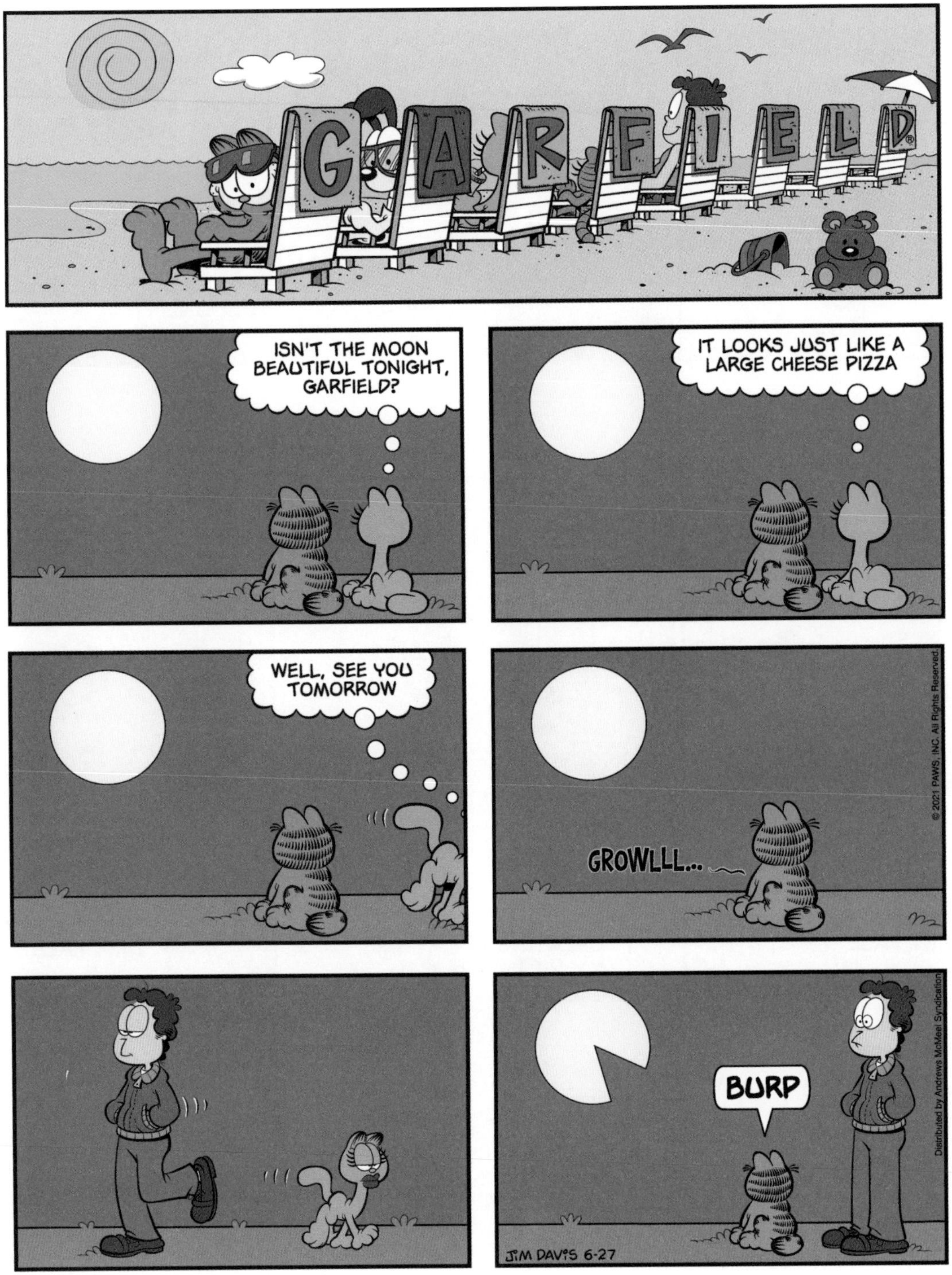
GARFIELD
ISN'T THE MOON BEAUTIFUL TONIGHT, GARFIELD?
IT LOOKS JUST LIKE A LARGE CHEESE PIZZA
WELL, SEE YOU TOMORROW
GROWLLL...
BURP
JIM DAVIS 6-27
© 2021 PAWS, INC. All Rights Reserved.
Distributed by Andrews McMeel Syndication

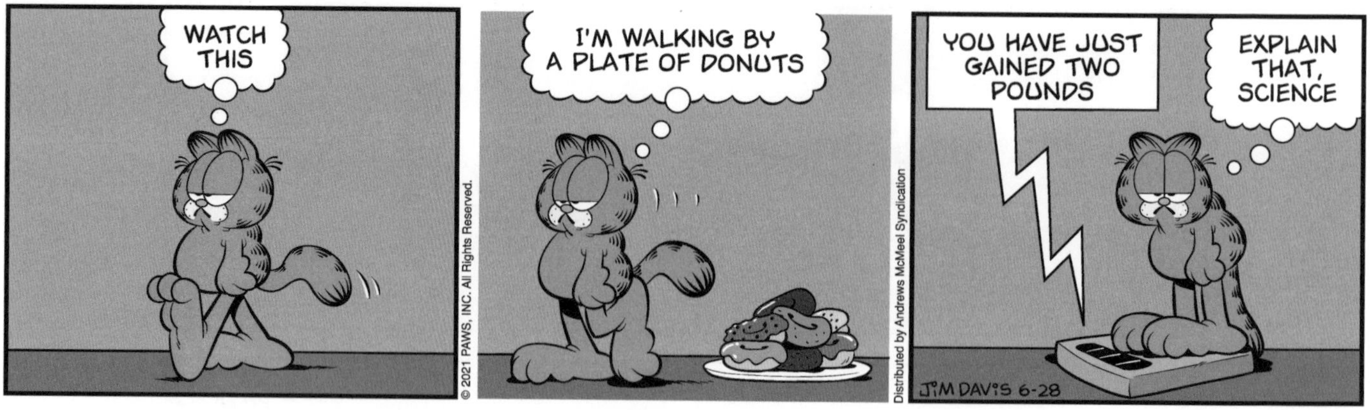
WATCH THIS
I'M WALKING BY A PLATE OF DONUTS
YOU HAVE JUST GAINED TWO POUNDS
EXPLAIN THAT, SCIENCE
© 2021 PAWS, INC. All Rights Reserved.
Distributed by Andrews McMeel Syndication
JIM DAVIS 6-28

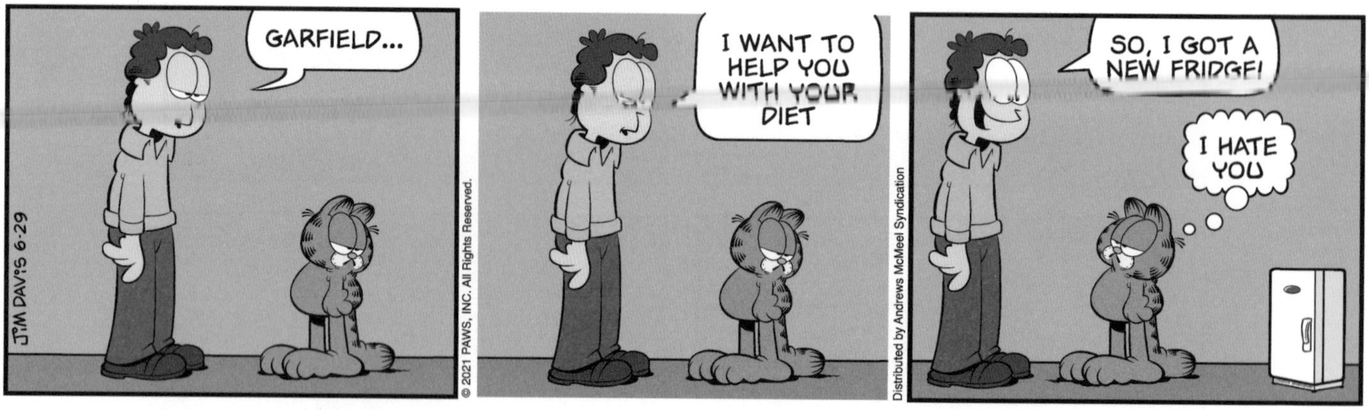
GARFIELD...
I WANT TO HELP YOU WITH YOUR DIET
SO, I GOT A NEW FRIDGE!
I HATE YOU
JIM DAVIS 6-29
© 2021 PAWS, INC. All Rights Reserved.
Distributed by Andrews McMeel Syndication

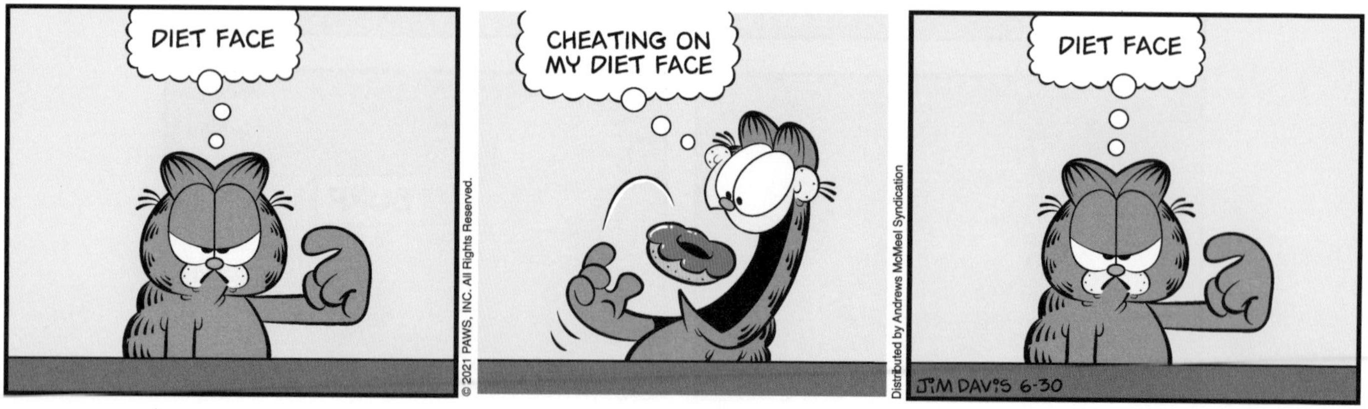
DIET FACE
CHEATING ON MY DIET FACE
DIET FACE
© 2021 PAWS, INC. All Rights Reserved.
Distributed by Andrews McMeel Syndication
JIM DAVIS 6-30

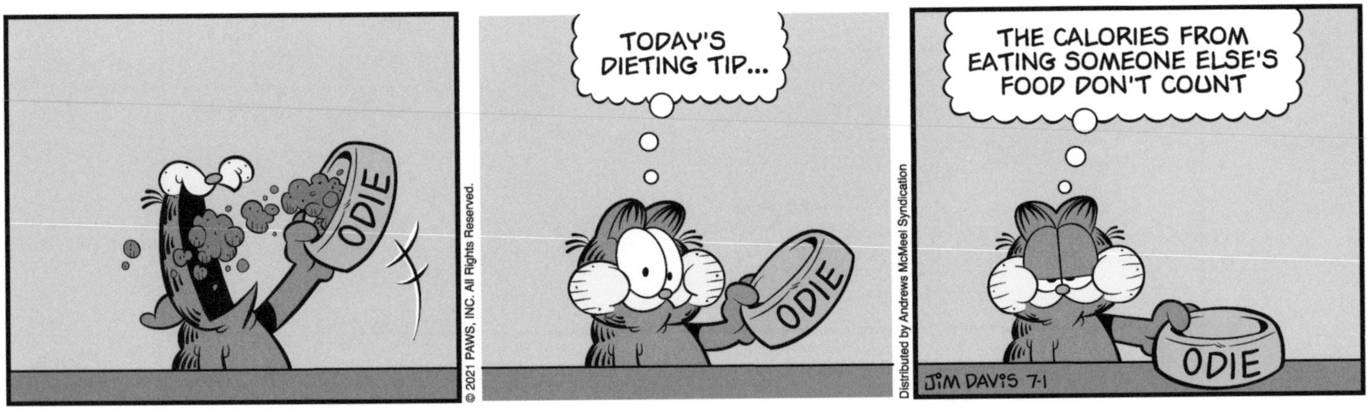
ODIE
© 2021 PAWS, INC. All Rights Reserved.
TODAY'S DIETING TIP...
ODIE
Distributed by Andrews McMeel Syndication
THE CALORIES FROM EATING SOMEONE ELSE'S FOOD DON'T COUNT
ODIE
JIM DAVIS 7-1

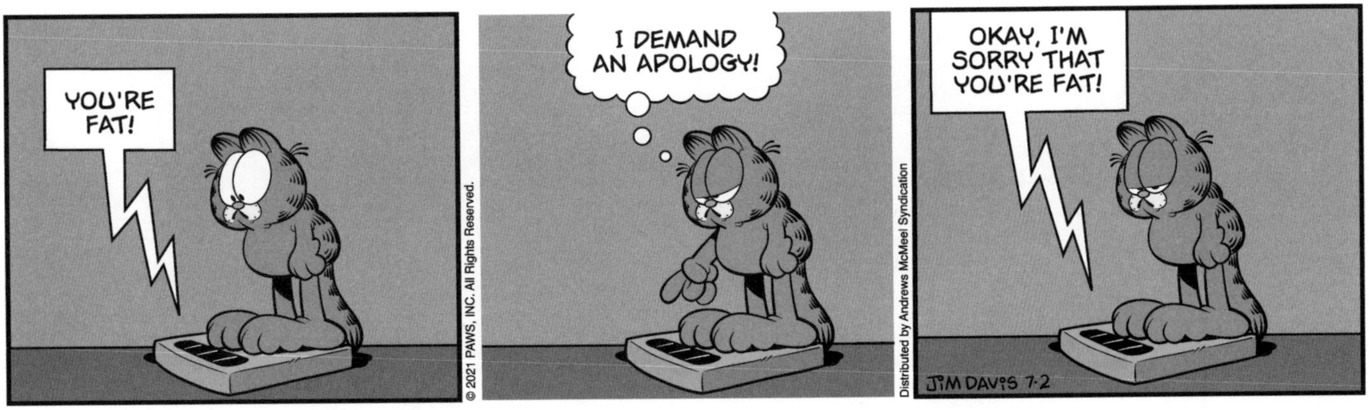
YOU'RE FAT!
© 2021 PAWS, INC. All Rights Reserved.
I DEMAND AN APOLOGY!
Distributed by Andrews McMeel Syndication
OKAY, I'M SORRY THAT YOU'RE FAT!
JIM DAVIS 7-2

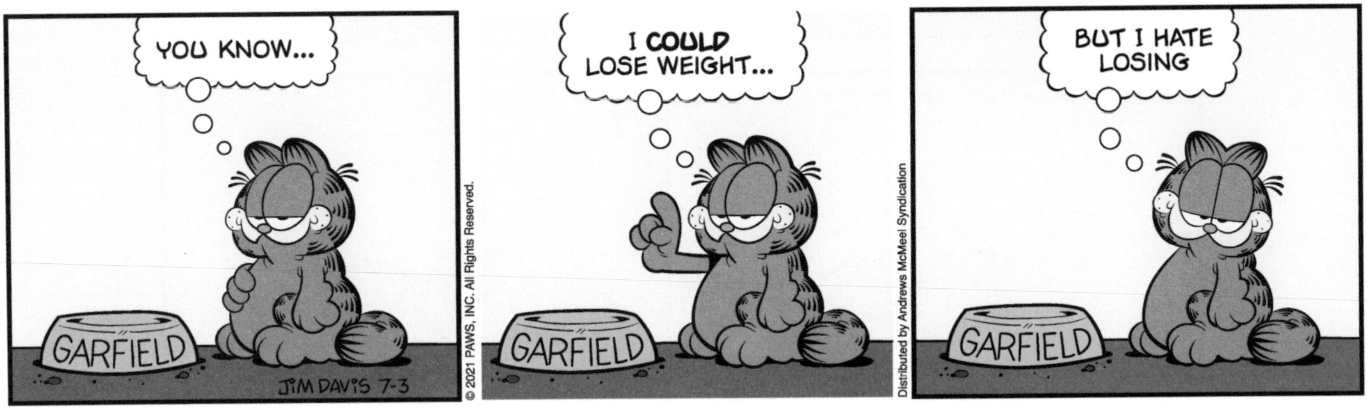
YOU KNOW...
GARFIELD
JIM DAVIS 7-3
© 2021 PAWS, INC. All Rights Reserved.
I COULD LOSE WEIGHT...
GARFIELD
Distributed by Andrews McMeel Syndication
BUT I HATE LOSING
GARFIELD

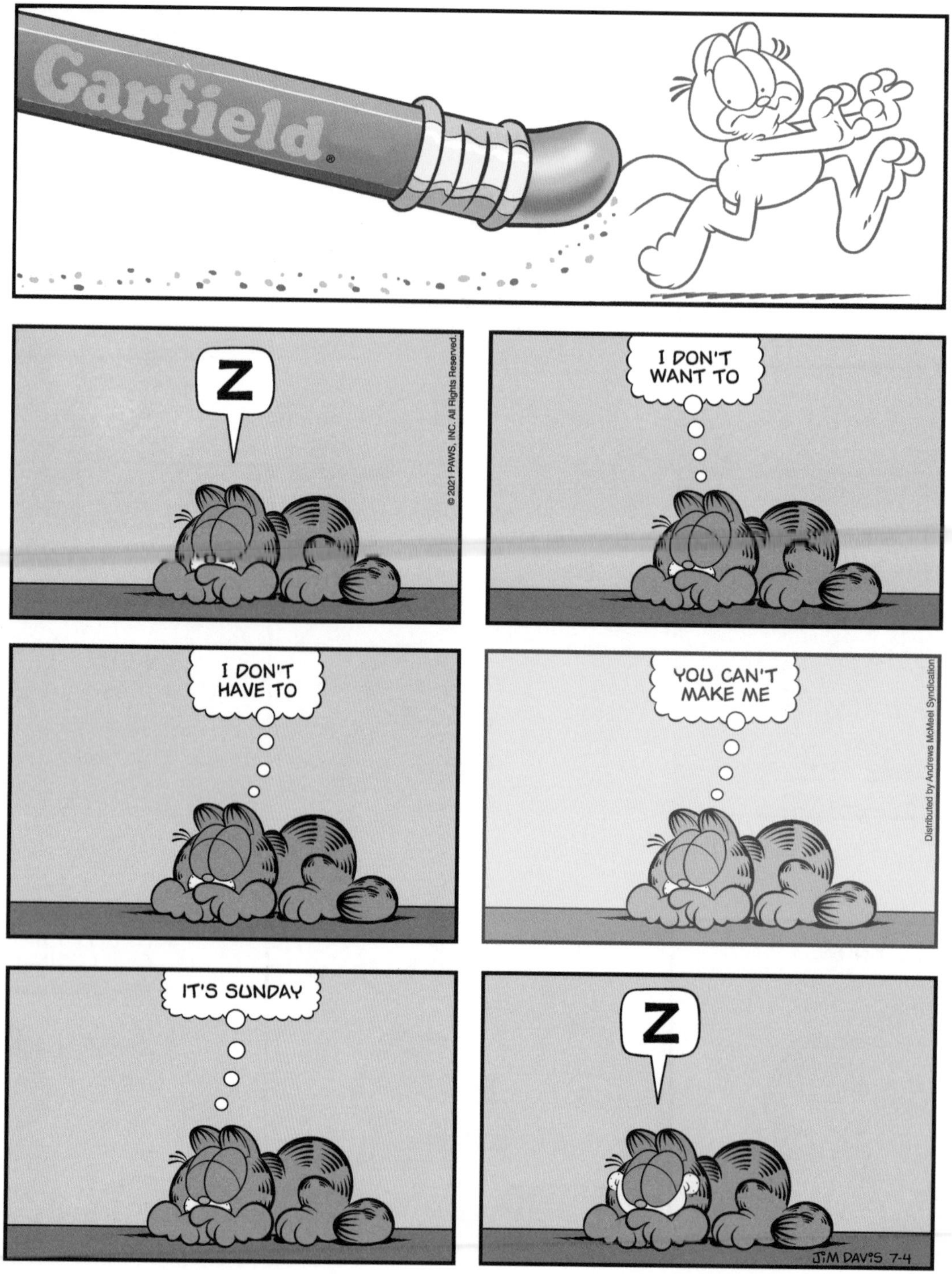
Garfield®
Z
© 2021 PAWS, INC. All Rights Reserved.
I DON'T WANT TO
I DON'T HAVE TO
YOU CAN'T MAKE ME
Distributed by Andrews McMeel Syndication
IT'S SUNDAY
Z
JIM DAVIS 7-4

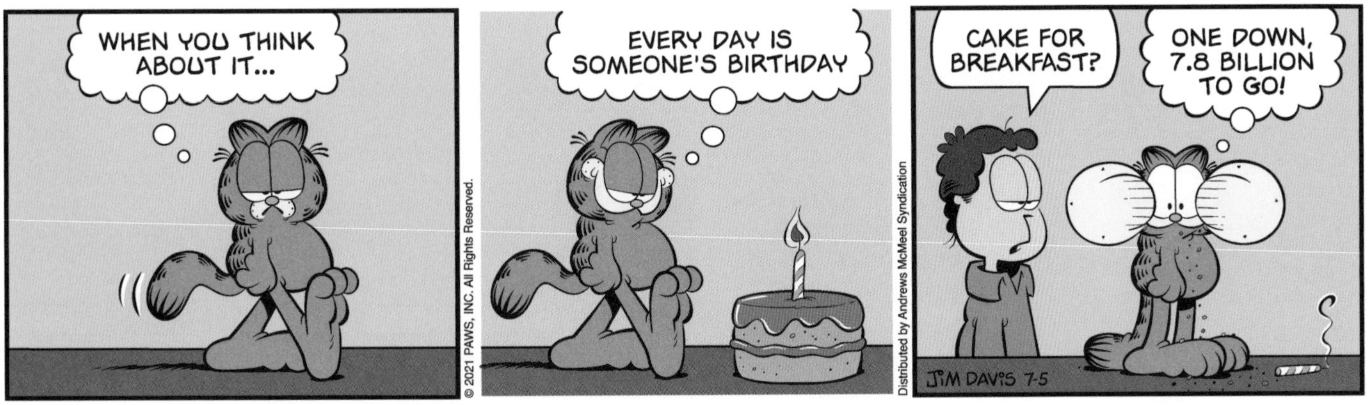
WHEN YOU THINK ABOUT IT...
EVERY DAY IS SOMEONE'S BIRTHDAY
CAKE FOR BREAKFAST?
ONE DOWN, 7.8 BILLION TO GO!
JIM DAVIS 7-5
© 2021 PAWS, INC. All Rights Reserved.
Distributed by Andrews McMeel Syndication

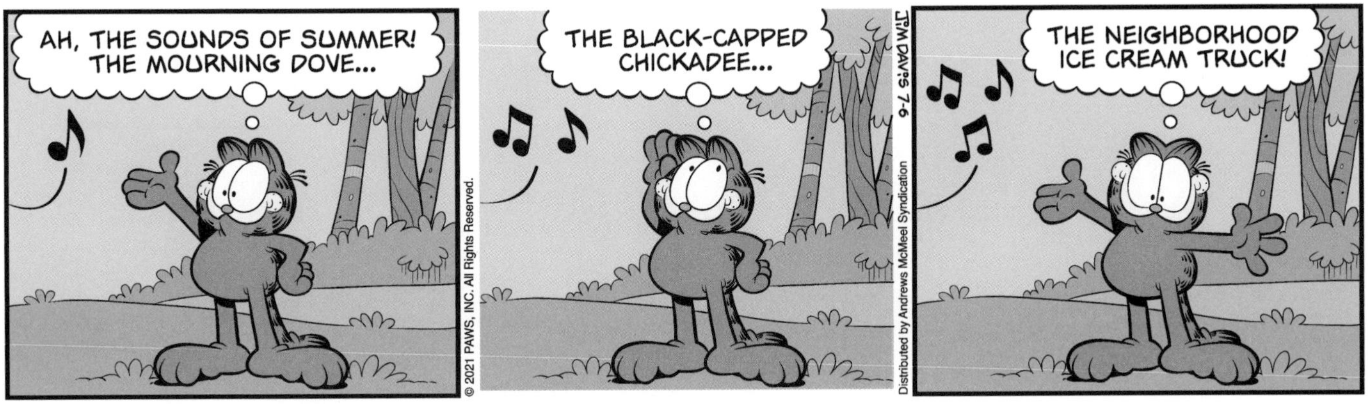
AH, THE SOUNDS OF SUMMER! THE MOURNING DOVE...
THE BLACK-CAPPED CHICKADEE...
THE NEIGHBORHOOD ICE CREAM TRUCK!
JIM DAVIS 7-6
© 2021 PAWS, INC. All Rights Reserved.
Distributed by Andrews McMeel Syndication

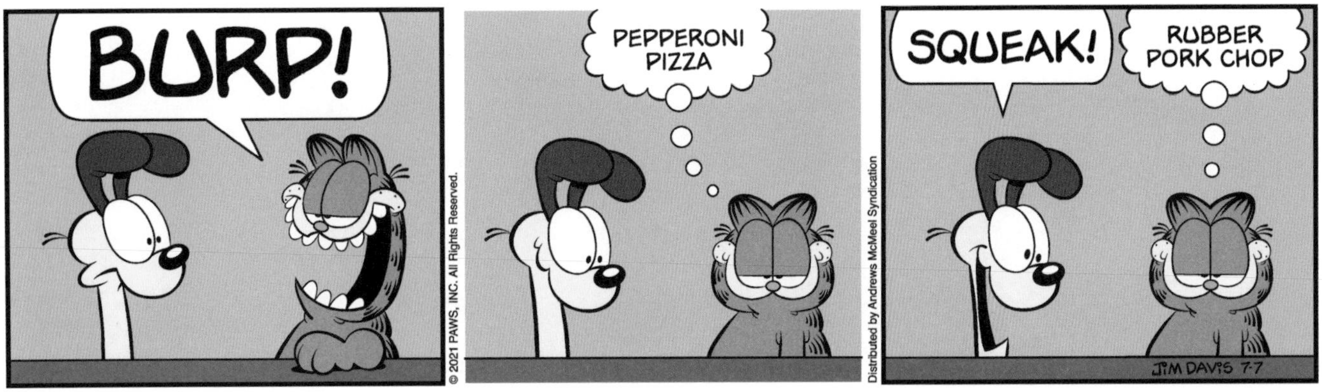
BURP!
PEPPERONI PIZZA
SQUEAK!
RUBBER PORK CHOP
JIM DAVIS 7-7
© 2021 PAWS, INC. All Rights Reserved.
Distributed by Andrews McMeel Syndication

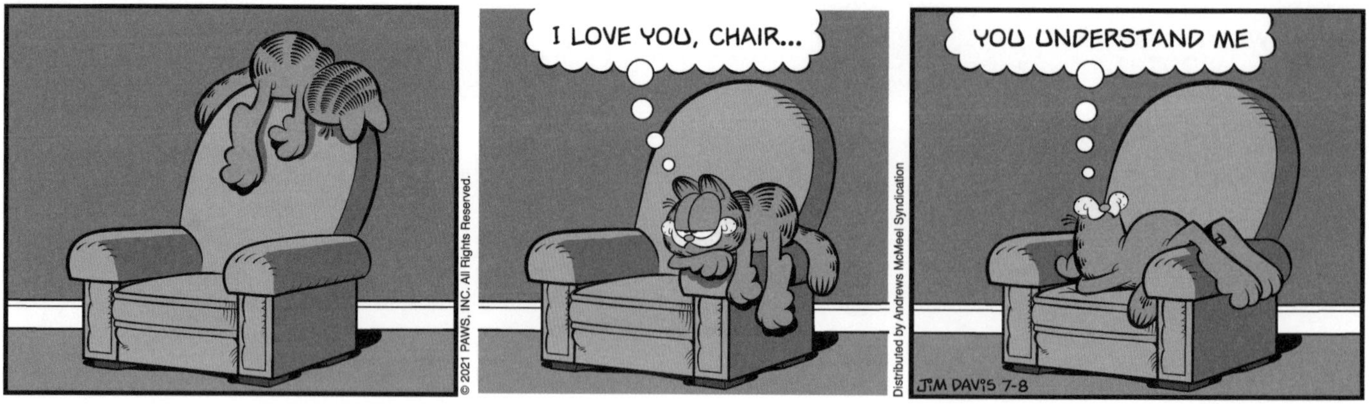

© 2021 PAWS, INC. All Rights Reserved.
I LOVE YOU, CHAIR...
Distributed by Andrews McMeel Syndication
YOU UNDERSTAND ME
JIM DAVIS 7-8

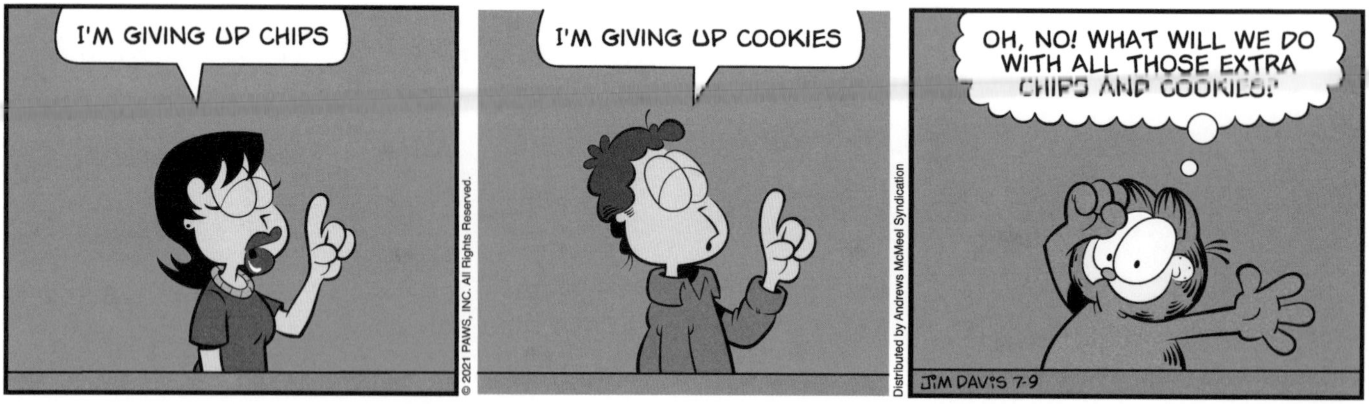

I'M GIVING UP CHIPS
© 2021 PAWS, INC. All Rights Reserved.
I'M GIVING UP COOKIES
Distributed by Andrews McMeel Syndication
OH, NO! WHAT WILL WE DO WITH ALL THOSE EXTRA CHIPS AND COOKIES?
JIM DAVIS 7-9

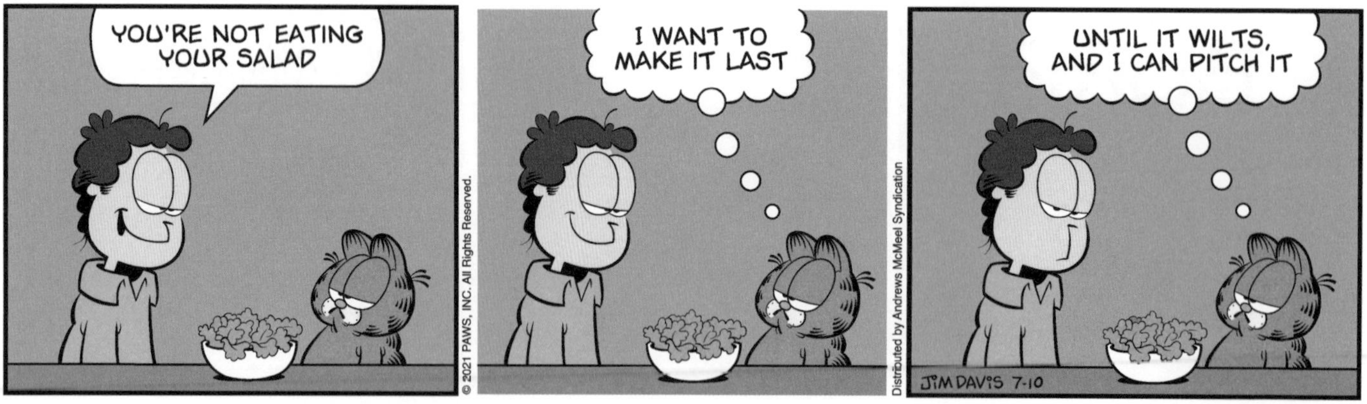

YOU'RE NOT EATING YOUR SALAD
© 2021 PAWS, INC. All Rights Reserved.
I WANT TO MAKE IT LAST
Distributed by Andrews McMeel Syndication
UNTIL IT WILTS, AND I CAN PITCH IT
JIM DAVIS 7-10

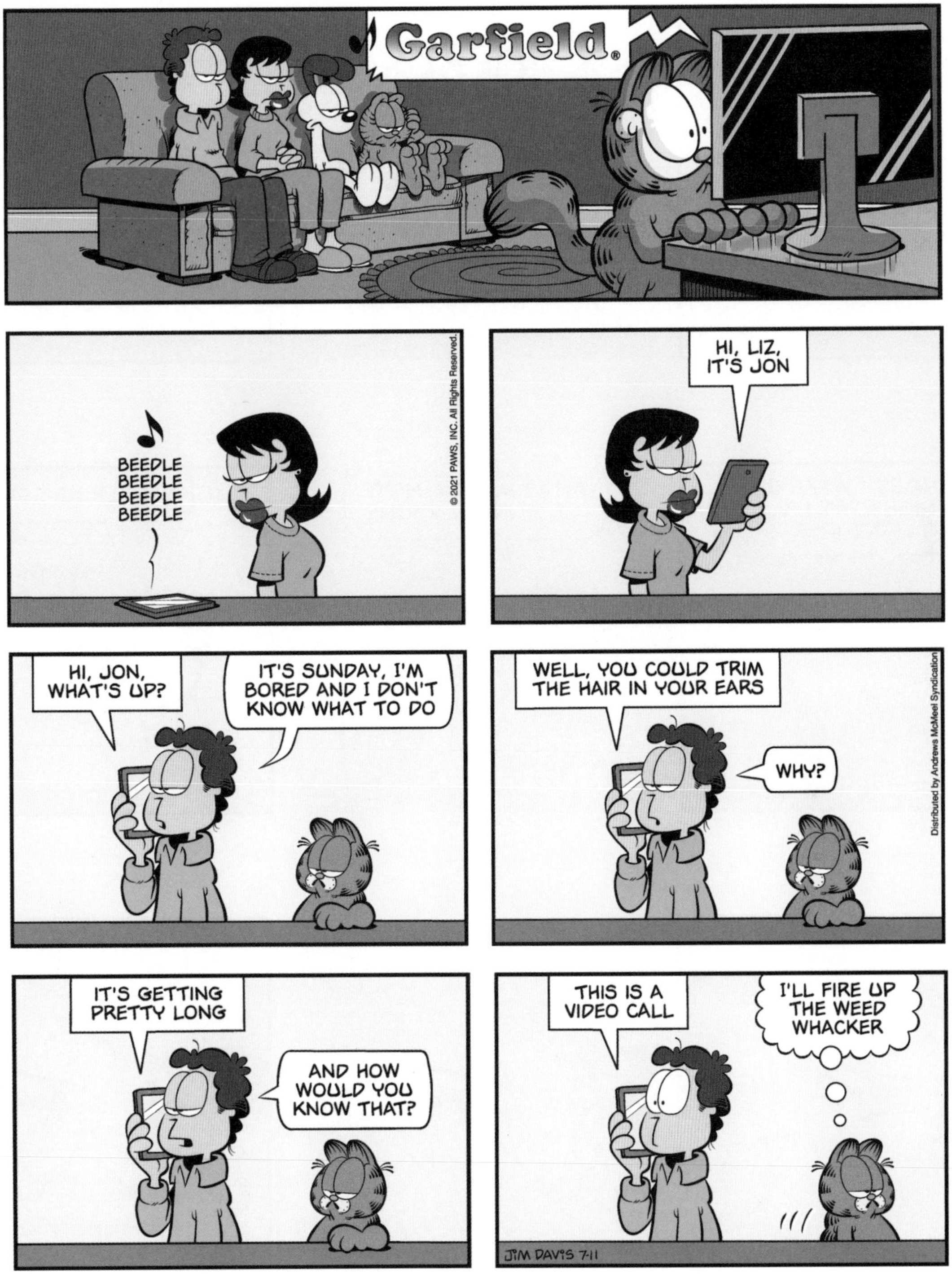
Garfield®
BEEDLE BEEDLE BEEDLE BEEDLE
© 2021 PAWS, INC. All Rights Reserved.
HI, LIZ, IT'S JON
HI, JON, WHAT'S UP?
IT'S SUNDAY, I'M BORED AND I DON'T KNOW WHAT TO DO
WELL, YOU COULD TRIM THE HAIR IN YOUR EARS
WHY?
Distributed by Andrews McMeel Syndication
IT'S GETTING PRETTY LONG
AND HOW WOULD YOU KNOW THAT?
THIS IS A VIDEO CALL
I'LL FIRE UP THE WEED WHACKER
JIM DAVIS 7-11

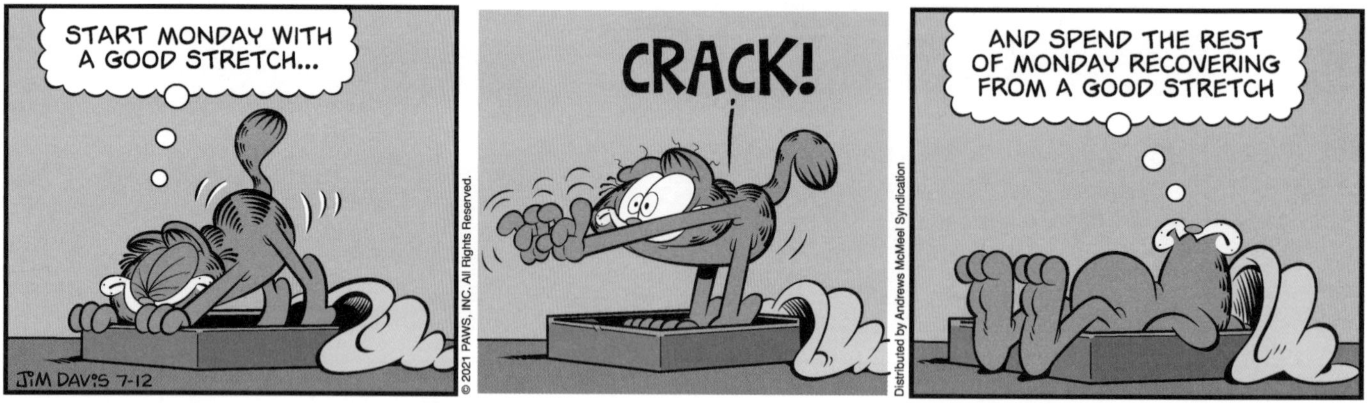
START MONDAY WITH A GOOD STRETCH...
JIM DAVIS 7-12
CRACK!
© 2021 PAWS, INC. All Rights Reserved.
AND SPEND THE REST OF MONDAY RECOVERING FROM A GOOD STRETCH
Distributed by Andrews McMeel Syndication

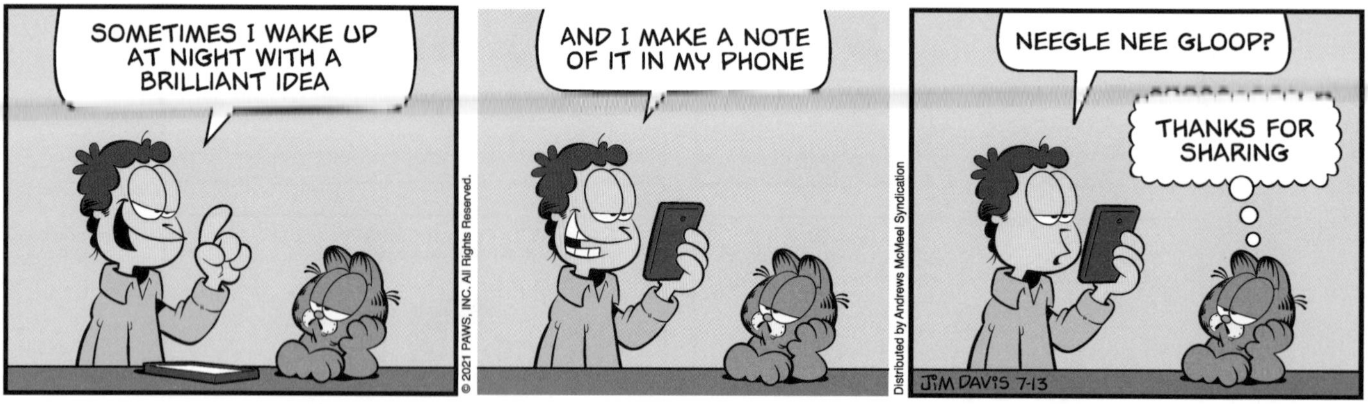
SOMETIMES I WAKE UP AT NIGHT WITH A BRILLIANT IDEA
© 2021 PAWS, INC. All Rights Reserved.
AND I MAKE A NOTE OF IT IN MY PHONE
Distributed by Andrews McMeel Syndication
NEEGLE NEE GLOOP?
THANKS FOR SHARING
JIM DAVIS 7-13

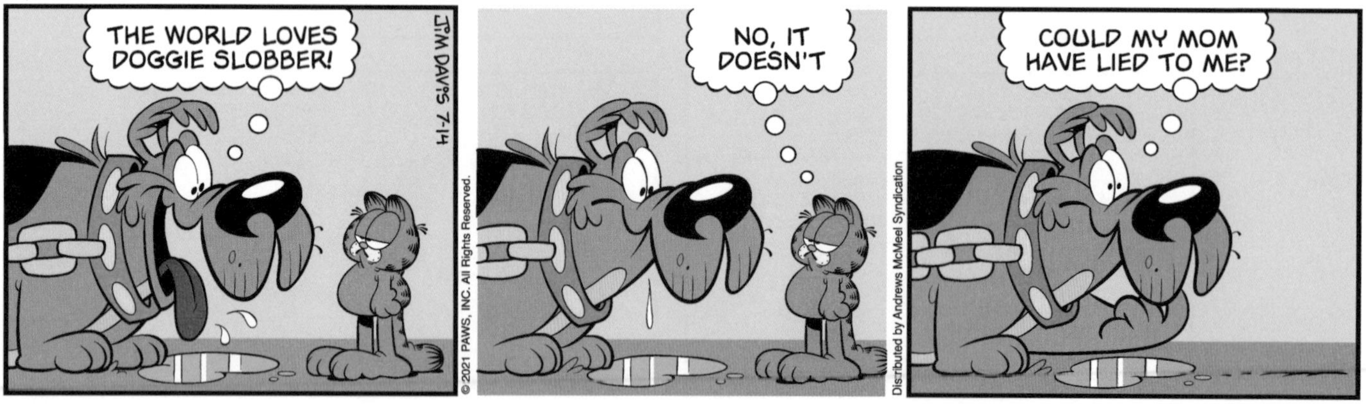
THE WORLD LOVES DOGGIE SLOBBER!
JIM DAVIS 7-14
© 2021 PAWS, INC. All Rights Reserved.
NO, IT DOESN'T
Distributed by Andrews McMeel Syndication
COULD MY MOM HAVE LIED TO ME?

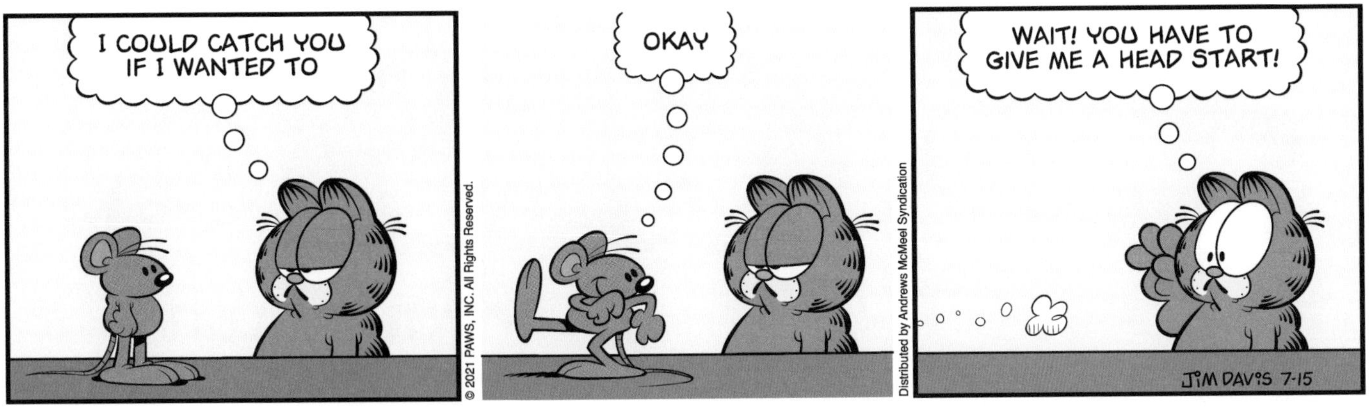
I COULD CATCH YOU IF I WANTED TO
© 2021 PAWS, INC. All Rights Reserved.
OKAY
Distributed by Andrews McMeel Syndication
WAIT! YOU HAVE TO GIVE ME A HEAD START!
JIM DAVIS 7-15

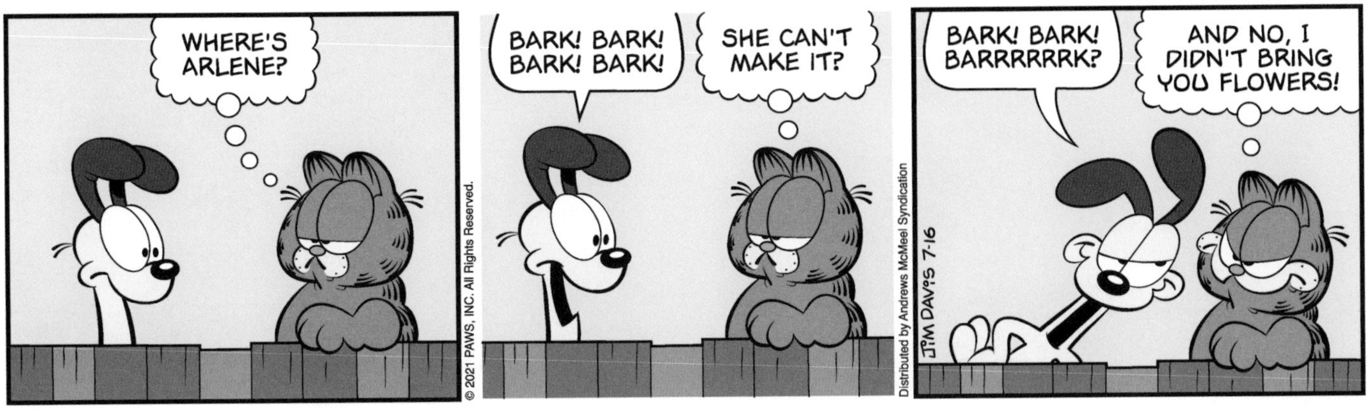
WHERE'S ARLENE?
© 2021 PAWS, INC. All Rights Reserved.
BARK! BARK! BARK! BARK!
SHE CAN'T MAKE IT?
Distributed by Andrews McMeel Syndication
JIM DAVIS 7-16
BARK! BARK! BARRRRRRK?
AND NO, I DIDN'T BRING YOU FLOWERS!

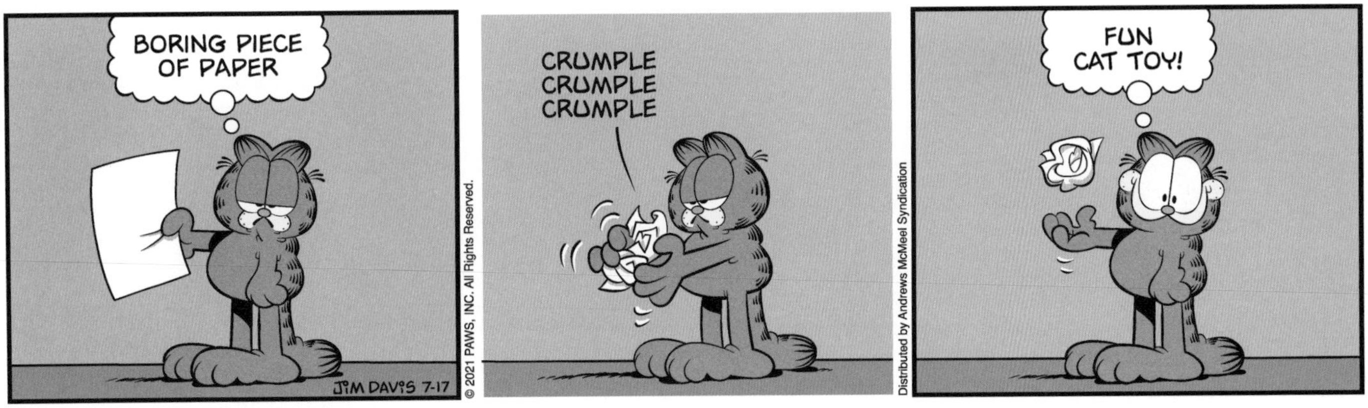
BORING PIECE OF PAPER
JIM DAVIS 7-17
© 2021 PAWS, INC. All Rights Reserved.
CRUMPLE CRUMPLE CRUMPLE
Distributed by Andrews McMeel Syndication
FUN CAT TOY!

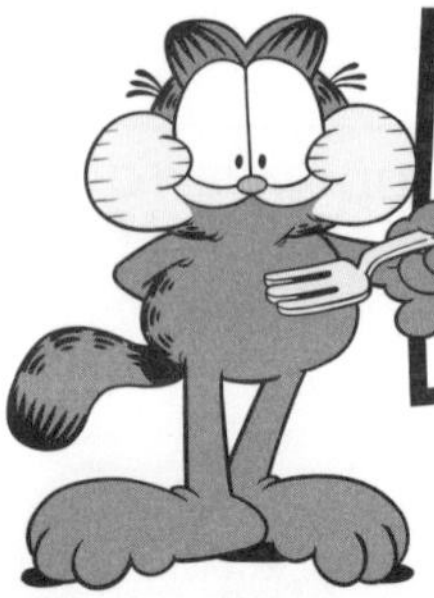

FUN THOUGHTS TO CHEW ON

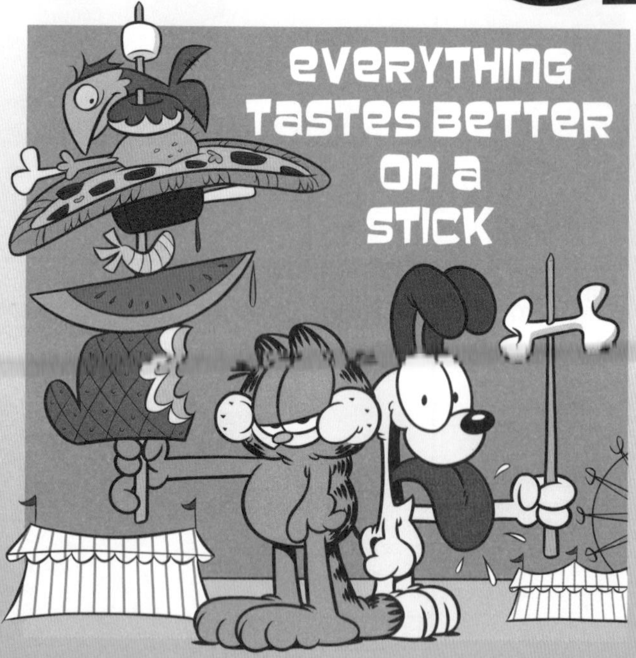
EVERYTHING TASTES BETTER ON A STICK

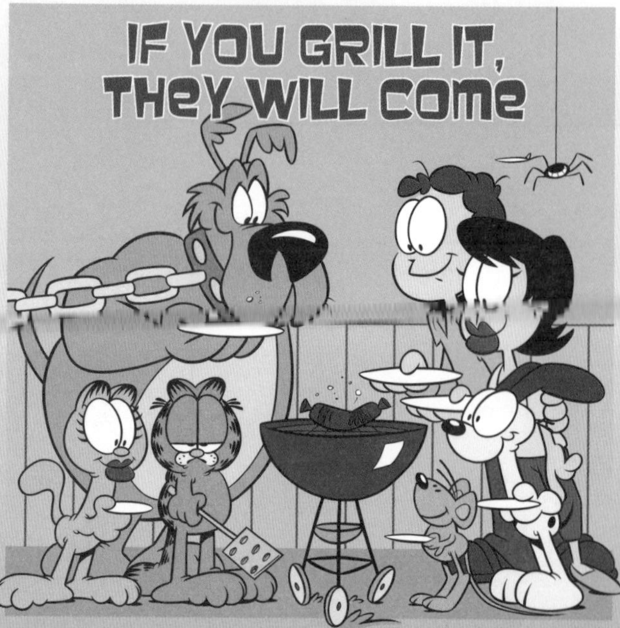
IF YOU GRILL IT, THEY WILL COME

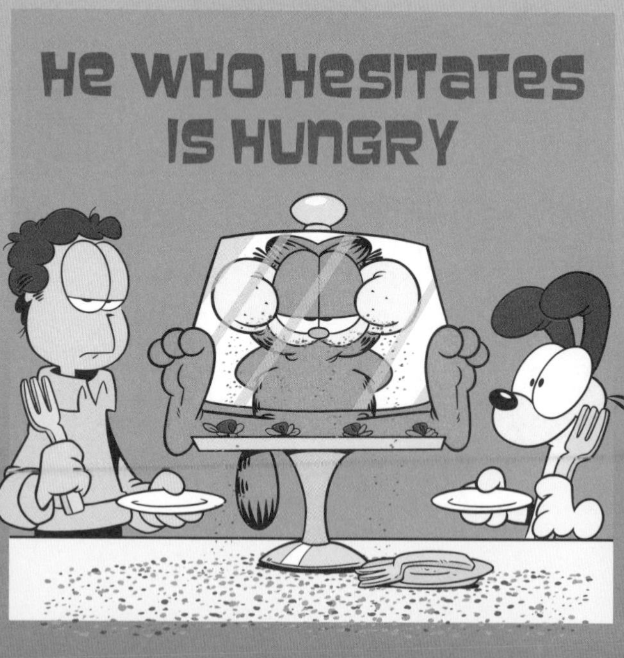
HE WHO HESITATES IS HUNGRY

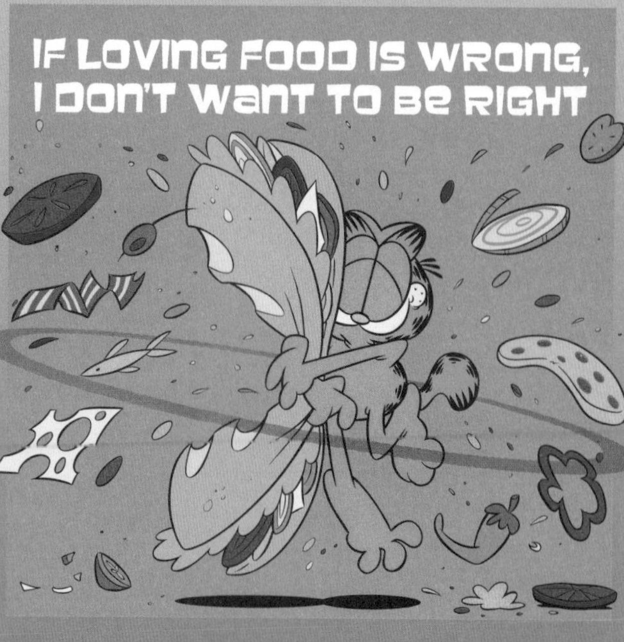
IF LOVING FOOD IS WRONG, I DON'T WANT TO BE RIGHT

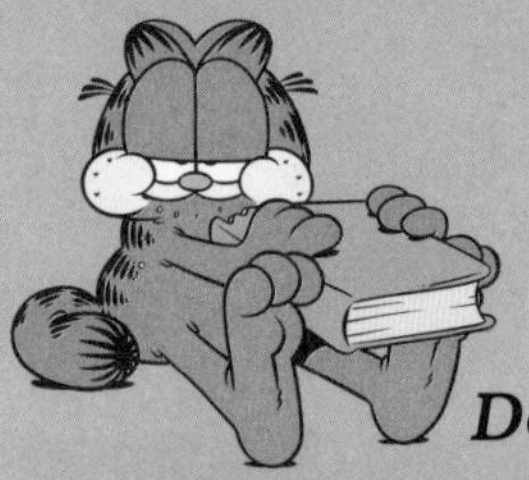

STRIPS, SPECIALS OR BESTSELLING BOOKS...
GARFIELD'S ON EVERYONE'S MENU.

Don't miss even one episode in the Tubby Tabby's hilarious series!

GARFIELD AT LARGE . . . . . (#1) 978-0-345-44382-3
GARFIELD GAINS WEIGHT . . . . . (#2) 978-0-345-44975-7
GARFIELD BIGGER THAN LIFE . . . . . (#3) 978-0-345-45027-2
GARFIELD WEIGHS IN . . . . . (#4) 978-0-345-45205-4
GARFIELD TAKES THE CAKE . . . . . (#5) 978-0-345-44978-8
GARFIELD EATS HIS HEART OUT . . . . . (#6) 978-0-345-46459-0
GARFIELD SITS AROUND THE HOUSE . . . . . (#7) 978-0-345-46463-7
GARFIELD TIPS THE SCALES . . . . . (#8) 978-0-345-46909-0
GARFIELD LOSES HIS FEET . . . . . (#9) 978-0-345-46467-5
GARFIELD MAKES IT BIG . . . . . (#10) 978-0-345-46468-2
GARFIELD ROLLS ON . . . . . (#11) 978-0-345-47561-9
GARFIELD OUT TO LUNCH . . . . . (#12) 978-0-345-47562-6
GARFIELD FOOD FOR THOUGHT . . . . . (#13) 978-0-345-47563-3
GARFIELD SWALLOWS HIS PRIDE . . . . . (#14) 978-0-345-91386-9
GARFIELD WORLDWIDE . . . . . (#15) 978-0-345-91754-6
GARFIELD ROUNDS OUT . . . . . (#16) 978-0-345-49169-5
GARFIELD CHEWS THE FAT . . . . . (#17) 978-0-345-49170-1
GARFIELD GOES TO WAIST . . . . . (#18) 978-0-345-49173-2
GARFIELD HANGS OUT . . . . . (#19) 978-0-345-49174-9
GARFIELD TAKES UP SPACE . . . . . (#20) 978-0-345-49178-7
GARFIELD SAYS A MOUTHFUL . . . . . (#21) 978-0-345-49179-4
GARFIELD BY THE POUND . . . . . (#22) 978-0-345-52558-1
GARFIELD KEEPS HIS CHINS UP . . . . . (#23) 978-0-345-52559-8
GARFIELD TAKES HIS LICKS . . . . . (#24) 978-0-345-52587-1
GARFIELD HITS THE BIG TIME . . . . . (#25) 978-0-345-52589-5
GARFIELD PULLS HIS WEIGHT . . . . . (#26) 978-0-345-52594-9
GARFIELD DISHES IT OUT . . . . . (#27) 978-0-345-52595-6
GARFIELD LIFE IN THE FAT LANE . . . . . (#28) 978-0-345-52600-7
GARFIELD TONS OF FUN . . . . . (#29) 978-0-345-52601-4
GARFIELD BIGGER AND BETTER . . . . . (#30) 978-0-345-52605-2
GARFIELD HAMS IT UP . . . . . (#31) 978-0-345-52606-9
GARFIELD THINKS BIG . . . . . (#32) 978-0-425-28516-9
GARFIELD THROWS HIS WEIGHT AROUND . . . . . (#33) 978-0-425-28559-6
GARFIELD LIFE TO THE FULLEST . . . . . (#34) 978-0-425-28564-0
GARFIELD FEEDS THE KITTY . . . . . (#35) 978-0-425-28569-5
GARFIELD HOGS THE SPOTLIGHT . . . . . (#36) 978-0-425-28574-9
GARFIELD BEEFS UP . . . . . (#37) 978-0-345-44109-6
GARFIELD GETS COOKIN' . . . . . (#38) 978-0-345-44582-7
GARFIELD EATS CROW . . . . . (#39) 978-0-345-45201-6
GARFIELD SURVIVAL OF THE FATTEST . . . . . (#40) 978-0-345-46458-3
GARFIELD OLDER AND WIDER . . . . . (#41) 978-0-345-46462-0
GARFIELD PIGS OUT . . . . . (#42) 978-0-345-46466 8
GARFIELD BLOTS OUT THE SUN . . . . . (#43) 978-0-345-46615-0
GARFIELD GOES BANANAS . . . . . (#44) 978-0-345-91346-3
GARFIELD LARGE & IN CHARGE . . . . . (#45) 978-0-345-49172-5
GARFIELD SPILLS THE BEANS . . . . . (#46) 978-0-345-49177-0
GARFIELD GETS HIS JUST DESSERTS . . . . . (#47) 978-0-345-91387-6
GARFIELD WILL EAT FOR FOOD . . . . . (#48) 978-0-345-49176-3
GARFIELD WEIGHS HIS OPTIONS . . . . . (#49) 978-0-345-49181-7
GARFIELD POTBELLY OF GOLD . . . . . (#50) 978-0-345-52244-3
GARFIELD SHOVELS IT IN . . . . . (#51) 978-0-345-52419-5
GARFIELD LARD OF THE JUNGLE . . . . . (#52) 978-0-345-52584-0
GARFIELD BRINGS HOME THE BACON . . . . . (#53) 978-0-345-52586-4
GARFIELD GETS IN A PICKLE . . . . . (#54) 978-0-345-52590-1
GARFIELD SINGS FOR HIS SUPPER . . . . . (#55) 978-0-345-52593-2
GARFIELD CAUTION: WIDE LOAD . . . . . (#56) 978-0-345-52596-3
GARFIELD SOUPED UP . . . . . (#57) 978-0-345-52598-7
GARFIELD GOES TO HIS HAPPY PLACE . . . . . (#58) 978-0-345-52602-1
GARFIELD THE BIG CHEESE . . . . . (#59) 978-0-345-52604-5
GARFIELD CLEANS HIS PLATE . . . . . (#60) 978-0-345-52608-3
GARFIELD CHICKENS OUT . . . . . (#61) 978-0-425-28515-2
GARFIELD LISTENS TO HIS GUT . . . . . (#62) 978-0-425-28557-2
GARFIELD COOKS UP TROUBLE . . . . . (#63) 978-0-425-28562-6
GARFIELD FEEDS HIS FACE . . . . . (#64) 978-0-425-28567-1
GARFIELD EATS AND RUNS . . . . . (#65) 978-0-425-28572-5
GARFIELD NUTTY AS A FRUITCAKE . . . . . (#66) 978-0-425-28576-3
GARFIELD SLURPS AND BURPS . . . . . (#67) 978-1-9848-1773-0
GARFIELD BELLY LAUGHS . . . . . (#68) 978-1-9848-1777-8
GARFIELD EASY AS PIE . . . . . (#69) 978-0-593-15640-7
GARFIELD GOES HOG WILD . . . . . (#70) 978-0-593-15642-1
GARFIELD WHAT LEFTOVERS? . . . . . (#71) 978-0-593-15644-5
GARFIELD LIVIN' THE SWEET LIFE . . . . . (#72) 978-0-593-15646-9
GARFIELD ROAD PIZZA . . . . . (#73) 978-0-593-15648-3

DVD TIE-INS

GARFIELD AS HIMSELF 978-0-345-47805-4
GARFIELD HOLIDAY CELEBRATIONS 978-0-345-47930-3
GARFIELD TRAVEL ADVENTURES 978-0-345-48087-3

AND DON'T MISS . . .

GARFIELD AT 25: IN DOG YEARS I'D BE DEAD 978-0-345-45204-7
GARFIELD'S JOKE ZONE/INSULTS 978-0-345-46263-3
GARFIELD FAT CAT 3-PACK/ VOL. 1 978-0-345-46455-2
GARFIELD FAT CAT 3-PACK/ VOL. 2 978-0-345-46465-1
GARFIELD FAT CAT 3-PACK/ VOL. 3 978-0-345-48088-0
GARFIELD FAT CAT 3-PACK/ VOL. 4 978-0-345-49171-8
GARFIELD FAT CAT 3-PACK/ VOL. 5 978-0-345-49180-8
GARFIELD FAT CAT 3-PACK/ VOL. 6 978-0-345-52420-1
GARFIELD FAT CAT 3-PACK/ VOL. 7 978-0-345-52588-8
GARFIELD FAT CAT 3-PACK/ VOL. 8 978-0-345-52599-4
GARFIELD FAT CAT 3-PACK/ VOL. 9 978-0-345-52607-6
GARFIELD FAT CAT 3-PACK/ VOL. 10 978-0-425-28558-9
GARFIELD FAT CAT 3-PACK/ VOL. 11 978-0-425-28566-4
GARFIELD FAT CAT 3-PACK/ VOL. 12 978-0-425-28578-7
GARFIELD FAT CAT 3-PACK/ VOL. 13 978-0-345-46460-6
GARFIELD FAT CAT 3-PACK/ VOL. 14 978-0-345-49175-6
GARFIELD FAT CAT 3-PACK/ VOL. 15 978-0-345-52585-7
GARFIELD FAT CAT 3-PACK/ VOL. 16 978-0-345-52592-5
GARFIELD FAT CAT 3-PACK/ VOL. 17 978-0-345-52603-8
GARFIELD FAT CAT 3-PACK/ VOL. 18 978-0-399-59440-3
GARFIELD FAT CAT 3-PACK/ VOL. 19 978-0-425-28561-9
GARFIELD FAT CAT 3-PACK/ VOL. 20 978-0-425-28571-8
GARFIELD FAT CAT 3-PACK/ VOL. 21 978-1-9848-1775-4
GARFIELD FAT CAT 3-PACK/ VOL. 22 978-0-593-15638-4
GARFIELD FAT CAT 3-PACK/ VOL. 23 978-0-593-15639-1
GARFIELD FAT CAT 3-PACK/ VOL. 24 978-0-593-15650-6
GARFIELD'S 20TH ANNIVERSARY COLLECTION 978-0-345-42126-5
SEASON'S EATINGS: A VERY MERRY GARFIELD CHRISTMAS . . . 978-0-345-47560-2
GARFIELD'S GUIDE TO EVERYTHING 978-0-345-46461-3
ODIE UNLEASHED! 978-0-345-46464-4
GARFIELD'S BOOK OF CAT NAMES 978-0-345-48516-8
THE GARFIELD JOURNAL 978-0-345-46469-9
LIGHTS, CAMERA, HAIRBALLS!: GARFIELD AT THE MOVIES 978-0-345-49134-3
30 YEARS OF LAUGHS AND LASAGNA 978-0-345-50379-4
GARFIELD MINUS GARFIELD 978-0-345-51387-8
GARFIELD FROM THE TRASH BIN 978-0-345-51881-1
GARFIELD LEFT SPEECHLESS 978-0-345-53058-5
MY LAUGHABLE LIFE WITH GARFIELD 978-0-345-52591-8
GARFIELD'S SUNDAY FINEST 978-0-345-52597-0
AGE HAPPENS: GARFIELD HITS THE BIG 4-0 978-0-345-52609-0
GARFIELD COMPLETE WORKS: VOLUME ONE: 1978 & 1979 . . . 978-0-425-28712-5
GARFIELD COMPLETE WORKS: VOLUME TWO: 1980 & 1981 . . . 978-0-425-28713-2

New larger, full-color format!

Home is where the stove is.